THE FALLING RATE OF PROFIT IN THE POSTWAR UNITED STATES ECONOMY

The Falling Rate of Profit in the Postwar United States Economy

Fred Moseley
Associate Professor of Economics
Mount Holyoke College

St. Martin's Press   New York

First published in the United States of America in **1991**

Printed in Great Britain

ISBN 0–312–06888–3

Library of Congress Cataloging-in-Publication Data
Moseley, Fred, 1946–
The falling rate of profit in the postwar United States economy/
Fred Moseley.
p.   cm.
Includes bibliographical references and index.
ISBN 0–312–06888–3
1. Profit—United States—History—20th century.   2. Capitalism–
–United States—History—20th century.   3. United States—Economic
conditions—1945–   4. Marxian economics.   I. Title.
HC110.P7M67 **1991**
338.5′16′097309045—dc20   91–25750
                                                                        CIP

To Paul Mattick, Sr.

Contents

List of Tables

List of Figures

Preface

The most important conclusion of Marx's theory of capitalism is that the rate of profit would tend to decline as a result of technological change. According to Marx's theory, the rate of profit varies inversely with the composition of capital and directly with the rate of surplus-value. Marx argued that both the composition of capital and the rate of surplus-value would increase as a result of technological change, thus having offsetting effects on the rate of profit. However, Marx argued further that the composition of capital would increase faster than the rate of surplus-value, so that the net effect would be a decline in the rate of profit.

The main purpose of this book is to subject these important conclusions of Marx's theory to a rigorous empirical test. Estimates of the three key Marxian ratios for the postwar US economy are derived which correspond as closely as possible to Marx's concepts as he defined them. These estimates are analyzed in order to determine whether or not the actual trends in these variables in the postwar US economy were in the directions suggested by Marx's theory.

There has been much theoretical controversy over Marx's theory of the falling rate of profit, but as yet very limited empirical research to test the validity of this theory. The earliest empirical studies of Marx's theory of the falling rate of profit (both for the US economy) were by Gillman (1958) and Mage (1963). For the postwar US economy, there have been two important prior empirical studies which have presented estimates of the three key Marxian variables: Weisskopf (1979) and Wolff (1979 and 1986). Both of these come to essentially the same conclusions concerning the trends in the Marxian variables. Both conclude that the rate of profit declined, as suggested by Marx's theory, but for a different reason than suggested by Marx's theory: because the rate of surplus-value declined, rather than because the composition of capital increased. These conclusions have been widely accepted by Marxian and radical economists.

However, this book argues that these prior estimates of the Marxian variables presented by Weisskopf and Wolff are not rigorous and reliable because the data categories used to derive them differ in significant respects from the definitions of these variables as formulated by Marx. It argues further that if more rigorous estimates are derived which correspond more closely to Marx's definitions, then the trends in the Marxian ratios are very different from these prior estimates and much more consistent with Marx's conclusions.

Chapter 1 presents a review of the theoretical controversies concerning Marx's theory of the falling rate of profit. The main conclusion here is that Marx's theory does not provide a definite prediction that technological change will always cause the rate of profit to decline, but it does offer plausible reasons why technological change might cause the rate of profit to decline under certain historical conditions. Whether or not Marx's theory is valid for a particular historical period, such as the postwar US economy, thus becomes an empirical question.

Chapter 2 discusses the major conceptual issues involved in the derivation of rigorous estimates of the Marxian variables. These conceptual issues are: (i) whether Marx's variables should be estimated in units of money or labor; (ii) whether or not Marx's variables refer to non-capitalist forms of production, as well as to capitalist production; (iii) whether or not Marx's concepts of constant capital and variable capital refer to the entire capital invested in the capitalist economy or instead refer only to the capital invested in production activities; (iv) whether or not Marx's concept of constant capital includes residential housing; and (v) whether taxes on wages should be considered as part of variable capital or surplus-value. My interpretation of these issues is contrasted with those of Weisskopf and Wolff.

Chapter 3 presents and analyzes my estimates of the Marxian variables based on the definitions discussed in Chapter 2. As stated above, the main conclusion is that the rate of profit declined significantly in the postwar US economy and for the reason suggested by Marx's theory, i.e. due to an increase in the composition of capital. These estimates are then compared with the prior estimates of Weisskopf and Wolff in order to determine which of the conceptual issues discussed in Chapter 2 contributed the most to the significant differences in the trends between my estimates and Weisskopf's and Wolff's estimates. It is found that the conceptual issue which is primarily responsible for these different trends is the issue of productive labor and unproductive labor (issue (iii) above). Thus the conclusions one reaches concerning the trends of the Marxian variables in the postwar US economy and concerning the causes of the decline of the rate of profit depend almost entirely on one's interpretation of Marx's distinction between productive and unproductive labor.

Chapter 4 is concerned with a separate, but related, question: the causes of the decline in the conventionally defined rate of profit, as opposed to the Marxian rate of profit as defined and analyzed in previous chapters. The main difference between the conventional and the Marxian rate of profit is that the former does not take into account Marx's distinction between productive and unproductive labor. In the postwar US economy, the conventional rate of profit declined even more than the Marxian rate of profit (approximately twice as much), and this decline would seem to be an important cause of the economic crisis of the 1970s and 1980s. The main conclusion of this chapter is that the most important cause of this decline in the conventional rate of profit was a very significant increase in the ratio of unproductive labor to productive labor, which almost doubled in the postwar US economy. This explanation of the decline in the conventional rate of profit is contrasted with the "profit squeeze" explanations presented by Weisskopf and Wolff, and a preliminary empirical test of these competing explanations is conducted.

Chapters 3 and 4 thus identify a very important phenomenon in the postwar US economy: the major increase in the ratio of unproductive labor to productive labor. This increase explains almost all the differences between the trends of my estimates and prior estimates of the Marxian ratios and, according to Marx's theory, was the most important cause of the decline in the conventional rate of profit. Chapter 5 presents a preliminary analysis of the underlying causes of this very important phenomenon. More detailed estimates of the different subgroups of unproductive labor are derived in order to determine which of these contributed the most to the overall increase of unproductive labor. Then the possible causes of each of the main subgroups is analyzed.

Finally, Chapter 6 reviews the main conclusions of this study, suggests important tasks for future research along these lines, and discusses the implications of these conclusions for the future trend in the conventional rate of profit and thus for a full and lasting recovery from the current economic crisis.

I am indebted to many people who have helped and encouraged and criticized me over the past ten years when working on the research that produced this book. This research project began as a Ph.D. dissertation at the University of Massachusetts under the direction of James Crotty. I have benefited ever since from the rigorous guidance he provided. I also benefited in the early stages from numerous discussions, and the related research of Anwar Shaikh. Special thanks are also due to Tom Weisskopf and Ed Wolff, who are in a sense the main "antagonists" of this book, and who have nevertheless been very helpful and encouraging to me all along (and very willing to provide me with some of their raw data). Although continuing to disagree with them on important issues, I have learned a great deal from their pioneering works on Marxian empirical research. Other colleagues who have given me the benefit of their comments and criticisms (without implicating any in the final product) include: Sam Bowles, Guglielmo Carchedi, Gerard Dumenil, Alan Freeman, Henry Gemery, Paolo Giussani, Mark Glick, Jon Goldstein, David Laibman, Paul Mattick Jr, Tom Michl, John Miller, Eduardo Ochoa, Angelo Reati, Frank Thompson, Ahmet Tonak, and John Weeks. I have also benefited greatly from four very capable students at Colby College who worked as my research assistants over several years: Toni Fredette, Bill Ralph, Randy Mitchell, and Joe Baker. Toni especially worked for me over the last three summers and was indispensable to the completion of the book.

I also thank Colby College for providing generous financial assistance for a sabbatical leave and research assistants and to Mount Holyoke College for a faculty research grant. I also thank three excellent research librarians at Colby, Sunny Pomerleau, Toni Katz, and Chuck Lincoln, who assisted me beyond the call of duty. This book incorporates material from articles previously published in the *Cambridge Journal of Economics*, *Review of Radical Political Economics*, *American Economic Review*, and *International Journal of Political Economy*. I am grateful to their editors and referees for comments and suggestions. Finally, very special thanks are due to my wife and best friend Patty Ramsey, the author of several books herself, who, in addition to years of encouragement and companionship, taught me the very important lesson of how to accept and apply the words "beyond the scope of this book", without which I would still be working on it.

FRED MOSELEY

Abbreviations of Marx's Works

The following abbreviations are used in references to Marx's works:

C.I   *Capital*, Volume 1
C.II   *Capital*, Volume 2
C.III   *Capital*, Volume 3
TSV.I   *Theories of Surplus-value*, Volume 1
TSV.II   *Theories of Surplus-value*, Volume 2
TSV.III   *Theories of Surplus-value*, Volume 3
G.   *The Grundrisse*
Cr.   *A Contribution to the The Critique of Political Economy*
MECW. 30   *Marx–Engels Collected Works*, Volume 30
SC.   *Selected Correspondence*

1 Marx's Theory of the Falling Rate of Profit

The most important conclusion of Marx's theory of capitalism is that the rate of profit would tend to decline over time as a result of technological change. Marx called his law of the tendency of the rate of profit to fall "in every respect the most important law of modern political economy" (G. 748). In a letter to Engels, Marx claimed that this law was one of his most important achievements over classical economics (SC. 194).[1]

However, Marx's law of the falling rate of profit has probably been the subject of more criticism than any other conclusion of his theory. The three main criticisms have been: (i) Marx did not conclusively prove that the composition of capital must necessarily increase; (ii) even if it is granted that the composition of capital does increase, Marx did not conclusively prove that it must necessarily increase faster than the rate of surplus-value; and (iii) aside from the above arguments, the decision rule of capitalists with regard to the introduction of new technology precludes a decline in the rate of profit, if the real wage is assumed to remain constant. This chapter will review the debate on these three issues and will also present my own conclusions concerning the validity of Marx's law of the falling rate of profit.[2]

Marx's theory of the falling rate of profit can be applied to three distinct time periods: long-run secular trends, medium-run long waves, and short-run cycles. It is not always clear which of these time periods Marx had in mind in his own discussions of the falling rate of profit. My interpretation is that Marx's conclusion applies first and foremost to a long wave period of expansion of thirty to forty years.[3] Marx's theory clearly suggests that during a long wave period of expansion, characterized by the absence of severe depressions, the rate of profit will decline as a result of ongoing technological change. His theory further suggests that the decline of the rate of profit will eventually cause the long wave period of expansion to end and to be followed by a severe depression and/or extended stagnation. During such depressions the rate of profit is increased, due primarily to the "devaluation of capital" which results from bankruptcies. Whether or

1

not these are a long-run secular tendency over more than one long wave for the rate of profit to decline, depends on whether the increase of the rate of profit during depressions is as large as its decline during expansions. Marx seems to have thought that the rate of profit would decline over the secular long run. However that may be, it is much clearer that there is a strong presumption in Marx's theory that the rate of profit would decline over long wave periods of expansion. Therefore, the primary empirical test of Marx's theory conducted in Chapter 3 will be for the post-World War II long-wave period of expansion from the mid-1940s to the mid-1970s.

1.1   INCREASE IN THE COMPOSITION OF CAPITAL?

1.1.1   Definition of the Composition of Capital

As is generally known, Marx defined the composition of capital in terms of three distinct but related ratios: the technical, the value, and the organic. However, the precise meanings of these three ratios are not universally agreed upon, especially the meaning of the organic composition. This subsection will briefly review these definitions.

The first ratio is the *technical* composition of capital (*TCC*), which is defined as the "real" ratio of the stock of the means of production (MP), measured in physical units, to the flow of labor employed in production (PL) during a given period (e.g. a year), measured in workers or days or hours:

$$TCC = MP \, / \, PL \qquad\qquad (1.1)$$

This ratio cannot be given a precise scalar meaning because the "means of production" consist of many different types of producer goods (buildings, equipment, raw materials, auxiliary materials, etc.) which cannot be meaningfully added together in physical terms, especially since technological change continually alters the types of goods being added together. Marx used the technical composition of capital in a less precise manner to loosely represent a given state of technology. He argued that technological change generally results in an increase in the technical composition of capital (see below), so that a change in technology can be loosely represented by in increase in the technical composition of capital.

The second ratio is the *value* composition of capital (*VCC*), which I define as the "money" ratio of the stock of constant capital (*C*) to the annual flow of variable capital (*V*),[4] i.e.

$$VCC = C/V \tag{1.2}$$

More precisely, I define constant capital as the replacement value of the stock of the means of production, measured in current prices and variable capital as the annual flow of the wages of production workers, also, of course, measured in terms of current prices. The theoretical issues involved in the precise definition of the concepts of constant capital and variable capital will be discussed at length in Chapter 2. These issues are very important for the derivation of rigorous estimates of these concepts, but they have very little bearing on the logic of Marx's theory of the falling rate of profit, and so will be ignored in this chapter.

Finally, the third ratio is the *organic* composition of capital (*OCC*), Marx's definition of which is notoriously ambiguous:

> There is a close correlation between the two [the technical composition and the value composition. FM]. I call the value composition of capital, in so far as it is determined by its technical composition and mirrors the changes in the latter, the organic composition of capital. (C.I, 762)

The difficulty with this definition is that it is not entirely clear what is meant by "a close correlation" and "in so far as it is determined by" and "mirrors changes". Many writers simply ignore the distinction between the organic composition and the value composition and define the organic composition as the ratio of constant capital to variable capital without qualification, i.e. as the value composition (e.g. Sweezy, 1968; Robinson, 1966; Gillman, 1958; Roemer, 1977; Weisskopf, 1979).

I interpret Marx's concept of the organic composition of capital in the following way: *the organic composition of capital is equal to the value composition of capital in so far as the latter is affected only by technological change* (C.III, 244–6; TSV.II, 379–4; TSV.III, 382–6). There are numerous other factors besides technological change which also affect the value composition of capital. The most important of these "other factors" are: the average real wage, the distribution of labor and capital across industries, the turnover time of capital, and the incidence of multiple shifts in the utilization of production facilities. Marx wished to ignore all these other factors in order to focus his analysis of the trend in the value composition of capital specifically and solely on the effects of technological change. The concept of the organic composition serves the purpose of focusing Marx's analysis in this way. In effect, the concept of the organic composition serves as an abbreviation for a set of *ceteris paribus* assumptions, i.e. that the other factors listed above remain constant.

This interpretation follows Mage (1963, pp. 68–74) and Cogoy (1973, pp. 56–8), although the only "other factor" discussed by Mage and Cogoy is a change in the average real wage, which changes variable capital in the denominator of the value composition of capital and hence changes the value composition itself in the opposite direction. In order to make the organic composition of capital invariant to changes in the real wage, Mage and Cogoy both suggest that the mathematical formulation which is most appropriate for the organic composition of capital is to replace variable capital in the denominator of the ratio with the sum of variable capital and surplus value, i.e. with the total new-value (N) produced during a given year; i.e.

$$OCC = C/(V + S) = C/N \tag{1.3}$$

Since this ratio is not affected by changes in the average real wage, one can relax the *ceteris paribus* assumption of a constant average real wage in the analysis of the trend of the organic composition of capital.

It should be pointed out that the organic composition of capital defined in this way (C/N) will in general not have exactly the same trend over time as the value composition (C/V). These two ratios will have the same trend only if the rate of surplus-value remains constant. The precise relation between these two ratios is given by the following equation:[5]

$$VCC/OCC = 1 + RS \tag{1.4}$$

where *RS* stands for the rate of surplus-value and is equal to the ratio of surplus-value to variable capital. Thus if the rate of surplus-value increases over a period of time, the value composition will increase faster than the organic composition. In this case, arguments which demonstrate an increasing value composition do not necessarily prove an increasing organic composition.

In addition, it should also be pointed out that, although this definition of the organic composition of capital is not affected by changes in the real wage, it is still affected by the remainder of the "other factors" listed above which also affect the value composition of capital besides technological change. Therefore, in the empirical analysis in Chapter 3, the effects of these other factors on the organic composition of capital must somehow be taken into account in order to test more rigorously Marx's hypothesis that technological change will cause the organic composition of capital to increase.

Fine and Harris (1979, chapter 4) have presented different definitions of the technical and the organic compositions of capital from the ones presented here. Fine and Harris define the technical composition of capital as the ratio of the quantity of the means of production *to the quantity of wage goods* (*MS*) (rather than to the quantity of productive labor employed, as in the definition presented above).[6] Mathematically:

$$TCC' = MP/MS \qquad (1.1')$$

Since *MS* is equal to the product of the quantity of productive labor and the average real wage (*WR*), the relation between Fine and Harris's definition of the technical composition of capital and the definition presented above is:

$$\frac{TCC'}{TCC} = \frac{MP/MS}{MP/PL} = \frac{PL}{MS}$$

or:

$$TCC' = TCC/WR$$

From this last equation, we can see that Fine and Harris's definition of the technical composition of capital (*TCC'*) depends not only on the level of technology, which determines the ratio *MP/PL* (or the *TCC*), but also on the average real wage. This definition seems clearly contrary to Marx's intentions.[7]

Further, Fine and Harris argue that the difference between the organic composition and the value composition is that for the organic composition the means of production and wage goods are evaluated in terms of the "old values" at the beginning of a period of technological change (V_0), and for the value composition the means of production and wage goods are evaluated in terms of the "new values" at the end of this period (V_t). Mathematically:

$$VCC'_t = \frac{MP_t}{MS_t} \times \frac{V_t^{mp}}{V_t^{ms}}$$

$$(1.2')$$

$$OCC'_t = \frac{MP_t}{MS_t} \times \frac{V_0^{mp}}{V_0^{ms}}$$

$$(1.3')$$

According to Fine and Harris, the purpose of the concept of the organic composition of capital is to focus the analysis on the "direct effect" of technological change on the ratio of the means or production to the means of subsistence (their technical composition of capital) and to abstract from the "indirect effects" of technological change on the relative values of the means of production and the means of subsistence.[8]

I argue, contrary to Fine and Harris, that the purpose of Marx's concept of the organic composition of capital is not to distinguish between the "direct" and "indirect" effects of technological change on the value composition of capital (the distinction between the technical and the organic compositions serve that purpose), but is instead to distinguish between the total (net) effect of technological change, on the one hand, and the effects of all other factors on the value composition of capital, on the other hand. According to my interpretation, the organic composition of capital serves to analyze both the "direct" and the "indirect" effects of technological change on the value composition of capital and explicitly to exclude from the analysis all other factors which also influence the value composition besides technological change.

Thus my estimates of the organic composition of capital presented in Chapter 3 will be of the current price ratio of the stock of constant capital to the annual flow of new-value produced, as suggested by Mage and Cogoy. The analysis in Chapter 3 will attempt to distinguish between the effect of technological change on this ratio from the effects of all other factors.

1.1.2 Tendency of the Organic Composition of Capital to Increase

Marx's argument concerning the tendency of the organic composition of capital to increase consists of two main points: first, Marx argued that the process of technological change generally results in an increase in the technical composition of capital for two reasons: (i) the machinery operated by an individual worker becomes bigger and more complex, consisting of more individual parts, and (ii) the quantity of raw materials processed by an individual worker increases as a consequence of the increased productivity which follows the technological change. Marx often used the example of the cotton industry (the most dynamic industry in the first half of the nineteenth century) to illustrate these points. In the late eighteenth century, a typical worker in the cotton industry operated a spinning wheel consisting of one spindle and processed 10 pounds of cotton per day. By the middle of the nineteenth century, a typical worker in the cotton industry operated an entire complex of machinery, consisting of hundreds of spindles and processed thousands of pounds of cotton per day (C.I, 509 and 772–3; C.III, 212; TSV.III, 364–6).

Secondly, Marx argued that this increase in the technical composition of capital would in turn result in an increase in the organic composition of capital. If the unit price of the means of production remained the same, this conclusion would be obvious and the increase in the organic composition would be proportional to the increase in the technical composition. However, Marx recognized that increases in productivity in industries which produce the means of production (Marx's "Department 1") would reduce the unit price of these means of production, so that the organic composition would not increase proportionally to the technical composition. But he asserted that in general the technical composition would increase faster than the productivity of labor in Department 1, so that the "cheapening of the elements of constant capital" would merely slow down the increase in the organic composition, not eliminate it altogether (C.I, 773–4; C.III, 226; TSV.II, 415; TSV.III, 366–9; G. 770–3). Marx provided no rigorous proof of this conclusion, but instead regarded it to be "self-evident" and "an incontrovertible fact".

Most of the criticisms of Marx's argument have been directed toward the second point. There has been very little dispute that technical change will in general result in an increase in the technical composition, even though the technical composition cannot be precisely defined. The main issue has been whether such an increase in the technical composition will in general result in an increase in the organic composition (i.e. the "cheapening" issue). It is well known that the necessary and sufficient condition for an increase in the organic composition is that the technical composition must increase faster than the productivity of labor in Department 1:

$$TCC^* > A_1^* \tag{1.5}$$

where an asterisk beside a variable indicates the time rate of change of this variable. Marx's critics argue that he provided no reasons why this condition would in general be fulfilled. Thus the trend in the organic composition of capital is "indeterminate".

Mage (1963, pp. 153–4), Lebowitz (1982), and Perelman (1985) have separately pointed out that Marx did provide at least one reason why this condition might be fulfilled: that the productivity of labor in agriculture and mining (industries in Department 1 which produce raw and auxiliary materials for the rest of the economy) would in general increase slower than the aggregate productivity of labor because natural conditions retard the increase of productivity in these industries (C.III, 56–7, 116–17, 231–4, 255, 748; TSV.III, 368–9). Algebraically:

$$A_1^* < A^* \qquad (1.6)$$

If it is further assumed that the aggregate technical composition of capital increases at the same rate as the aggregate productivity of labor, i.e. that

$$TCC^* = A^* \qquad (1.7)$$

then the inequality (1.5) obviously follows.

A second possible cause of an increase in the organic composition of capital, not specifically mentioned by Marx, is that the productivity of labor in the rest of Department 1, which produces buildings and producer equipment, may increase slower than the aggregate productivity of labor. One reason why this might be true is that buildings and producer equipment are generally produced in smaller quantities, so that the economies of scale are smaller than in mass-produced consumer goods. Another reason might be that these means of production are constantly changing in design and are often made to special order, so that there is less "learning by doing". Of course, the fact that these products are frequently changing in design also means that it is very difficult to compare productivity in these industries in different periods and thus to define the rate of increase of productivity in these industries precisely. But leaving this difficulty aside, the possibility of a slower rate of increase of productivity in these industries seems to merit further study.

A third possible cause of an increase in the organic composition of capital besides slower productivity growth in these two parts of

Department 1 is that the technical composition of capital may increase faster than the aggregate productivity of labor, i.e. instead of the equality (1.7), we have:

$$TCC^* > A^* \tag{1.8}$$

In other words, productivity increases may require greater than proportional increases in the quantity of means of production per worker. In this case, the inequality (1.5) follows, even though $A_1^* = A^*$. Marx seemed to have assumed that (1.8) would in general be true, but he did not provide an explicit analysis of the relation between these two "real" ratios.

Thus a more complete (or "determinant") theory of the trend in the organic composition of capital requires a better understanding of these three key relationships just discussed: (i) the relation between the productivity of labor in the production of raw and auxiliary materials and the aggregate productivity of labor; (ii) the relation between the productivity of labor in the production of buildings and equipment and the aggregate productivity of labor; and (iii) the relation between the aggregate productivity of labor and the aggregate technical composition of capital. However, these relations seem to be more technological than economic in nature. There seems to be little that economic theory (Marxian or otherwise) can offer as an explanation of the likely trends in these relations.

An additional argument for an increasing organic composition of capital ignores the technical composition of capital (and the productivity of labor) altogether and focuses instead on the relation between the rate of capital accumulation and the rate of growth of the labor force (Mage, 1963, pp. 155–7; Yaffe, 1972, pp. 17–19; and Hunt, 1983, pp. 137–9). The organic composition of capital is by definition equal to the stock of constant capital divided by the annual flow of new-value ($OCC = C/N$). The annual flow of new-value is in turn equal to:

$$N = mHD(PL) \tag{1.9}$$

where m represents the value added per hour[9]
      H represents the number of hours per working day
      D represents the number of working days per year.
and PL represents the number of production workers employed.

If m, H, and D are all assumed to remain constant, then

$$N^* = (PL)^* \tag{1.10}$$

and

$$OCC^* = (C/PL)^* = C^* - (PL)^* \tag{1.11}$$

Thus the organic composition of capital will increase if and only if $C^* > (PL)^*$.

It is argued further that the essence of capitalism is the expansion of capital. Thus it is inherent in capitalism that capital will be expanded as rapidly as possible. By definition, the maximum rate of capital accumulation ($C^* = \Delta C/C$) is the rate of profit ($RP = S/C$), since $\Delta C < = S$. The actual rate of capital accumulation may be assumed to be some constant fraction (a) of the rate of profit, i.e. $C^* = a(RP)$. On the other hand, the rate of growth of the labor force is limited in the long run by the rate of increase of the population, which is generally considered to be approximately 2 per cent per year. Thus the organic composition of capital will increase if and only if:

$$a(RP) > .02$$

It is argued that for plausible values of a and RP, this inequality will be true. In other words, since it is generally possible for capital to expand faster than the labor force, it will expand faster and the organic composition of capital will increase.

My conclusion from the above is that the criticism of Marx that he failed to prove rigorously that the organic composition of capital must increase is largely justified. However, Marx did provide at least one possible reason why the organic composition might increase: that the productivity of labor in agriculture and mining would increase slower than in the rest of the economy. Furthermore, other possible (but not inevitable) causes of an increase in the organic composition not explicitly mentioned by Marx include: the productivity of labor in construction and producer goods industries might increase slower than in the rest of the economy; the quantity of means of production per worker might increase faster than the productivity of labor; and the expansionist drive of capitalism might cause capital to increase faster than the labor force. These possible causes certainly do not prove the necessity of an increasing organic composition of capital, but they are perhaps plausible reasons to expect that the organic composition will tend to increase. For the purposes of further analysis, it will be assumed in the next section that the organic composition of capital does increase, i.e. that *ceteris paribus* technological change causes the value composition of capital to increase.

1.2 COMPOSITION OF CAPITAL INCREASE FASTER THAN THE RATE OF SURPLUS-VALUE?

1.2.1 Marx's Argument

According to Marx's theory, the rate of profit (RP) is defined as the ratio of the annual flow of surplus-value (S) to the accumulated stock of constant capital invested (C),[10] and depends on the composition of capital (inversely) and the rate of surplus-value (RS) (directly):

$$RP = \frac{S}{C} = \frac{S/V}{C/V} = \frac{RS}{VCC} \tag{1.12}$$

With a constant rate of surplus-value, an increase in the composition of capital would obviously cause the rate of profit to fall. However, the negative effect of an increase in the composition of capital may be partially or totally offset by the positive effect of an increase in the rate of surplus-value.

According to Marx's theory, the trend in the rate of surplus-value depends primarily on the relative rates of increase of the productivity of labor in the production of wage-goods and the average real wage.[11] If the productivity of labor increases (due to technological change) faster than the average real wage, then the rate of surplus-value will increase (C.I, Part 4). Marx argued that this condition would in general be fulfilled primarily because of the downward pressure exerted on the real wage by a secularly increasing reserve army of unemployed workers (C.I, Part 7). Thus Marx argued that the rate of surplus-value would generally increase as a secular tendency.[12]

Thus technological change has "contradictory effects" on the two determinants of the rate of profit: it results in an increase in the composition of capital which has a negative effect on the rate of profit, but also causes an increase in the rate of surplus-value which has a positive effect on the rate of surplus value. Thus the net effect on the rate of profit depends on the relative rates of increase of the composition of capital and the rate of surplus-value. This is the second important issue mentioned in the introduction to this chapter: does the composition of capital increase faster than the rate of surplus-value?

Some critics have argued that Marx failed to take into account this tendency of the rate of surplus value to increase in his analysis of the rate of profit (e.g. Sweezy, 1968, chapter 6; Robinson, 1966, chapter 5). This criticism has been convincingly refuted by Rosdolsky (1977, pp. 398–411). He called attention to important passages in the Grundrisse and in Volumes 1 and 3 of *Capital* in which Marx explicitly took into account increases in the rate of surplus-value in his analysis of the rate of profit, arguing that these increases in the rate of surplus-value would be dominated by increases in the composition of capital, i.e. that increases in the rate of surplus-value may "check but not prevent" the decline in the rate of profit.

Marx's arguments in these passages were usually not expressed precisely in terms of the composition of capital and the rate of surplus-value, but rather in terms of the related variables of the stock of constant capital per production worker ($C_a = C/PL$) and the flow of surplus-value per worker per day ($S_a = S/D(PL)$):

$$RP = \frac{S}{C} = \frac{S/L}{C/PL} = \frac{DS_a}{C_a} \tag{1.13}$$

According to this formulation, since D is assumed to remain constant, the trend in the rate of profit depends on the relative rates of increase of S_a and C_a. It has already been demonstrated above (pp. 9–10) that, under Marx's assumptions of constant m, H, and D, the trend of C_a will be the same as the trend in the organic composition of capital.

S_a will have a slightly different trend from the rate of surplus-value, but these two variables will always change in the same direction. Since D is assumed to remain constant and $L^* = N^*$ (see above, pp. 9–10), S_a will always change proportionally to the ratio of surplus-value to new-value, which may be called the share of surplus-value ($SS = S/N$ and $S_a^* = SS^*$). The share of surplus-value will always change in the same direction as the rate of surplus-value, with the percentage change in the former always less than the percentage change in the latter.[13]

Thus, Marx's analysis of the relative rates of increase of constant capital per worker and surplus-value per worker per day is equivalent to an analysis of the relative rates of increase of the organic composition of capital and the share of surplus-value (rather than the rate of surplus value).[14] The rate of profit will decline if and only if C_a increases faster than S_a, or if the organic composition of capital increases faster than the share of surplus-value.

Marx's argument was essentially that S_a has an "insurmountable limit" – the length of the working-day – but C_a does not have a definite limit, and thus C_a will eventually increase faster than S_a. The main point in this argument is that the percentage increase in S_a that results from a given percentage increase in the productivity of labor would diminish over time, even if the real wage remains constant. This point follows straightforwardly from Marx's labor theory of value, and will be derived algebraically below (p. 14). Marx argued the point by means of numerical examples. For example, if the rate of surplus-value is 1.0, then a 100 per cent increase in the productivity of labor will reduce variable capital by half (assuming a constant real wage) and will increase S_a by 50 per cent. At a later stage of development, with a rate of surplus-value of 2.0, then an equivalent 100 per cent increase in the productivity of labor will once again reduce variable capital by half, but since surplus-value is already two-thirds of the value added produced in a given working day, S_a will increase only 17 per cent (see especially G. 333–41.)

However, Marx's argument in these passages is incomplete because he does not explicitly relate the other determinant of the rate of profit – C_a – to given percentage increases in productivity. In other passages, Marx suggested that the percentage increase in capital per worker would in general be less than the percentage increase in the productivity of labor (i.e. that the elasticity of C_a with respect to productivity would be less than one) (G. 346–7; C.III, 260). However, Marx does not attempt to determine this relation more precisely, nor determine whether it is likely to increase or decrease over time. The implication seems to be that since the percentage increase in S_a diminishes over time, it would sooner or later be smaller than the percentage increase in C_a. But there is no explicit analysis of the precise relationships involved nor of the precise point at which the percentage increase in S_a becomes smaller than the percentage increase in C_a.

1.2.2 Formal Model with Constant Real Wage

Marx's analysis can be formalized and extended in the following manner.[15] It follows from Marx's labor theory of value that S_a is positively related to the productivity of labor. More precisely, if the productivity of labor is defined as output per hour (A'), then:

$$
\begin{aligned}
S_a &= mL_s \\
&= m(H - L_n) \\
&= m(H - B/A')
\end{aligned}
\tag{1.14}
$$

where m and H are defined as above and:

L_s represents surplus-labor-time
L_n represents necessary-labor-time, and
B represents the average real wage of production workers.

If the productivity of labor is alternatively defined as output per worker per day (A), then $A' = A/H$ and substitution yields:

$$
S_a = mH(1 - BA^{-1})
\tag{1.15}
$$

The derivative of S_a with respect to A is:

$$
dS_a/dA = mHBA^{-2}
\tag{1.16}
$$

The elasticity of S_a with respect to A (E_{SA}) is then given by:

$$
E_{sa} = (dS_a/dA)/(S_a/A) = (mHBA^{-2})/(mH(A^{-1} - BA^{-2}))
\tag{1.17}
$$

which simplifies to:

$$
E_{sa} = B / (A - B)
\tag{1.18}
$$

From this equation we can see that the elasticity of S_a with respect to A varies inversely with A, i.e. that E_{sa} will diminish over time as productivity increases, as in Marx's numerical analysis above.

Further, since $L_n = B/A'$ or $B = A'L_n$, it follows that:

$$
\begin{aligned}
E_{sa} &= A'L_n / (A'H - A'L_n) \\
&= L_n / (H - L_n) = L_n/L_s = mL_n / mL_s = V/S \\
&= 1/RS
\end{aligned}
\tag{1.19}
$$

Thus we arrive at the interesting conclusion that *the elasticity of S_a with respect to productivity is equal to the inverse of the rate of surplus* *value*, which is a precise mathematical expression of Marx's intuition in the passages cited above.

Now we consider C_a, the other determinant of the rate of profit. Since C_a is assumed to increase as a result of technological change, C_a is also positively related to the productivity of labor. More precisely, in keeping with Marx (above), we assume that the percentage rate of change of C_a is equal to some positive (and constant) fraction (k) of the percentage rate of change of A (i.e. that changes in C_a are proportional to changes in A):

$$C_a^* = kA^* \tag{1.20}$$

where $0 < k < 1$. In this case, the elasticity of C_a with respect to A is equal to the constant k ($E_{sa} = k$).

The trend in the rate of profit will depend on the relative magnitudes of E_{sa} and E_{ca}. If $E_{sa} < E_{ca}$, then the rate of profit will decline, and vice versa. The relation between these two elasticities is illustrated in Figure 1.1.

Figure 1.1 E_{SA} and E_{CA} with constant real wages

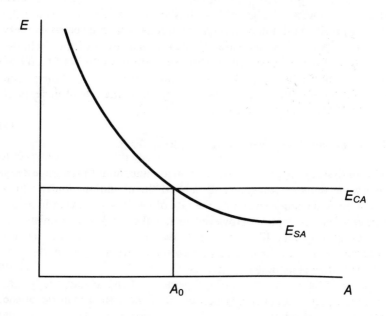

Moreover, we can determine what the rate of surplus-value will be at the point of intersection between the E_{sa} and E_{ca} curves; I call this the "break-even" rate of surplus-value, RS_0. At the point of intersection, $E_{sa} = E_{ca}$. Since $E_{sa} = 1/RS$ and $E_{ca} = k$, at the point of intersection we have:

$$1/RS_0 = k$$
or
$$RS_0 = 1/k \tag{1.21}$$

Thus the "break-even" rate of surplus-value varies inversely with k. If k were close to 1, then RS_0 would be close to 1, i.e. at a fairly early stage in the history of capitalism (Marx seemed to have assumed that the rate of surplus-value was approximately equal to 1 in the mid-nineteenth century.) On the other hand, if k were close to zero, then RS_0 would be very large, and probably so large that it has not yet been reached.

It should be emphasized that the above argument does not prove the necessity that technological change with a constant real wage will always cause the rate of profit to fall in all periods of time. Rather, this argument proves the possibility (based on Marx's assumptions) that technological change with a constant real wage might cause the rate of profit to fall under certain conditions, and that the probability of this negative effect increases over time as a result of the declining elasticity of the surplus-value per worker with respect to productivity. Whether or not this negative effect occurs during a given time period depends on the value of the parameter k, i.e. on the rate of increase of C_a (or of the organic composition of capital).

1.2.3 Formal Model with Increasing Real Wage

The analysis in the previous subsection assumed that the average daily real wage remains constant and derived the conditions under which technological change will cause the rate of profit to decline even under this extreme assumption. However, in actual capitalist economies, it is of course not very likely that the average real wage will remain constant. How are the conclusions of the above analysis modified if the real wage is assumed to increase?

Let us assume that the rate of increase of the average daily real wage is equal to a constant fraction (b) of the rate of increase of the productivity of labor:

$$B^* = bA^* \tag{1.22}$$

where $0 < b < 1$. Integration of this equation yields:

$$B = cA^b \tag{1.23}$$

where c is the factor of proportionality based on the initial values of B and A at the beginning of the period of analysis.

In this case, S_a is equal to:

$$S_a = mH(1 - B/A) = mH(1 - cA^{b-1}) \tag{1.24}$$

and the derivative of S_a with respect of A is:

$$dS_a/dA = (1-b)mHcA^{b-2} \tag{1.25}$$

and the elasticity of S_a with respect to A is:

$$E_{sa} = (1 - b)\,(c/(A^{1-b} - c)) \tag{1.26}$$

It can be seen from this equation that E_{sa} varies inversely with the productivity of labor as in the constant real wage case. We can also see that E_{sa} in this increasing real wage case will always be less than E_{sa} in constant real wage case $(= B/(A - B))$, since $(1 - b) < 1$. This is illustrated in Figure 1.2 by a leftward shift in the E_{sa} curve.

Partial differentiation of E_{sa} with respect to b shows that E_{sa} varies inversely with b, as one would expect. If b were close to zero, then E_{sa} would be close to $B/(A - B)$ as in the constant real wage case. At the other extreme, if b were close to 1 (i.e. the rate of increase of the real wage almost equal to the rate of increase of productivity), then E_{sa} would be close to zero (i.e. almost no increase in S_a as a result of increases in productivity).

Substitution of $c = BA^{-b}$ into equation (1.26) and further simplification yields:

$$E_{sa} = (1 - b)\,(B/(A - B)) \tag{1.27}$$

Since it was shown above that $B/(A - B) = 1/RS$, this last equation is equivalent to:

$$E_{sa} = (1 - b)\,(1/RS) \tag{1.28}$$

We can see from this equation that E_{sa} is smaller in this case than in the constant real wage case $(= 1/RS;$ see equation 1.19).

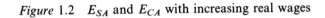

Figure 1.2 E_{SA} and E_{CA} with increasing real wages

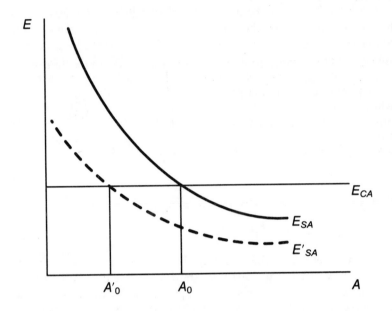

Finally, we can determine for this increasing real wage case the "break-even" rate of surplus-value at the point of intersection between the E_{sa} and E_{ca} curves, where $E_{sa} = E_{ca}$:

$$(1 - b)(1/RS_0) = k$$

or

$$RS_0 = (1 - b)/k \qquad (1.29)$$

We can see from this equation that RS_0 is smaller in this case than in the constant real wage case. This is illustrated in Figure 1.2 by the shift to the left in A_0 (a smaller RS_0 is associated with a lower level of productivity). In general, we can see that RS_0 varies inversely with b as well as k. If b were close to zero, then RS_0 would be close to $1/k$, as in the constant real wage case. At the other extreme, if b were close to one and k were not close to 0, then RS_0 would be close to zero. In other words, if the real wage increased almost as fast as productivity and k were not close to 0, then the "break-even" rate of surplus-value (or level of productivity) would occur at a very early stage in the history of capitalism, after which further technological change would cause the rate of profit to decline.

Table 1.1 shows the "break-even" rate of surplus value for various hypothetical values of the parameters k and b in equation (1.29). Suppose, for example, that the value of b were 0.50, i.e. that real wages increase half as fast as the productivity of labor. If, at the same time, k were fairly low (e.g. $k = 0.25$, or capital per worker increases 25 per cent as fast as the productivity of labor), then $RS_0 = 2.00$, which is probably close to the current rate of surplus value. On the other hand, if k were higher (e.g. $k = 0.50$), then RS_0 would be only 1.00, a rate of surplus value which was probably reached in the nineteenth century.

Table 1.1   "Break-even" rate of surplus-value for different values of k and b

		k			
		0.10	0.25	0.50	0.75
	0.25	7.50	3.00	1.50	1.00
b	0.50	5.00	2.00	1.00	0.67
	0.75	2.50	1.00	0.50	0.33

The main conclusion of the above analysis is that technological change which increases the composition of capital will *eventually* (but perhaps only in the very long run) cause the rate of profit to decline, because the elasticity of surplus value per worker with respect to productivity diminishes over time and the elasticity of capital per worker with respect to productivity is assumed to remain more or less constant. The precise point at which the rate of profit will start to decline depends on the values of the parameters k and b.

We have assumed throughout the above analysis that the parameters k and b remain constant, at least over a long-wave period of expansion. However, it may be that these parameters actually exhibit "long-wave cycles". For example, these parameters may be characteristically low during the early decades of a long wave period of expansion, and then rise during the later decades, for various reasons which remain largely unknown at this time. Changes in the parameters k and b would obviously change the "break-even" rate of surplus-value, and thus change the trend in the rate of profit.

Unfortunately, we know very little at this time about the determinants of the values of the parameters k and b, especially k. Thus the net effect of technological change on the rate of profit according to Marxian theory remains very much "indeterminate." But some progress had been made in this analysis: We have identified more precisely the factors which determine the "break-even" level of productivity, at which point further technological change would cause the rate of profit to decline.

1.3 OKISHIO'S THEOREM

1.3.1 The Theorem

A more recent criticism of Marx's theory of the falling rate of profit is different from the traditional criticisms discussed above. It does not explicitly consider the trends in the composition of capital and the rate of surplus value, but instead analyzes the rate of profit in terms of a linear production model, whereby the rate of profit is determined simultaneously with the prices of commodities by a system of equations which represent the technical conditions of production in each industry. This criticism was actually initiated by Okishio in 1961 (and in some respects as far back as 1907 by Bortkiewitz), but began to be widely discussed only in the 1970s. The most influential articles along these lines have been Roemer (1977 and 1979) and van Parijs (1980). Van Parijs considers this criticism so devastating that it "deprives all other criticisms of their relevance".

The original Okishio Theorem was based on two important restrictive assumptions: that the real wage remains constant and the capital consists only 'of circulating capital (i.e. no fixed capital).[16] The theorem starts from the point of view of individual capitalists and asks the question: under what conditions would an individual capitalist introduce new technology? In other words, what is the "decision rule" of capitalists with regard to the introduction of new technology? In the assumed case of only circulating capital, the capitalists' "decision rule" is that new technology would be introduced only if it reduces the costs of production at prevailing prices, thus enabling the innovating capitalist to earn temporary super profits. Okishio proves, using linear algebra, that technological change which satisfies this condition will never lower the equilibrium (general) rate of profit, and will raise the equilibrium rate of profit if the innovation takes place in a "basic goods" industry.

Roemer (1979) generalized Okishio's Theorem to two special cases of fixed capital (while maintaining the assumption of a constant real wage): one in which fixed capital lasts forever (i.e. does not depreciate), and the other in which the rate of profit analyzed is not the actual one but is instead the "von Neumann rate of profit" (the minimum rate for which there exists a positive price vector which satisfies a generalized von Neumann equation system). Roemer assumes that capitalists have a somewhat different decision rule in the case of fixed capital: they introduce new technology only if it raises their transitional rate of profit. This condition is not the same as the "lower cost" criterion in the fixed capital case, because it is possible to have technological change which simultaneously reduces per unit costs and increases per unit investment, the latter causing the transitional rate of profit to decline. Roemer proves that if all goods are "basic goods", then technological change with fixed capital which satisfies the "higher transitional rate of profit" criterion will always raise the equilibrium rate of profit, as long as the real wage remains constant.

1.3.2 Criticisms

The first set of criticisms of the Okishio Theorem concerns the assumption of a constant real wage. Laibman (1982a) argues that a constant rate of exploitation should instead be assumed because the latter is a better indicator of "class struggle neutrality". Lipietz (1986) also argues that a constant rate of exploitation should be assumed because a constant real wage would result in realization problems, quite apart from the falling rate of profit. These criticisms implicitly or explicitly acknowledge that the Okishio Theorem is valid on its own assumptions, but argue that the assumption of a constant real wage is unrealistic. Laibman proves (for both the circulating capital case and the non-depreciating fixed capital case) that, with a constant rate of exploitation, technological change which satisfies the "lower cost" criterion may reduce the equilibrium rate of profit. Lipietz proves (for the circulating capital only case) that, with a constant rate of exploitation, technological change which satisfies the "lower cost" criterion and is in addition labor saving (or capital using) will always reduce the equilibrium rate of profit.

Foley (1986b, p. 139) argues that most capitalist economies are characterized neither by constant real wages nor by a constant rate of surplus-value, but instead fall within an "intermediate range" in which the real wage increases, but slower than productivity increases, so that the rate of surplus-value also increases. Foley contends that for these actual capitalist economies "it is not possible to say *a priori* whether the process of technological change will raise or lower the profit rate". Under these circumstances, the effect of technological change on the rate of profit becomes a question which can be answered only by empirical investigation.

The second set of criticisms has been directed toward Roemer's generalization of the Okishio Theorem with reference to the case of fixed capital. Shaikh (1978a and 1980) argues that the decision rule of capitalists in the fixed capital case is not the "higher transitional rate of profit" criterion, but is instead the "lower cost" criterion. Shaikh argues that intense ("warlike") competition among capitalists forces them to implement new technology which lowers per unit costs, even though this new technology might lower their transitional rate of profit because cost-reducing innovations require large amounts of investment in fixed capital. Capitalists in effect have no choice in this matter; in order to survive the competitive struggle, they must do whatever is necessary to lower production costs.[17] Shaikh shows by means of a numerical example that if the "lower cost" criterion is assumed, then it is possible that technological change which satisfies this condition will lower the innovating capitalist's transitional rate of profit, and thus will presumably lower the equilibrium rate of profit (although Shaikh does not demonstrate this last point).

Alberro and Persky (1981) argue that even if the "higher transitional rate of profit" criterion is adopted so that technological change increases the equilibrium rate of profit, the actual rate of profit might still decline because the actual rate which results might be lower than the new equilibrium rate of profit due to unanticipated technological change – which causes recently implemented technology to be scrapped (or at least to be devalued) prematurely. Thus the expected stream of future profits on which the new equilibrium rate of profit is based never materializes, and the actual rate of profit is lower than the equilibrium rate of profit.

A similar criticism is made by Reuten and Williams (1989), who emphasize that Roemer's generalization about fixed capital assumes that *all* firms adopt the new more productive technique. The above criticisms of Roemer also implicitly make this assumption. However, Reuten and Williams argue that, in the actual capitalist economy, capital has already been invested in the existing technology and will be lost if this is scrapped prematurely and the new technology adopted. Under these conditions, firms will adopt the new technology only if the expected increase in the rate of profit is greater than the losses which would result from the early obsolescence of the old technology. Firms for which this condition is not satisfied will not innovate and will suffer a decline in their rate of profit, due to their relatively lower productivity. Reuten and Williams argue that the net result of such partial innovation is that the average rate of profit in a given industry and in the economy as a whole tends to decline (even though the rate of profit increases for the innovating firms).

Finally, Salvadori (1981) argues that Roemer's proofs for the cases of non-depreciating fixed capital and the von Neumann rate of profit do not apply to depreciating capital and the actual rate of profit. Salvadori points out that "it is not surprising that technical change cannot lower the von Neumann rate of profit since such change reduces the set of which the von Neumann rate of profit is the minimum" (ibid., p. 60). Salvadori presents a numerical example for the case of depreciating fixed capital and generalized joint production in which the actual rate of profit declines as a result of technical change, even with a constant real wage.

The outcome of this debate so far seems to be that Okishio's Theorem is valid on its own assumptions, but that these assumptions are generally not valid for actual capitalist economies, especially the assumption of a constant real wage and the restricted cases of fixed capital.

1.3.3 Evaluation

The present author is in general agreement with the criticisms of the Okishio Theorem reviewed in the previous subsection, primarily that its assumptions are not valid for actual capitalist economies. We will see in Chapter 3 below that the postwar US economy fell within Foley's "intermediate range", characterized by both increasing real wages and an increasing rate of surplus-value, for which the Okishio Theorem and its derivatives make no definite prediction about the effect of technological change on the rate of profit. Thus the empirical results presented in Chapter 3 should provide valuable empirical evidence concerning the effect of technological change on the rate of profit in these "intermediate" circumstances.

However, there remains from the above discussion the following question, which although it has little or no empirical significance does seem to be theoretically significant: in the case of a constant real wage, is it at least theoretically possible for technological change to cause the rate of profit to fall? The analysis presented in section 1.2.2 above suggests an affirmative answer to this question, i.e. that there are some values for the parameter k for which technological change with a constant real wage will eventually cause the rate of profit to fall. However, the Okishio Theorem discussed in section 1.3.1 concludes that the answer to this question is negative under all circumstances.

The reason for these contradictory conclusions may be that the Okishio Theorem is not generalisable in the case of fixed capital, as the critics discussed above argue. Another possible and more fundamental reason for these contradictory conclusions may be that Marx's theory cannot be accurately represented by linear production models, as utilized in the Okishio debate. If so, then conclusions reached using linear production models do not necessarily apply to Marx's theory. An exploration of this possibility would require a thorough discussion of a number of fundamental methodological issues, such as: (i) whether the aggregate amount of profit (or surplus-value) in the economy as a whole is determined prior or subsequent to the determination of the amount of profit in each industry; (ii) whether the aggregate rate of profit is determined prior to or simultaneously with the determination of the prices of individual commodities; and (iii) whether Marx's analysis of the determination of prices of production (in C.III, Part 2) is "incomplete" and "inconsistent", as charged by Bortkiewitz in 1907 and many others since then.[18] Such an examination would require a book by itself. I intend to return to these controversies in subsequent work.

1.4 CONCLUSION

The main conclusion of this chapter is that Marx's theory does not provide a definite prediction concerning the trend in the rate of profit. However, Marx's theory does provide a number of plausible reasons why the rate of profit might decline under certain historical conditions.[19] Whether or not Marx's theory is valid for a particular historical period (such as the post-World War II period) thus becomes an empirical question.

The next two chapters are concerned with this empirical question: is Marx's theory of the falling rate of profit valid for the postwar US economy? Estimates of the rate of profit and its two proximate determinants, the rate of surplus-value and the composition of capital, will be presented and analyzed in Chapter 3 in order to determine whether or not the trends in these variables were in the directions suggested by Marx's theory. First, however, we must examine the conceptual issues involved in the derivation of estimates of these Marxian variables. Chapter 2 discusses these conceptual issues.

2 Conceptual Issues in the Estimation of the Marxian Variables

We have seen in Chapter 1 that according to Marx's theory, the rate of profit depends on the composition of capital and the rate of surplus-value, and that these three variables are defined in terms of three fundamental magnitudes: constant capital, variable capital, and surplus-value. This chapter discusses the major conceptual issues involved in the estimation of these fundamental Marxian magnitudes. My interpretation of these issues will be contrasted with the interpretation of Weisskopf and Wolff in their earlier empirical studies of the Marxian variables. In Chapter 3, the effect of the different interpretations of these conceptual issues on the trends of the Marxian ratios will be examined.

There are five major conceptual issues involved in the precise definition of Marx's concepts of constant capital, variable capital, and surplus value and thus in the estimation of the three Marxian ratios. These five issues may be briefly stated as follows:

1. Do the concepts of constant capital, variable capital, and surplus-value refer to observable quantities of *money* (or prices) or to observable quantities of *labor*?
2. Do the concepts of constant capital and variable capital refer only to *capitalist production*, or also to various forms of *non-capitalist production* (mainly government production, but also household production and institutional production)?
3. Do the concepts of constant capital and variable capital refer only to the capital invested in *production activities* in capitalist enterprises or also to the capital invested in *non-production activities*?
4. Does the concept of constant capital include the value of *residential housing*?
5. Are the *taxes paid by workers* out of their wages a part of variable capital or surplus-value?

These five conceptual issues will be discussed in turn in the following sections.

26

2.1 MONEY OR LABOR UNITS

The first issue involved in the estimation of the Marxian variables is whether the observable reality to which Marx's concepts of constant capital, variable capital, and surplus-value refer are quantities of money or quantities of labor. I argue that these Marxian concepts refer to observable quantities of money. These concepts are components of the more general concept of capital. Thus the precise definitions of these components follow from the definition of the general concept of capital.

The concept of capital is central to Marx's theory, as the title of his book suggests. Marx emphasized the fundamental importance of the concept of capital in the following passage:

> The exact development of the concept of capital is necessary, since it is the fundamental concept of modern economics, just as capital itself, whose abstract, reflected image is its concept, is the foundation of bourgeois society. The sharp formulation of the basic presuppositions of the relation must bring out all the contradictions of bourgeois production, as well as the boundary, where it drives beyond itself. (G. 331)[1]

Marx introduced his concept of capital in part 2 of volume 1 of *Capital* which is entitled "The Transformation of Money into Capital". As this title suggests, Marx's concept of capital is defined in terms of money. In chapter 4 ("The General Formula for Capital"), Marx defines capital as money which passes through its own characteristic form of circulation which distinguishes money as capital from money as a mere means of exchange.

The first distinguishing characteristic of money which functions as capital is that the commodities purchased with this money are later resold (in one form or another) in order to recover the original money expended. In Marx's words, the money originally "thrown into circulation" is later "withdrawn from circulation" through the sale of commodities. By contrast, money which functions as a mere means of exchange is used to purchase commodities which are consumed by the buyer; therefore, this money is not later recovered through the sale of commodities. The process undergone by money which functions as capital was described by Marx as "buying in order to sell" and was expressed symbolically as $M-C-M$, where M stands for money, C for commodities, and $(-)$ for an act of exchange between money and commodities:

> $M–C–M$, the transformation of money into commodities, and the reconversion of commodities into money: buying in order to sell. Money which describes the latter course in its movement is transformed into capital, and from the point of view of its function, already is capital. (C.I, 248)

The second distinguishing characteristic of money which functions as capital is that the sum of money recovered through the sale of commodities is greater than the original sum of money expended. More money is withdrawn from circulation than was thrown into it in the beginning. Marx described the process through which money is transformed into capital more completely as "buying in order to sell dearer" and expressed this process symbolically as $M–C–M'$, where $M' = M + \Delta M$: 'The cotton originally bought for \$100 is for example resold at \$100 + \$10, i.e. \$110. The complete form of this process is therefore $M–C–M'$, where $M' = M + \Delta M$, i.e. the original sum advanced plus an increment' (C.I, 251).[2]

Thus we see that Marx's concept of capital is defined in terms of money, as money expended in order to make more money.[3] Similarly, the concepts of constant capital, variable capital, and surplus-value are defined as the theoretically significant components of the total sum of money which functions as capital. In chapter 4, Marx defines the concept of surplus-value as the increment of money (ΔM) withdrawn from circulation over and above the initial sum of money thrown into circulation: "This increment or excess over the original value I call 'surplus-value.' The value originally advanced, therefore, not only remains intact while in circulation, but increases its magnitude, adds to itself, or is valorized. And this movement converts it into capital" (C.I, 251–2).[4]

Similarly, the concepts of constant capital and variable capital are defined in chapter 8 of volume 1 as two components of the initial sum of money which is invested as capital. Constant capital is defined as the sum of money which is used to purchase the means of production (buildings, equipment, raw and auxiliary materials), while variable capital is defined as the sum of money which is used to purchase labor-power.

This distinction between constant capital and variable capital is derived from Marx's theory of value and surplus-value. According to this theory, the money used to purchase the means of production is transferred to the price of the final product (either all in one period in the case of raw and auxiliary materials, or over a number of periods in the case of buildings and equipment). However, no surplus-value is produced as a result of this transfer of a given sum of money. In Marx's words, the sum of money used to purchase the means of production "does not undergo any quantitative alteration in the process of production". For this reason, Marx called this component of the initial money-capital "constant" capital.

On the other hand, the money used to purchase labor-power is not transferred to the price of the product. Instead, this sum of money is replaced in the process of production by labor itself, i.e. by a "value creating power". This labor produces value which is greater than the sum of money used to purchase labor-power. In this way, the sum of money exchanged for labor-power "does undergo a quantitative alteration of value in the process of production". For this reason, Marx called this second component of the initial money-capital "variable" capital.[5]

Both concepts of constant capital and variable capital may be considered either as a stock of advanced capital or as a flow of capital consumed during a given period of production. Each of these concepts is relevant to different aspects of Marx's theory. The flow of constant capital is relevant to the determination of the price of commodities, since this magnitude becomes one component of the price of commodities. The flow of variable capital is relevant to the determination of the amount of surplus value, since this latter amount is equal to the difference between the new-value component of the price of commodities and the variable capital consumed in the production of these commodities. Finally, the stocks of constant capital and variable capital are relevant to the determination of the rate of profit, since the sum of these amounts is the denominator in the rate of profit.[6]

It should also be noted that both the stock and the flow of constant capital is evaluated in Marx's theory in terms of the current replacement cost of the means of production, not in terms of the actual historical cost of these means of production. In other words, constant capital is evaluated in terms of the amount of money that would have to be invested during the current period to purchase the existing means of production, not the actual amount of money spent to purchase these means of production in past periods. If the average productivity of labor in the production of the means of production increases or decreases, or if the value of money increases of decreases, then the replacement cost of the means of production will decrease or increase correspondingly, and so will the current value of the stock and flow of constant capital (C.I, 317–19; C.III, 139–41; TSV.II, 200–3 and 427–8).

Thus I conclude that Marx's concepts of constant capital, variable capital, and surplus-value are defined in terms of sums of money which function as capital. In principle, these concepts correspond to entries in the income statements and balance sheets of capitalist firms. Foley (1982a, 1982b) also emphasizes the correspondence between Marx's concepts of capital and its components and the money magnitudes in the financial accounts of capitalist firms.

Wolff argues, to the contrary, following the Sraffa-based interpretation of Marx's theory, that the observable phenomena to which Marx's concepts of constant capital, variable capital, and surplus-value refer are quantities of labor contained in different bundles of goods. Specifically, Wolff argues that constant capital refers to observable quantities of labor contained in producer-goods, that variable capital refers to observable quantities of labor contained in wage-goods, and that surplus value refers to observable quantities of labor contained in surplus-goods. Therefore, according to Wolff, the estimation of the key Marxian variables involves the derivation of estimates of the quantities of labor contained in these three bundles of goods.

I recognize, of course, that quantities of labor play an important role in Marx's theory. Indeed, Marx's theory of value and surplus value is based on the fundamental assumption that the quantities of money which circulate as capital are determined fundamentally by the quantities of labor contained in commodities (C.I, chapter 1). However, these quantities of labor which are assumed to determine quantities of money or prices are defined by Marx in units of homogeneous *abstract labor*, which is not directly observable as such. Abstract labor is defined by Marx to be labor without special skills and of average intensity (C.I, chapter 1.1 and 1.2; Rubin, 1972, chapters 14–15; Sweezy, 1968, chapter 3). By contrast, the actual concrete labor which can be observed and counted within capitalist enterprises consists of many different levels of skills and is of varying degrees of intensity. Therefore, the quantities of actual labor required to produce commodities will in general not be equal to the quantity of abstract labor contained in commodities, and the former may not even be a good approximation of the latter.

Wolff's estimates of the quantities of labor contained in producer-goods, wage-goods, and surplus-goods are in terms of quantities of actual, concrete labor. No attempt is made to convert quantities of actual labor, with different skills and levels of intensity, into equivalent quantities of abstract labor. One hour of each person employed is counted as equivalent to one hour of all other persons employed. Thus I argue that Wolff's estimates are not reliable estimates of the quantities of abstract labor contained in commodities.

Indeed, it even appears to be impossible in principle to derive reliable estimates of quantities of abstract labor. In order to do so, one would need one set of reduction coefficients that would convert quantities of different types of skilled labor into equivalent quantities of unskilled labor, and another set of reduction coefficients that would convert quantities of labor of above or below average intensity into equivalent quantities of labor of average intensity. Marx provided no such sets of reduction coefficients. Instead, he simply took these reduction coefficients as given but unknown (C.I, chapter 1.1 and 1.2), as had Smith and Ricardo before him (Smith, 1965, chapter 8; Ricardo, 1977, chapter 1). A number of Marxist economists since Marx have adopted a rule for converting skilled labor into unskilled labor first suggested by Hilferding which is based on the labor required to train skilled labor (Hilferding, 1949, chapter 1; Rubin, 1972, chapter 15; Sweezy, 1968, chapter 3; Rowthorn, 1974; Roncaglia, 1974). However, this rule has been criticized by other Marxist economists (Rosdolsky, 1977, chapter 31; Tortasada, 1977; Harvey 1985) and no general consensus has emerged. No one has yet suggested reliable ways to measure different intensities of labor. Thus it appears to be impossible in principle to convert observable quantities of actual labor into equivalent quantities of abstract labor for purposes of estimation. If this is true, then Marx's variables cannot be estimated in terms of quantities of abstract labor, but only in terms of quantities of money, which Marx argued is the "necessary form of appearance" of quantities of abstract labor (C.I, chapter 1.3; Rosdolsky, 1977, chapter 5; Elson, 1979; Weeks, 1981, chapters 1 and 2; de Vroey, 1981; Lipietz, 1982a, 1986; Mohun, 1984–5; Foley, 1986b, chapter 2). In any case, whether or not abstract labor is unobservable in principle, Wolff's estimates of quantities of actual labor are not reliable estimates of quantities of abstract labor.

Weisskopf adopts an intermediate interpretation of this issue, as do many others. He argues that Marx's concepts most rigorously refer to observable quantities of labor, but that estimates in terms of money are none the less reliable estimates of these concepts, and are much easier to derive. Thus, Weisskopf's estimates are in terms of money, as are mine.

2.2 NON-CAPITALIST PRODUCTION

The second issue involved in the estimation of the Marxian variables is whether the concepts of constant capital and variable capital refer only to capitalist production, or also include the sums of money expended in non-capitalist forms of production to purchase means of production and labor-power. The main form of non-capitalist production in Marx's time was household production, i.e. the production of household services by domestic servants. Today, of course, the main form of non-capitalist production is government production, i.e. the production of public services by government employees.[7] Non-profit institutions are another form of non-capitalist production in the contemporary US economy.

It follows directly from Marx's definition of capital presented in the preceding section that the sums of money used to purchase means of production and labor-power in non-capitalist forms of production are not capital, because both distinguishing features of capital discussed above are missing in the case of non-capitalist production. In the first place, these sums of money are not recovered through the sale of commodities because the products produced are not sold on the market (i.e. are not "commodities" in Marx's sense). More important-ly, no increment of money or profit is recovered in these non-capitalist forms of production. In other words, these sums of money do not undergo the unique process of circulation which is characteristic of capital. In order to distinguish these forms of money expended in non-capitalist forms of production from capital, Marx referred to these sums of money as "revenue" (C.I, 1038–49; TSV.I, 389–414; Mattick, 1969; Yaffe, 1972; Cogoy, 1987). Since these sums of money are not capital, they obviously are not constant capital and variable capital.

Wolff (1987b) maintains that a defensible argument can be made for including the government sector in the definitions of constant capital and variable capital, even though he acknowledges that this argument is not decisive. Wolff offers several reasons for including the government sector: (i) Many government services are the same as services produced by capitalist enterprises (e.g. health, education, utilities, etc.); (ii) Governments in effect "sell" their services because they are financed by taxes, even though the recipients of the services are not always the payers of the taxes, at least not in the same proportions; and (iii) Governments expand just like capitalist enter-prises. Wolff acknowledges that an argument against including the government sector is that no profit is obtained in this sector. He concludes that "there is no definitive answer to whether government capital should be included" in the definition of capital. In this most recent paper, Wolff presents two sets of estimates of constant capital and variable capital, one which includes the government sector and another which excludes it. In earlier papers, Wolff presented only one set of estimates which included the government sector.

I argue, to the contrary, that according to Marx's definition of capital in *Capital*, there is no ambiguity: capital is money expended in order to make more money. If more money is not the purpose and the normal outcome of the expenditure of money, then this money does not function as capital. None of the arguments advanced by Wolff alters this fundamental distinction. One could also dispute Wolff's argument that the financing of government services by taxes is essentially the same as a market exchange, but this is unnecessary because the fundamental distinction of profit/no-profit remains in any case. Marx's reason for defining capital in this precise way was that the main purpose of his theory was to explain how the expenditure of money as capital led to the recovery of a greater sum of money, and to relate the amount of profit recovered to the amount of capital expended, i.e. to determine the magnitude and the rate of profit. If the definition of capital were broadened to include government expenditures, then the rate of profit would relate the amount of profit in part to money which plays no role in the generation of this profit.

Wolff (1987b) also makes a similar argument for including the non-profit institutions sector of the economy in the definitions of constant capital and variable capital, and in this case all the estimates he presents include the non-profit institutions sector. My response is similar to the case of the government sector. Even though non-profit institutions usually sell their products as commodities and through these sales recover the money expended to purchase means of production and labor-power (unlike government agencies), these institutions none the less do not recover more money than was expended, i.e. they do not recover a profit (by definition). Thus the money expended by these non-profit institutions is not capital. Again, if the definition of capital were broadened to include the expenditures by non-profit institutions, then the denominator of the rate of profit would include money which played no role in the generation of profit, the numerator in the rate of profit.

Wolff's estimates of variable capital also include the household sector of the economy, although no argument is presented for this interpretation.

Weisskopf does not present an explicit discussion of this issue, but his estimates of constant capital and variable capital do not include sums of money expended in these non-capitalist forms of production, similar to my estimates.

2.3 NON-PRODUCTION CAPITAL (PRODUCTIVE LABOR/ UNPRODUCTIVE LABOR)

The third issue involved in the estimation of the Marxian variables is whether the concepts of constant capital and variable capital refer to all the capital invested in capitalist enterprises or instead refer only to the capital invested in production activities. I argue that Marx's concepts of constant capital and variable capital refer only to the capital invested in *production activities*, where "production" is defined fairly broadly to include such activities as transportation and storage. However, the definition of "production" specifically does not include the following two types of activities within capitalist enterprises:

1. *Circulation activities* related to the exchange of commodities and money, including such functions as sales, purchasing, accounting, check processing, advertising, debt/credit relations, insurance, warranties, legal counsel, securities exchange, etc.
2. *Supervisory activities* related to the control and surveillance of the labor of production workers, including such functions as the transmission of orders, the direct supervision of production workers, the supervision of supervisors, etc. up to top management, the creation and processing of production and payroll records for individuals and groups of employees, etc.

This distinction between production and non-production activities within capitalist enterprises is based on Marx's theory of value and surplus-value. Marx assumed that the value of commodities is determined by the quantity of past and current abstract labor which is required to *produce* these commodities, not including the labor and materials required to perform the functions of circulation and supervision (C.I, chapter 1). From this fundamental assumption, it follows that the past labor contained in the means of production and consumed in the production process adds to the value of the commodities produced, and the current labor employed in production both adds to the value of the commodities and produces surplus-value (C.I, chapter

7). Since, according to this theory, the capital invested in the material and labor inputs to capitalist production results in the production of value and surplus-value, Marx referred to this capital as "productive capital".

However, according to Marx's theory, the (past and current) labor required to perform the non-production functions of circulation and supervision, although entirely necessary within the capitalist mode of production, none the less do not add to the value of commodities and hence do not result in the production of surplus-value.

According to Marx, circulation labor does not add to the value of commodities because commodities enter the process of circulation with their values already determined (by the labor required to produce them). The function of circulation labor is to transform the physical state of existence of this predetermined amount of value, from the price of commodities to money, or vice versa. No additional value is produced in this transformation of a given amount of value (C.I, chapters 3 and 5; C.II, chapter 6; C.III, chapter 17; MECW. 30, 21–33).

> [C]ommodities enter the process of exchange with a determinate price (Cr. 87).

> The value of a commodity is expressed in its price before it enters into circulation, and it is therefore a pre-condition of circulation, not its result . . . If we consider this in the abstract . . . all that happens in exchange . . . is a metamorphosis, a mere change in the form of the commodity . . . This change of form does not imply any change in the magnitude of the value . . . This form exists first as the price of the commodity offered for sale, then as an actual sum of money, which was, however, already expressed in the price, and lastly as the price of an equivalent commodity. (C.I, 260)

> The general law is that all costs of circulation which arise only from changes in the form of commodities do not add to their value. They are merely expenses incurred in the realization of value or its conversion from one form into another. (C.II, 225–6)

Also according to Marx, supervisory labor does not add to the value of commodities because this labor is not technically necessary for production, but instead is made necessary because of the antagonistic relation between capitalists and workers over the intensity of the labor of workers (C.I, 448–51; C.III, 382–90; TSV.III, 353–61 and 495–506; MECW. 30, 262, 387, 413). Marx referred to supervisory labor, which is necessary to ensure that production workers maintain an acceptable level of intensity of labor, as the "labor of exploiting", as opposed to "exploited labor". In Marx's discussion of Smith's theory of value, he remarked that Smith had already refuted the idea that the labor of supervision adds to the value of commodities (TSV.I, 81).

> The exploitation of labor costs labor. Insofar as the labor performed by the industrial capitalist is rendered necessary only because of the contradiction between capital and labor, it enters into the cost of his overseers . . . These costs, like the greater part of the trading expenses, belong to the incidental expenses of capitalist production. (TSV.III, 355–6)

Marx acknowledged that some part of the labor of managers and supervisors is technically necessary for production to the extent that they perform the functions of planning and coordinating production activities. This part of the labor of managers and supervisors Marx considered to be productive labor which produces value and surplus-value. However, Marx argued that only a small percentage of the labor of managers and supervisors is devoted to these productive functions and that most of their labor is devoted instead to the unproductive function of controlling the labor of production workers. Marx pointed to the examples of cooperative factories in England, which had largely eliminated managers and supervisors, to demonstrate how little of their labor is actually necessary for production (C.I, 448–50; C.III, 383–8; TSV.III, 355–6 and 495–506).

Capital must, of course, be invested in both material and labor to carry out the unproductive functions of circulation and supervision, but this capital none the less does not result in the production of value and surplus-value. For this reason, Marx referred to the capital invested in these unproductive functions as "unproductive capital" (C.II, part 1; TSV.I, addendum 12). Since this unproductive capital produces no value, it cannot be recovered out of value which it produces. Instead, according to Marx's theory, this unproductive capital is recovered, together with a profit, out of the surplus-value produced by productive labor employed in capitalist production (C.III, chapter 17).

The capital spent to meet those costs (including the labor done under its control) belongs under the *faux frais* of capitalist production. They must be replaced from the surplus-value and constitute, as far as the entire capitalist class is concerned, a deduction from the surplus-value. (C.II, 226)

Marx's concepts of productive capital and unproductive capital are parallel to his more widely discussed concepts of productive labor and unproductive labor. Productive labor is labor employed in capitalist production which produces value and surplus-value. Unproductive labor is labor employed in the unproductive functions of circulation and supervision within capitalist enterprises (Rubin, 1972, chapter 19; Gillman, 1958; Mage, 1963; Gough, 1972; Yaffe, 1973; Braverman, 1974, chapter 19; Shaikh, 1978b; Leadbeater, 1985; Moseley, 1982, chapter 4; Foley, 1986b).[8, 9] Criticisms of Marx's concepts of productive labor and unproductive labor are considered in the Appendix to this chapter.

It follows from the above definitions of productive capital and unproductive capital that the concepts of constant capital and variable capital refer only to productive capital. It was shown above that the distinction between constant capital and variable capital is derived from the different roles performed by the means of production and the labor-power utilized in capitalist production in the creation of value and surplus-value. The means of production transfer their value to the value of the products; hence the capital used to purchase these means of production is called constant capital. On the other hand, the labor utilized in capitalist production creates additional value which is the source of surplus-value; hence the capital used to purchase labor-power is called variable capital.

This distinction obviously does not apply to the capital which is not exchanged for the inputs to production. The value of the means of circulation and the means of supervision is not transferred to the value of the product; hence the capital used to purchase these materials does not function as constant capital. Similarly, the labor utilized in circulation and supervision does not produce value or surplus-value; hence the capital used to purchase this labor-power does not function as variable capital. Of course, the unproductive capital invested in circulation and supervision may be divided, for some purposes, into the capital exchanged for materials and the capital exchanged for labor-power. But this distinction is irrelevant to the production of value and surplus-value and thus to the distinction between constant capital and variable capital.

Weisskopf and Wolff do not take into account Marx's distinction between productive capital and unproductive capital in their empirical studies of Marxian theory.[10] In later works, they both justify their interpretation by noting that their primary aim was not to derive rigorous estimates of the Marxian variables, but was instead to explain the changes in the conventional rate of profit, because this rate of profit is a more direct determinant of capital investment. However, both studies are presented, at least in part, as empirical tests of the predictions of Marx's theory (e.g. rising composition of capital and falling rate of profit). For this purpose, one should take into account Marx's distinction between productive capital and unproductive capital. Furthermore, even if one's primary aim is to explain the conventional rate of profit, that in itself is no reason to ignore Marx's distinction between productive capital and unproductive capital. The trend in the conventional rate of profit can be analyzed in terms of Marx's concepts, including the concepts of productive capital and unproductive capital. Such an analysis of the conventional rate of profit is presented in Chapter 4.

2.4   RESIDENTIAL HOUSING

The fourth issue involved in the estimation of the Marxian variables is whether the concept of constant capital includes the value of residential housing. I argue that constant capital does not include the value of residential housing because residences are not means of production utilized in capitalist production, but are instead means of consumption. This distinction is most obvious in the case of owner-occupied residences. The money expended to purchase owner-occupied residences is not later recovered through the sale of commodities, and hence is not capital. Since it is not capital, it cannot be constant capital. In the case of tenant-occupied residences, the money expended to purchase (or build) apartment buildings, etc. is capital, but it is not productive capital, because these residences are not means of production used to produce commodities. This capital is similar to the "unproductive capital" invested in the functions of circulation or supervision. From this perspective, the only difference between a house and a pizza is that a pizza is consumed immediately and a house is consumed over many years. The durability of a house makes it possible for capitalist enterprises to rent houses as well as to sell them. But even though a house is rented, it remains a means of consumption, not a means of production used to produce commodities for the market. Weisskopf's estimates of constant capital include the value of residential housing. Since Weisskopf's estimates are for the Non-Financial Corporate Business sector of the economy, rather than for the Business sector as a whole, and since almost all of the residential housing in this sector is tenant occupied, Weisskopf's estimates in effect include only tenant-occupied residences.[11] No theoretical justification is presented for including the value of these residences in constant capital.

Wolff's estimates of constant capital do not include the value of residential housing, similar to my estimates.

2.5 TAXES ON WAGES

The fifth and final issue involved in the estimation of the Marxian variables is whether the taxes on the wages of (productive) workers should be considered a part of variable capital or surplus-value. This issue was not discussed by Marx himself. The analysis in *Capital* abstracts altogether from the effects of government policies on capitalist production. Thus in an empirical test of Marx's theory, this issue should be decided in a way most consistent with the overall analytical framework of Marx's theory.

I have argued above that the analytical framework of Marx's theory is the *circulation of capital*, the expenditure of money as a means of making more money ($M–C–M'$). From this point of view, variable capital should be defined as the total amount of money expended to purchase productive labor-power, including the portion which is taxed by the government. The total amount of this money is expended as capital and must be recovered out of the value produced by productive labor before any surplus-value can be appropriated. The fact that a portion of the money expended as capital to purchase productive labor-power does not actually provide income for workers is irrelevant to the function of this money as capital and hence as variable capital. The collection of taxes by the government is a subsidiary operation which falls outside the circulation of capital. No matter how the total sum of money expended to purchase productive labor-power is subsequently divided between income for workers and revenue for the government, the entire sum must be recovered before any surplus-value is appropriated, not just the portion of it which remains after taxes as the disposable income of workers. Thus this entire sum of money functions as variable capital.

Wolff defines variable capital instead as the after-tax wages of workers and thus treats taxes on wages as a part of surplus-value. The implicit justification for this definition is that variable capital should be defined from the point of view of the *disposable income of workers*. I argue, to the contrary, that variable capital should be defined instead from the point of view of the circulation of capital.

Shaikh (1978b) also argues that taxes on wages should be considered a part of surplus-value, but goes a step further than Wolff and defines the income provided to productive workers by the government (in money or in kind) as a part of variable capital (and hence as a deduction from surplus-value). Shaikh divides all government expenditures into eleven categories and each category is included or excluded from variable capital on the basis of the criterion of whether or not these expenditures provide income for productive workers. From the point of view of the disposable income of workers, Shaikh's definition of variable capital is more consistent than Wolff's, since these government expenditures do provide income for workers. However, from the point of view of the circulation of capital, these government expenditures are clearly not capital, since this money is not recovered together with a surplus-value through the sale of commodities, and hence are not variable capital. We reached a similar conclusion above with respect to the government expenditures used to purchase the labor power of government employees.

It should be noted that although taxes and government expenditures do not affect the *definition* of variable capital, they may affect the *determination* of the amount of variable capital. Marx assumes in *Capital* that the amount of variable capital per worker is equal to the price of the average quantity of wage goods consumed per worker. On this assumption, the amount of variable capital is determined by two factors: the quantity of wage goods and the price of these wage goods. However, once taxes on wages and government expenditures for workers are introduced, the determination of the amount of variable capital may also depend on these latter two factors. If it is assumed that the overall quantity of wage goods is not affected by the imposition of taxes on wages or by government expenditures for workers, then the amount of variable capital per productive worker will vary directly with the taxes on wages and inversely with the

government expenditures for workers.[12] However, this more complicated determination of the amount of variable capital does not affect
the definition of variable capital, which remains the amount of money
expended as capital to purchase productive labor-power. This precise
sum of money must be recovered through the sale of commodities
before any surplus-value is appropriated.

Weisskopf defines variable capital to include the taxes paid by
workers, as I do. However, Weisskopf states in the conclusion of
his paper that a complete analysis of the class struggle over the
distribution of income should take into account taxes and government expenditure. This statement seems to suggest that such a
complete study would require an alteration of the definitions of of
variable capital and surplus-value. I argue, to the contrary, that the
primary purpose of Marx's theory is not to analyze the distribution of
income, but rather to analyze the expansion of capital. For this latter
purpose, the definitions of variable capital and surplus-value are not
affected by taxes and government expenditures.

2.6 SUMMARY

To summarize, the definitions of the basic Marxian variables adopted
in this book are as follows.

Constant capital is the accumulated stock of money invested in the
means of production utilized in capitalist production (evaluated in
current prices). Constant capital does *not* include the money expended
to purchase the means of production utilized in non-capitalist forms
of production, nor does it include the money expended to purchase
the means of circulation and the means of supervision utilized within
capitalist enterprises.

Variable capital is the annual flow of money invested in the labor-
power utilized within capitalist production. As such, it is the before-
tax wages of productive workers. Variable capital does *not* include the
wages of non-capitalist employees, nor does it include the wages of
employees in capitalist enterprises utilized in the unproductive functions of circulation and supervision.

Surplus-value is the difference between the annual flow of new-value
produced by productive labor and the annual flow of variable capital.
As such, it includes not only the various types of property income
(profit, interest, and rent), but also the labor and material costs of the
unproductive functions of circulation and supervision.

Thus I argue that Marx's theory of the falling rate of profit refers to the *before-tax money rate of profit on productive capital in the private capitalist economy*. This theory is not about the rate of profit as it is conventionally defined, which does not distinguish between productive capital and unproductive capital. The main differences between the "Marxian" rate of profit and the "conventional" rate of profit are: (i) surplus-value, the numerator in the Marxian rate of profit, includes the annual costs of unproductive capital, and profit, the numerator in the conventional rate of profit, does not include these unproductive costs; and (ii) the stock of productive capital, the denominator in the Marxian rate of profit, does not include the capital invested in the unproductive functions of circulation and supervision, and the stock of capital, the denominator in the conventional rate of profit, does include this unproductive capital.[13] An empirical test of Marx's theory of the falling rate of profit should be in terms of the rate of profit as Marx defined it, not in terms of the conventional rate of profit.

It might be argued that such an empirical test of Marx's theory is of limited interest because the conventional rate of profit is a more important determinant of business investment and thus of general economic conditions than the Marxian rate of profit. I agree that the conventional rate of profit is a more direct determinant of the rate of capital accumulation than the Marxian rate of profit.[14] However, I maintain that an empirical test of Marx's theory is still of considerable interest, at least as a scholarly exercise. Given the long, often heated, and inclusive theoretical debate over Marx's theory of the falling rate of profit, an empirical test of the actual Marxian rate of profit in the postwar US economy should be of some interest. In addition, we will see in chapter 4 that the two determinants of the Marxian rate of profit, the composition of capital and the rate of surplus-value, are also determinants of the conventional rate of profit.

Table 2.1 presents a capsule summary of the interpretations of the four major conceptual issues, discussed above, adopted by myself, Wolff, and Weisskopf. For purposes of further comparison, Table 2.1 also includes the interpretations of these issues adopted by Gillman (1958) and Mage (1963), two important earlier Marxian empirical studies of the US economy.

In chapter 3, my estimates of the Marxian variables will be compared in detail with those of Wolff and Weisskopf, in order to determine the effects of the different interpretations of each of these conceptual issues on the trends of the estimates of the Marxian variables.

Table 2.1   Interpretations of conceptual issues

	Moseley	Wolff	Weisskopf	Gillman	Mage
1. Labor or money?	money	labor	labor[1]	money	both[2]
2. Include non-capitalist production?	no	yes	no	no	no
3. Distinguish non-production capital?	yes	no	no	yes[3]	yes[4]
4. Include residential housing?	no	no	yes	no	no
5. Taxes on wages?	variable capital	surplus value	variable capital	variable capital	neither

1. Weisskopf's interpretation is that Marx's concepts most rigorously refer to observable quantities of labor, but that estimates in terms of money are none the less reliable approximations; thus his estimates are in terms of money.
2. Mage presents two sets of estimates, one in units of current prices and one in units of labor-hours, but argues that the latter are more rigorously correct.
3. Gillman distinguishes between productive and unproductive capital invested in labor-power, but not in means of production.
4. Mage also distinguishes between productive and unproductive capital invested in labor-power, but not in means of production. In addition, Mage considers the wages of unproductive labor to be a part of constant capital, rather than surplus value.

Appendix: Recent Criticisms of Marx's Concepts of Productive Labor and Unproductive Labor

Marx's definitions of productive and unproductive labor have been criticized by a number of writers. This Appendix briefly considers some important recent criticisms.

Hunt (1979) argues that Marx's writings on concepts of productive and unproductive labor are inconsistent with respect to the following three questions: (i) is the usefulness of the product a criterion for the distinction between productive and unproductive labor? (ii) is the material or immaterial nature of the product a criterion of the distinction between productive and unproductive labor? and (iii) should commercial labor be considered productive or unproductive labor?

Hunt's criticisms have been convincingly answered by Leadbeater (1985) with a detailed textual analysis of Marx's writings, which need not be repeated here.[15] Although there are some ambiguities in Marx's many writings on the subject, most of which are preliminary drafts, the evidence is overwhelming and generally accepted (even by most critics) that Marx employed consistent definitions with respect to all three issues raised by Hunt, even if the justifications for these definitions are not always clear and accepted. The criterion for the distinction between productive and unproductive labor is whether the labor produces surplus value, not the usefulness of the product.[16] Similarly, the distinction between material and immaterial products is also irrelevant to the distinction between productive and unproductive labor; surplus value is also produced through the capitalist production of services. And commercial labor is considered to be unproductive labor because it is assumed that the value of commodities is determined prior to the circulation process, and thus that no value is created as a result of this process. Hunt even agrees that no value and surplus-value is produced in exchange, but maintains that this assumption is not related to Marx's definition of unproductive labor. Hunt states:

> Marx's demonstration that exchange can never be a source of surplus-value for society as a whole is certainly one of the important cornerstones of his analysis of capitalism. I fully agree with this demonstration and accept all its implications; moreover, I believe that failure to understand Marx on this point generally leads to the acceptance of the neo-classical marginal productivity theory of distribution. But I do not believe that Marx's definitions of productive and unproductive labor help to make this impor-

44

tant distinction between the sphere of production and the sphere of circulation. (Hunt, 1979, p. 321)

If the theoretical principle that no value is produced in exchange and all its implications are accepted, then whether or not Marx used the concept of unproductive labor to express this assumption is only a secondary question of terminology. I am primarily interested in the theoretical principle and its implications, which will be analyzed in succeeding chapters.

More substantially, Hunt goes on to argue that it is often difficult in practice to distinguish between the sphere of production and the sphere of circulation, this difficulty leading to a contradiction between Marx's treatment of circulation labor as unproductive labor and the general principle that the nature of the use-value produced is immaterial as to whether a particular kind of labor is productive or unproductive. Hunt uses the example of advertising firms. He argues that advertising firms produce a commodity, just like manufacturing firms. The nature of the use-value of advertising is obviously different from that of manufactured goods, but this difference, according to Marx, should be irrelevant to the determination of productive or unproductive labor. Therefore, these advertising workers should be considered as employed in the sphere of production and should also be considered productive labor.

However, this argument applies only to those labor activities which actually produce a commodity and is thus relevant only to a small portion of the total circulation labor (less than 10 per cent). In addition to advertising firms, it would also apply to accounting firms, data processing firms, and the like (which are usually classified as "business services"). However, it is not valid to generalize from this argument, as Hunt does, to all circulation labor, the vast majority of which is employed in selling commodities produced by others (e.g. those employed in wholesale and retail trade).

Furthermore, I contend that Hunt's argument is not valid even for advertising and these other business services. Marx's treatment of these services as unproductive labor is based on the *function* performed by this labor. The fact that this function becomes a commodity does not alter its unproductive nature.

Harrison (1973) does not question the internal consistency of Marx's definitions, but he does criticize Marx's concept of unproductive labor on two main points: (i) the concept of unproductive labor destroys the unity of exploitation between productive and unproductive workers because it implies that unproductive workers are not quantitatively exploited; and (ii) the concept of unproductive labor renders the "transformation problem" insoluble, i.e. prices of production no longer bear a determinant relation to values.

With regard to Harrison's first criticism, Marx also argued that unproductive workers are quantitatively exploited, in the sense that they generally perform surplus labor, i.e. they perform more labor than is required to produce their wage-goods (C.II, 209–10). However, Marx also argued that the precise nature of the quantitative exploitation of unproductive workers is different from that of productive workers, in the sense that their surplus labor is not manifested in the monetary form of surplus-value, because they perform different functions for capital, the functions of circulation and supervision, which Marx assumed to be unproductive of value and surplus-value for the reasons discussed above.[17] Therefore, a critique of Marx's concept of unproductive labor should consist of a direct critique of Marx's analysis of the unproductive functions of circulation and supervision, rather than an ad hoc appeal to the "unity of the notion of exploitation".

A complete response to Harrison's second criticism would require a full discussion of the "transformation problem", which is clearly beyond the scope of this book. As mentioned in chapter 1, (notes 2 and 18), my interpretation of the "transformation problem" differs from the standard Bortkiewicz–Sweezy–Sraffa interpretation (which Harrison follows), and is based on Mattick Sr (1972), Mattick Jr (1981), and Carchedi (1984, 1988). In Moseley (1982, chapter 3), I provide a detailed response to Harrison's second criticism, based on my interpretation of the "transformation problem". My conclusion is that the concept of unproductive labor does not make the "transformation problem" insoluble, but only adds an additional element to the determination of prices of production, besides value and the distribution of surplus-value across industries: the distribution of unproductive labor across industries. This additional element can easily be incorporated into the formal mathematical determination of prices of production. Marx himself discussed the general method of incorporating merchant capital into the determination of prices of production in chapter 17 of volume 3 of *Capital*. Although Fine (1973) seems to accept the more common Bortkiewicz–Sweezy–Sraffa interpretation of the "transformation problem", he also argues that the incorporation of unproductive labor into the determination of prices of production is simply a matter of adding a new set of equations, which expresses the distribution of unproductive labor across industries, to the usual system of equations which expresses values and the composition of capital across industries.

Laibman (1982b) makes the same two criticisms as Harrison and also argues that Marx's treatment of commercial labor as unproductive is untenable because much of this commercial labor would remain necessary in a socialist economy (e.g. bookkeeping and sales). However, this argument imputes to Marx a different theoretical basis for the unproductive nature of commercial labor from Marx's own: that unproductive labor is labor which would not be necessary in socialism.[18] But we have seen above that Marx's own basis for considering commercial labor as unproductive labor is the assumption that the price of commodities is determined prior to circulation (i.e. that price is "a precondition of circulation, not its result"), and that the circulation process merely results in a change of physical form of a given amount of value.

Finally, de Vroey (1982) argues that non-production labor employed in capitalist economies should also be considered as productive labor because it is private labor which is not regulated directly by society, but is instead indirectly regulated through the market exchange of products, just like production labor. This argument seems to imply that, if non-production labor did not produce value, it could not be indirectly regulated through the market. De Vroey bases his argument on the notion of "abstract labor", following in the tradition of Rubin (1972). However, Rubin himself accepted Marx's distinction between productive and unproductive labor (chapter 19).

More importantly, Rubin argued that labor in capitalist economies is not actually regulated through market exchange, but is instead regulated through the distribution of capital (chapter 18). In other words, the distribution of labor across industries and between functions depends on the distribution of capital, which in turn is regulated by the rate of profit. This conception of the regulation of labor through the regulation of capital is completely compatible with Marx's distinction between productive and unproductive functions. Unproductive labor is regulated through the distribution of unproductive capital, which is invested in order to perform unproductive functions and which receives the average rate of profit, even though these functions themselves do not produce value and surplus-value. Thus it is not necessary to postulate that non-production labor produces value in order to explain how this labor is regulated in a capitalist economy.

In conclusion, I contend that these criticisms of Marx's concepts of productive labor and unproductive labor are not persuasive and that these concepts were consistently defined by Marx and are free from logical contradictions. Therefore, in an empirical test of Marx's theory of the falling rate of profit, the estimates of the Marxian variables should take into account this fundamental distinction.

However, beyond the question of logical consistency is the question of validity. The validity of Marx's concepts cannot be decided on the basis of theoretical arguments alone. Ultimately, the validity of these concepts depends on their ability to explain and predict important empirical phenomena. In chapter 4, we will see that Marx's concepts lead to a new explanation of the decline in the conventional rate of profit in the postwar US economy and that this explanation is more consistent with the empirical evidence than competing explanations of this phenomena.

3 Estimates of the Marxian Variables for the Postwar US Economy

This chapter presents estimates of the rate of surplus-value, the composition of capital, and the rate of profit for the postwar US economy, based on the definitions of these concepts discussed in the previous chapter. The first three sections will examine the estimates of each of these three Marxian variables for the period 1947–77 in order to determine the extent to which the trends in these variables during this period were in the directions hypothesized by Marx, as discussed in Chapter 1.

Estimates presented in the first three sections end in the year 1977 for two reasons. First, it is my judgment that in the mid-1970s the US economy entered a qualitatively new phase, from a long-wave phase of expansion and prosperity to a long-wave phase of stagnation and crisis.[1] Thus it seems desirable to first test Marx's theory for the phase of expansion and prosperity, the phase to which Marx's theory of the falling rate of profit most clearly applies (see Chapter 1, pp. 1–2). The specific year 1977 is selected as the end year because the economy in 1977 was in a similar phase of the cycle as in 1947, the initial year for which many of the data series used to derive these estimates of the Marxian variables are available. Secondly, ending the period in the mid-1970s also facilitates comparison of my estimates with the two main prior sets of estimates of the Marxian variables for the postwar US economy by Weisskopf and Wolff. Weisskopf's estimates end in 1975 and Wolff's estimates end in 1976.

The fourth and fifth sections of this chapter present a detailed comparison of my estimates of the Marxian variables with these other two prior sets of estimates. These two sections will determine which of the conceptual issues discussed in Chapter 2 contributed the most to the differences between the trends of my estimates and the trends of Weisskopf's and Wolff's estimates. The final section of this chapter presents my estimates of the Marxian variables for the more recent period of stagnation from 1977 to 1987.

It should be emphasized that Marx's theory most rigorously applies to the world capitalist economy as a whole, not to an individual national economy (Mattick Sr, 1959). Therefore, it is not entirely legitimate to test Marx's theory on the basis of estimates derived for a single national economy, in this case the US economy. However, the task of deriving estimates of the Marxian variable for the entire world economy is overwhelming and perhaps impossible (because the necessary raw data may not exist). Therefore I follow the familiar procedure of restricting my empirical analysis to a single national economy. The possible biases in the trends of the Marxian variables which may result from this procedure are discussed in Appendix C, section C.2.

3.1 RATE OF SURPLUS-VALUE

We have seen in Chapter 1 that the rate of surplus value (RS) is defined as the ratio of the annual flow of surplus-value (S) to the annual flow of variable capital (V), i.e. $RS = S/V$. The annual flow of surplus value is in turn equal to the difference between the annual flow of new-value (N) and the annual flow of variable capital; i.e. $S = N - V$. Thus the rate of surplus-value can then be expressed as $RS = (N - V)/V$, and can be estimated in terms of these two absolute magnitudes: new-value and variable capital.

The Marxian concept of *new-value* is roughly analogous to the national income accounting concept of the net product of the Business sector, but with two important differences: (i) the net product of the Business sector includes various "imputations" which do not correspond to goods actually produced and sold on the market by business enterprises (the most important of these imputations by far – 80 per cent – is made to account for the "housing services" of owner-occupied homes); (ii) the net product of the Business sector does not include the unproductive depreciation costs of structures and equipment utilized in the functions of circulation and supervision. Thus the basic procedure used to derive estimates of new-value in this book is to subtract "imputations" from and add unproductive depreciation costs to the net product of the Business sector.[2]

A further complication is that part of the new-value produced in the Business sector is the result of the labor of self-employed proprietors and partners who perform productive functions (mainly farmers, construction workers, and doctors). This "proprietor value" is neither variable capital nor surplus-value. Therefore, it is subtracted from "gross new-value" to obtain "net new-value", which is equal to the sum of variable capital and surplus-value.

The specific sources and methods used to derive estimates of new-value are described in Appendix B, section B.1.

It is much more difficult to derive estimates of *variable capital* because a distinction must be made between the wages of productive labor (variable capital) and the wages of unproductive labor. The data for "total employee compensation" in the Business sector of the US National Income and Product Accounts are for all employees; no distinction is made between employees engaged in production activities and employees engaged in non-production activities. Therefore, some method must be used to estimate the percentage of the compensation of employees which is paid to workers engaged in production activities. The method used to estimate this percentage varies from industry to industry because the relevant data which exist vary from industry to industry. The primary sources of data used to estimate this percentage are the *Census of Manufactures*, which distinguishes between "production workers" and "other employees", and the *Bureau of Labor Statistics Current Establishment Survey,* which distinguishes between "non-supervisory employees" and "other employees". The specific sources and methods used to derive estimates of variable capital are described in Appendix B, section B.2. Detailed estimates of variable capital by industry are presented in Appendix A, Table A.1.

Annual estimates of new-value, variable capital, surplus-value, and the rate of surplus-value from 1947 to 1977 derived by these methods are presented in Table 3.1. The possible bias in the trend of the estimates of the rate of surplus-value is discussed in Appendix C, section C.1.

These estimates show that *the rate of surplus-value increased modestly but significantly in the postwar US economy*. According to these estimates, the rate of surplus-value increased 17 per cent over this period, from 1.40 in 1947 to 1.63 in 1977. Measured in terms of five-year moving averages, the rate of surplus-value increased 15 per cent from an average of 1.42 in 1947–51 to an average of 1.64 in 1973–7.[3] The existence of a trend in the rate of surplus-value for this period was tested by regressing the natural logarithm of the rate of surplus-value against time as the independent variable.[4] The coefficient of time was positive (0.0066) and statistically significant at the 1 per cent level (t-statistic = 6.16), thus indicating a positive trend.

Table 3.1   The rate of surplus-value

	N	V	S	RS	Index
1947	169.6	70.8	98.9	1.40	100.0
1948	183.0	77.7	105.3	1.35	96.9
1949	185.3	74.2	111.1	1.50	107.1
1950	199.0	82.2	116.8	1.42	101.6
1951	233.3	95.5	137.8	1.44	103.2
1952	245.3	101.7	143.6	1.41	101.1
1953	257.9	109.5	148.4	1.35	97.0
1954	256.0	104.2	151.8	1.46	104.3
1955	282.3	112.4	169.9	1.51	108.2
1956	293.8	120.4	173.3	1.44	103.0
1957	309.3	123.9	185.5	1.50	107.2
1958	308.2	119.2	189.0	1.59	113.5
1959	338.9	129.7	209.2	1.61	115.4
1960	351.1	133.9	217.2	1.62	116.1
1961	360.4	134.6	225.8	1.68	120.1
1962	390.7	143.9	246.7	1.71	122.7
1963	413.3	152.3	261.1	1.71	122.7
1964	442.9	162.3	280.6	1.73	123.8
1965	479.7	175.6	304.1	1.73	124.0
1966	525.5	192.9	332.5	1.72	123.3
1967	549.1	201.6	347.5	1.72	123.4
1968	596.4	221.8	374.5	1.69	120.8
1969	634.6	242.2	392.4	1.62	115.9
1970	654.3	250.4	403.9	1.61	115.4
1971	705.5	260.2	445.3	1.71	122.5
1972	780.6	292.3	488.3	1.67	119.6
1973	864.9	333.6	531.4	1.59	114.0
1974	900.6	352.5	548.1	1.55	111.3
1975	989.0	365.4	623.6	1.71	122.1
1976	1104.7	415.0	689.7	1.66	119.0
1977	1235.3	469.2	766.1	1.63	116.9

Notation and Sources

N   New-value (billions of current dollars) (flow), see Appendix B, section B.1
V   Variable capital (billions of current dollars) (flow), see Appendix B, section B.2, detailed estimates by industry in Appendix A, Table A.1
S   Surplus-value (billions of current dollars) ($= N - V$) (flow)
RS   Rate of surplus-value ($= S/V$)

According to Marx's theory, the absolute level of the rate of surplus-value is equal to the ratio of surplus-labor-time to necessary-labor-time (C.I, chapter 9). If we assume an eight-hour working day, these estimates of the rate of surplus-value suggest that at the beginning of the postwar period, necessary-labor-time (the time necessary for the average productive worker to produce a value equivalent to his/her wage) was approximately three and one-third hours and surplus-labor-time (the time during which the average productive worker produces surplus-value for capitalists) was four and two-thirds hours. By 1977, necessary-labor-time had declined to approximately three hours and surplus-labor-time had increased to about five hours.

These results are broadly consistent with Marx's hypothesis that the rate of surplus-value would tend to increase over time. However, the approximately 15 per cent increase in the rate of surplus-value over three decades is perhaps less than might be expected on the basis of Marx's theory. These results raise the question: why did the rate of surplus-value not increase faster in the postwar US economy, more in line with Marx's expectations? A closer examination of these estimates of the rate of surplus-value reveals that all of the overall increase occurred in the first half of the period, from the late 1940s to the mid-1960s. After the mid-1960s, the rate of surplus-value essentially leveled off (and even declined slightly). Thus the question of the causes of the less-than-expected increase in the rate of surplus-value over the whole period may be rephrased as: why did the rate of surplus-value stop increasing in the mid-1960s?

It is possible that at least part of this sharp slowdown in the rate of surplus-value beginning in the mid-1960s was due to the effect of different capacity utilization rates, because the capacity utilization rate in the mid-1960s was significantly higher than the postwar average (for Manufacturing, 87.3 per cent in 1963–7 compared to an average of 83.1 per cent for the whole period). Thus if the rate of surplus-value were significantly and positively related to the capacity utilization rate, as is the conventional ratio of profit to wages, then part of the increase in the rate of surplus-value from the late-1940s to the mid-1960s would be due to the increase in the capacity utilization rate during this period.

To test the dependence of the rate of surplus-value on the capacity utilization rate, I regressed the rate of surplus-value against time and the capacity utilization rate. The somewhat surprising result was that, in contrast to the conventional profit-to-wages ratio, the rate of surplus-value was not significantly dependent on the capacity utilization rate. (The coefficient of the capacity utilization rate was -0.0009, with a t-statistic of -0.26.) Presumably the reason for this difference between the rate of surplus-value and the conventional profit–wages ratio is that the number of production workers (and hence the amount of variable capital) tends to vary over the cycle more or less proportionally with the quantity of output (and hence with the amount of surplus-value), in contrast to the total number of all (business) employees (and hence the total amount of wages) which tends to vary over the cycle less than proportionally with the quantity of output (and hence with the amount of profit), because the number of non-production workers varies less over the cycle. In any case, the slowdown in the rate of surplus-value since the mid-1960s was apparently not due to the effect of a decline in the capacity utilization rate.

In order to analyze further the causes of the leveling off of the rate of surplus-value, I decomposed the rate of surplus-value, as follows:

$$RS = \frac{S}{V} = \frac{N-V}{V} = \frac{N}{V} - 1 \tag{3.1}$$

and

$$\frac{N}{V} = \frac{Q/PL}{RV/PL} \frac{P_n}{P_v} = \frac{PR}{WR} \frac{P_n}{P_v} \tag{3.2}$$

where the letters refer to the following variables:

Q total real output ($= N / P_n$)
P_n price index for total output
RV total real wage of productive labor ($= V / P_v$)
P_v price index for wage-goods
PL total hours of productive labor
PR productivity of productive labor
WR average real wage of productive labor.

Thus, according to this decomposition, the rate of surplus-value varies directly with the productivity of productive labor, inversely with the average real wage of productive labor, and directly with the price ratio P_n/P_v. If this price ratio remains constant, then the trend in the rate of surplus-value will depend on the relative rates of increase in the productivity of productive labor and the average real wage of productive labor.

Annual estimates of these three determinants of the rate of surplus-value were derived for the period of study. Estimates of the productivity of productive labor and the average real wage of productive labor were derived by dividing respectively the total real output and the total real wage of productive labor (both measured in constant dollars) by the total hours of productive labor. The hours of productive labor were estimated from BLS data on the hours of "production workers" for the Manufacturing, Mining, and Construction industries and of "non-supervisory employees" for the other industries. The specific sources and methods used to estimate the hours of productive labor are described in Appendix B, section B.4.

Estimates of the productivity of productive labor, the average real wage of productive labor, and the price ratio P_n/P_v are presented in Tables 3.2, 3.3 and 3.4, respectively. According to these estimates, the main cause of the leveling off of the rate of surplus-value after 1965 was a significant slowdown in productivity growth, from an annual average rate of increase of 3.36 per cent in 1947–65 to an average rate of 2.03 per cent in 1965–77.[5] The price ratio P_n/P_v remained essentially constant throughout both periods and the average real wage increased at approximately the same average rate in both periods (2.57 in 1947–65 and 2.37 in 1965–77).

I also tested for a cyclical effect on the productivity of productive labor and the average real wage of productive labor by regressing each variable against time and the capacity utilization rate. As with the rate of surplus-value, the surprising results of these regressions were that neither of these variables was significantly dependent on the capacity utilization rate, in contrast to the conventional estimates of productivity and the real wage. (For the productivity of productive labor, the coefficient of the capacity utilization rate was 0.012 with a t-statistic of 1.38, and for the average real wage of productive labor of productive labor, the coefficient of the capacity utilization rate was 0.004, with a t-statistic of 1.37.) Thus the conclusion stated in the previous paragraph is not altered by a consideration of cyclical effects.

These estimates also show that the underlying cause of the secular increase in the rate of surplus-value is that for the entire period, productivity increased at a faster rate than real wages (at an annual rate of 2.82 per cent, compared to 2.49 for real wages). However, all this faster increase in productivity occurred prior to 1965; after 1965, productivity and real wages increased at approximately the same rate.

Finally, these estimates also show that the postwar US economy exhibited characteristics of what Foley (1986a, 1986b) has described

Table 3.2 Productivity of productive labor

	N	P_n	Q	PL	PR	Index
1947	169.6	53.3	318.3	59.7	5.33	100.0
1948	183.0	57.0	321.1	60.3	5.32	99.8
1949	185.3	56.5	328.0	56.5	5.81	108.8
1950	199.0	57.4	346.7	59.2	5.86	109.9
1951	233.3	61.6	378.9	62.3	6.08	113.9
1952	245.3	62.4	393.1	62.7	6.27	117.6
1953	257.9	63.0	409.4	63.6	6.44	120.6
1954	256.0	63.7	401.9	59.8	6.72	125.9
1955	282.3	64.7	436.4	62.2	7.01	131.4
1956	293.8	66.8	439.8	62.9	6.99	131.0
1957	309.3	69.0	448.3	61.6	7.28	136.4
1958	308.2	70.0	440.3	57.6	7.64	143.2
1959	338.9	71.4	474.7	60.5	7.84	147.0
1960	351.1	72.4	484.9	59.9	8.09	151.7
1961	360.4	72.9	494.3	58.8	8.41	157.7
1962	390.7	74.0	528.0	60.1	8.78	164.6
1963	413.3	74.8	552.6	60.8	9.09	170.3
1964	442.9	75.5	586.6	61.6	9.53	178.6
1965	479.7	76.9	623.8	63.9	9.76	183.0
1966	525.5	79.2	663.5	66.2	10.03	188.0
1967	549.1	81.4	674.5	65.5	10.29	193.0
1968	596.4	84.5	705.7	66.6	10.60	198.7
1969	634.6	88.5	717.1	68.4	10.48	196.5
1970	654.3	92.5	707.3	66.7	10.60	198.8
1971	705.5	96.6	730.3	65.8	11.09	207.9
1972	780.6	100.0	780.6	68.5	11.40	213.7
1973	864.9	105.4	820.6	71.5	11.48	215.2
1974	900.6	115.0	783.2	71.2	11.00	206.3
1975	989.0	125.8	786.2	66.6	11.81	221.3
1976	1104.7	131.9	837.5	69.0	12.13	227.4
1977	1235.3	139.3	886.7	71.2	12.45	233.3

Average annual rates of change of PR

1947–65	3.36%
1965–77	2.03%
1965–72	2.22%
1972–77	1.76%
1947–77	2.82%

Notation and Sources

N New-value (billions of current dollars) (flow), see Appendix B, section B.1
P_n Implicit price deflator for the Business sector, US National Income and Product Accounts, Table 7.6
Q Real output (billions of 1972 dollars) ($= N/P_n \times 100$) (flow)
PL Productive labor (billions of hours), see Appendix B, section B.4b
PR Productivity of productive labor ($= Q/PL$) (1972 dollars per hour)

Table 3.3   Average real wage of productive labor

	V	P_v	RV	PL	WR	Index
1947	70.8	52.9	133.8	59.7	2.24	100.0
1948	77.7	56.0	138.8	60.3	2.30	102.6
1949	74.2	55.8	133.0	56.5	2.35	105.0
1950	82.3	56.9	144.6	59.2	2.44	109.0
1951	95.5	60.6	157.6	62.3	2.53	112.8
1952	101.7	62.0	164.0	62.7	2.62	116.7
1953	109.5	63.2	173.3	63.6	2.72	121.5
1954	104.2	63.7	163.6	59.8	2.73	121.9
1955	112.4	64.4	174.5	62.2	2.80	125.1
1956	120.4	65.6	183.6	62.9	2.92	130.1
1957	123.9	67.8	182.7	61.6	2.97	132.3
1958	119.2	69.2	172.3	57.6	2.99	133.3
1959	129.7	70.6	183.8	60.5	3.04	135.4
1960	133.9	71.9	186.2	59.9	3.10	138.6
1961	134.6	72.6	185.4	58.8	3.15	140.6
1962	143.9	73.7	195.3	60.1	3.25	144.8
1963	152.3	74.8	203.6	60.8	3.35	149.3
1964	162.3	75.9	213.8	61.6	3.47	154.9
1965	175.6	77.2	227.5	63.9	3.56	158.7
1966	193.0	79.4	243.0	66.2	3.67	163.8
1967	201.6	81.4	247.6	65.5	3.78	168.5
1968	221.8	84.6	262.2	66.6	3.94	175.6
1969	242.2	88.4	274.0	68.4	4.01	178.7
1970	250.4	92.5	270.7	66.7	4.06	181.0
1971	260.2	96.5	269.6	65.8	4.09	182.6
1972	292.3	100.0	292.3	68.5	4.27	190.4
1973	333.6	105.7	315.6	71.5	4.41	196.9
1974	352.5	116.4	302.9	71.2	4.26	189.8
1975	365.4	125.3	291.7	66.6	4.38	195.3
1976	415.0	131.7	315.1	69.0	4.56	203.5
1977	469.2	139.3	336.8	71.2	4.73	210.9

Average annual rates of change of WR
1947–65   2.57%
1965–77   2.37%
1965–72   2.60%
1972–77   2.04%
1947–77   2.49%

Notation and Sources
    V   Variable capital (billions of current dollars) (flow), see Appendix B, section B.2, detailed estimates by industry in Appendix A, Table A.1
  P_v Implicit price deflator for Personal Consumption Expenditure US National Income and Product Accounts, Table 7.4
  RV Real variable capital (billions of 1972 dollars) ($= V/P_v \times 100$) (flow)
  PL Productive labor (billions of hours), see Appendix B, section B.4b
  WR Real wage of productive labor ($= RV/PL$) (1972 dollars per hour)

Table 3.4   Price ratios

	P_n/P_v	P_c/P_v	P_c/P_n
1947	1.01	1.04	1.03
1948	1.02	1.03	1.01
1949	1.01	1.02	1.01
1950	1.01	1.08	1.07
1951	1.02	1.07	1.05
1952	1.01	1.04	1.03
1953	1.00	1.03	1.03
1954	1.00	1.02	1.02
1955	1.00	1.03	1.02
1956	1.02	1.07	1.05
1957	1.02	1.08	1.06
1958	1.01	1.06	1.05
1959	1.01	1.05	1.04
1960	1.01	1.04	1.03
1961	1.00	1.02	1.02
1962	1.00	1.01	1.01
1963	1.00	1.00	1.00
1964	0.99	0.99	1.00
1965	1.00	0.99	1.00
1966	1.00	0.99	0.99
1967	1.00	0.99	0.99
1968	1.00	0.99	0.99
1969	1.00	0.99	0.99
1970	1.00	0.99	0.99
1971	1.00	1.00	1.00
1972	1.00	1.01	1.01
1973	1.00	1.02	1.03
1974	0.99	1.05	1.06
1975	1.00	1.08	1.08
1976	1.00	1.08	1.08
1977	1.00	1.08	1.08

Notation and Sources

P_n Implicit price deflator for the Business sector, US National Income and Product Accounts, table 7.6

P_v Implicit price deflator for Personal Consumption Expenditure, US National Income and Product Accounts, table 7.4

P_c Implicit price deflator for means of production, see Appendix B, section B.4, detailed estimates in Appendix A, Table A.4

as an "intermediate zone", between the two extreme assumptions in the debate over the Okishio Theorem of constant real wages, on the one hand, and a constant rate of surplus-value, on the other hand (see

Chapter 1, section 1.3). The postwar US economy exhibited neither constant real wages nor a constant rate of surplus-value. Instead, real wages increased significantly but at a slower rate than the productivity of labor, so that the rate of surplus-value increased along increasing real wages. According to Foley, for economies falling within this intermediate range, nothing can be concluded *a priori* about the effect of technological change on the rate of profit. Thus the estimates of the rate of profit presented later in this chapter should provide valuable empirical evidence concerning the effect of technological change on the rate of profit under these intermediate circumstances.

3.2 COMPOSITION OF CAPITAL

We saw in Chapter 1 that Marx's concept of the composition of capital consists of three distinct but related ratios: the technical composition of capital, the value composition of capital, and the organic composition of capital. Estimates of all three ratios were derived and are presented in this section.

The main additional estimate required in order to derive estimates of these ratios is the stock of *constant capital*, which is the sum of fixed constant capital and circulating constant capital. Estimates of fixed constant capital were derived from data published by the BEA for the private non-residential fixed capital stock of the US. Briefly, fixed constant capital was estimated as the current value of the buildings and equipment used for production activities, not including the buildings and equipment used for circulation and supervision activities. Circulating constant capital was estimated as the current value of business inventories. The specific sources and methods used to derive estimates of constant capital are described in Appendix B, section B.3A. Detailed estimates of constant capital by industry are presented in Appendix A, Table A.2.

3.2.1 Technical Composition of Capital

The technical composition of capital (TCC) was defined in Chapter 1 as the real ratio of the quantity of means of production (MP) to the quantity of productive labor (PL), i.e. $TCC = MP / PL$. The quantity of means of production was calculated by dividing the nominal value of constant capital by a composite price deflator for the means of production, which is a weighted average of the price deflator for

Table 3.5   Technical composition of capital

	C	P_c	MP	PL	TCC	Index	ATCC	Index
1947	253.5	54.8	462.6	59.7	7.75	100.0	6.71	100.0
1948	279.5	57.8	483.6	60.3	8.02	103.4	7.03	104.9
1949	282.5	56.9	496.2	56.5	8.88	113.3	6.71	100.1
1950	323.6	61.2	528.5	59.2	9.16	115.2	7.99	119.2
1951	360.7	64.9	555.4	62.3	9.06	114.9	8.36	124.7
1952	375.2	64.4	582.5	62.7	9.39	119.9	8.69	129.7
1953	390.2	65.0	599.9	63.6	9.51	121.6	9.32	139.1
1954	400.0	65.1	614.7	59.8	10.34	132.5	8.98	133.9
1955	433.3	66.1	655.2	62.2	10.59	135.8	10.13	151.1
1956	477.5	70.1	680.9	62.9	10.82	139.5	10.31	153.7
1957	505.4	73.2	690.4	61.6	11.21	144.6	10.37	154.7
1958	516.7	73.2	705.5	57.6	12.24	157.8	10.27	153.2
1959	536.5	74.1	724.2	60.5	11.97	154.3	10.87	162.1
1960	550.6	74.5	739.1	59.9	12.34	159.1	11.04	164.6
1961	563.0	74.0	760.6	58.8	12.94	166.9	11.28	168.2
1962	585.2	74.5	785.8	60.1	13.07	168.5	11.94	178.1
1963	607.1	74.9	810.7	60.8	13.33	171.9	12.48	186.1
1964	636.4	75.4	843.8	61.6	13.71	176.8	13.13	195.8
1965	687.6	76.7	896.6	63.9	14.03	180.9	13.96	208.2
1966	754.9	78.7	959.4	66.2	14.50	187.0	14.65	218.4
1967	812.9	80.8	1006.0	65.5	15.35	198.0	14.92	222.5
1968	891.6	83.9	1062.5	66.6	15.95	205.8	15.56	232.1
1969	985.1	88.0	1120.0	68.4	17.49	211.2	15.94	237.8
1970	1073.0	92.0	1166.6	66.7	18.43	225.6	16.08	239.8
1971	1171.2	96.5	1213.3	65.8	18.47	237.7	16.78	250.2
1972	1276.4	100.9	1264.6	68.5	18.93	238.2	17.53	261.4
1973	1463.2	108.1	1353.2	71.5	20.86	244.1	18.53	276.4
1974	1807.9	121.8	1484.5	71.2	21.83	269.0	19.89	296.6
1975	1969.1	135.5	1453.5	66.6	21.77	281.5	19.51	290.9
1976	2135.6	142.1	1503.2	69.0	22.13	280.8	20.12	300.1
1977	2361.6	149.8	1576.5	71.2	22.85	285.4	21.00	313.2

Average annual rates of change of	TCC	ATCC
1947–65	3.09%	4.07%
1965–77	3.80%	3.40%
1965–72	3.91%	3.25%
1972–77	3.65%	3.62%
1947–77	3.38%	3.81%

Notation and Sources

C   Constant capital (billions of current dollars), see Appendix B, section B.3a, detailed estimates by industry in Appendix A, Table A.2

P_c Implicit price deflator for means of production, see Appendix A, Table A.4

MP   Means of production (billions of 1972 dollars) ($= C/P_c \times 100$)

PL   Productive labor (billions of hours), see Appendix B, section B.4b

TCC   Technical composition of capital ($= MP/PL$)

ATTC   Adjusted technical composition of capital: see text

buildings and equipment and the price deflator for inventories.[6] The quantity of productive labor was estimated by the hours of "production workers" and "non-supervisory employees", as described above.

Annual estimates of these variables are presented in Table 3.5. Over the whole period from 1947 to 1977, the technical composition of capital increased 175 per cent. Measured in terms of five-year averages from 1947–51 to 1973–7, the increase was 145 per cent. Thus the technical composition of capital increased very substantially over this period, as expected.

These estimates also show that there was an acceleration in the average annual rate of increase in the technical composition of capital from the period prior to 1965 (3.29 per cent) to the period after 1965 (3.80 per cent). However, it is likely that at least part of this acceleration in the technical composition was due to the relatively higher rates of capacity utilization in the mid-1960s. It seems plausible that the technical composition of capital varies inversely with the capacity utilization rate, since, for example, a cyclical expansion probably results at least in part in businesses rehiring production workers without adding new buildings and equipment. I tested this hypothesis by regressing the technical composition of capital against time and the capacity utilization rate. The results of this regression show that the coefficient of the capacity utilization rate was indeed negative (-0.131) and significant at the 1 per cent significance level (t-statistic $= -4.93$). I then used this regression coefficient to adjust the estimates of the technical composition for different rates of capacity utilization, employing a method previously used by Feldstein and Summers (1977) and by Bosworth (1982) to adjust estimates of the rate of profit.[7] These cyclically adjusted estimates of the technical composition of capital are also shown in Table 3.5. These adjusted estimates show no acceleration in the average annual rate of increase from the pre-1965 period to the post-1965 period (and even a significant decline from 4.07 per cent in 1947–65 to 3.40 in 1965–77), thus suggesting that all the acceleration in the unadjusted estimates was due to this capacity utilization effect.[8]

3.2.2 Value Composition of Capital

The value composition of capital (VCC) was defined in Chapter 1 as the money or nominal ratio of the stock of constant capital (C) to the annual flow of variable capital (V) (both measured in units of current dollars), i.e. $VCC = C / V$.[9] Estimates of constant capital and variable

Table 3.6   Value composition of capital

	C	V	VCC	Index	AVCC	Index
1947	253.5	70.8	3.58	100.0	3.21	100.0
1948	279.5	77.7	3.60	100.4	3.25	101.2
1949	282.5	74.2	3.81	106.3	3.07	95.6
1950	323.6	82.3	3.94	109.8	3.60	112.2
1951	360.7	95.5	3.78	105.4	3.58	111.5
1952	375.2	101.7	3.69	103.0	3.48	108.3
1953	390.2	109.5	3.56	99.4	3.53	109.9
1954	400.0	104.2	3.84	107.2	3.38	105.2
1955	433.3	112.4	3.85	107.6	3.71	115.8
1956	477.5	120.4	3.96	110.7	3.78	117.9
1957	505.4	123.9	4.08	113.9	3.78	117.8
1958	516.7	119.2	4.33	121.0	3.63	113.2
1959	536.5	129.7	4.14	115.4	3.74	116.7
1960	550.6	133.9	4.11	114.8	3.65	113.7
1961	563.0	134.6	4.18	116.8	3.59	111.9
1962	585.2	143.9	4.07	113.5	3.66	114.2
1963	607.1	152.3	3.99	111.3	3.68	114.8
1964	636.4	162.3	3.92	109.5	3.72	115.8
1965	687.6	175.6	3.92	109.3	3.89	121.3
1966	754.9	193.0	3.91	109.2	3.96	123.5
1967	812.9	201.6	4.03	112.6	3.88	120.9
1968	891.6	221.8	4.02	112.2	3.88	120.9
1969	985.1	242.2	4.07	113.5	3.91	121.9
1970	1073.0	250.4	4.29	119.6	3.78	117.8
1971	1171.0	260.2	4.50	125.7	3.91	122.7
1972	1276.4	292.3	4.37	121.9	4.03	125.6
1973	1463.2	333.6	4.39	122.5	4.25	132.3
1974	1807.9	352.5	5.13	143.2	4.78	149.1
1975	1969.1	365.4	5.39	150.4	4.56	142.2
1976	2135.6	415.0	5.15	143.7	4.56	142.1
1977	2361.6	469.2	5.03	140.5	4.63	144.4

Average annual rates of change of	VCC	AVCC
1947–65	0.49%	1.07%
1965–77	2.09%	1.45%
1965–72	1.56%	0.50%
1972–77	2.84%	2.78%
1947–77	1.13%	1.22%

Notation and Sources

C   Constant capital (billions of current dollars) (stock), see Appendix B, section B.3a, detailed estimates by industry in Appendix A, Table A.2

V   Variable capital (billions of current dollars) (flow), see Appendix B, section B.2, detailed estimates by industry in Appendix A, Table A.1

VCC   Value composition of capital (= C/V)

AVCC   Cyclically adjusted value composition of capital: see text

capital were derived by the methods described above. Annual estimates of these magnitudes and of the value composition of capital are
presented in Table 3.6. The possible bias in the trend of these estimates of the value composition of capital is discussed in Appendix C,
section C.1.

These estimates show that *the value composition of capital increased
41 per cent over the whole period*, from 3.58 in 1947 to 5.03 in 1977. In
terms of five-year averages, the value composition of capital increased
34 per cent over this period, from 3.74 in 1947–51 to 5.02 in 1973–7.
Regressing the natural logarithm of the value composition of capital
against time, the coefficient of time is positive (0.0096) and statistically significant at the 1 per cent level (t-statistic = 7.81), thus
indicating a strong positive trend.

These results are, of course, consistent with Marx's hypothesis of a
rising value composition of capital. However, as in the case of the rate
of surplus-value, the extent of the increase in the value composition of
capital over a thirty year period of expansion is perhaps less than
might be expected on the basis of Marx's theory.

Closer examination of the two components of the stock of constant
capital – fixed capital and circulating capital – reveals an important
reason for the smaller increase in the value composition of capital:
circulating constant capital increased at a much slower rate than fixed
constant capital, approximately 60 per cent as fast over the whole
period (see Appendix A, Table A.3). If the value composition of
capital is divided into two components corresponding to these two
components of constant capital, one finds that the fixed capital
component of the value composition of capital increased 63 per
cent, more in line with Marx's expectations, while the circulating
capital component did not increase at all, and even declined slightly
(5 per cent). Thus the much slower growth of circulating constant
capital significantly retarded the increase in the overall value composition of capital.

For further analysis of the proximate causes of the slower increase
of circulating constant capital, both circulating constant capital (CC)
and fixed constant capital (FC) were decomposed into their real and
price components, as follows:

$$CC = RCC \times P_{cc}$$

$$FC = RFC \times P_{fc}. \tag{3.3}$$

This decomposition shows that there are two possible causes of the slower increase of circulating constant capital: slower increase of real circulating capital (the quantity of raw materials and other intermediate goods) compared to real fixed capital (the quantity of structures and equipment), and/or slower increase of the price index for circulating capital compared to the price index for fixed capital.

Examination of the estimates of these variables reveals that both of these possible causes were partially responsible for the slower increase of circulating constant capital in the postwar US economy (see Appendix A, Table A.4). Real circulating capital increased approximately 80 per cent as fast as real fixed capital and the price index for circulating capital increased approximately 60 per cent as fast as the price index for fixed capital. Thus the slower increase in the price index for circulating capital accounted for most of the slower increase in the nominal value of circulating capital. The significance of the price index for circulating constant capital will be discussed later in connection with the organic composition of capital.

The estimates of the value composition of capital also show a significant acceleration in the average annual rate of increase in the value composition of capital from the pre-1965 period (0.49 per cent) to the post-1965 period (2.09 per cent). In order to determine how much of this acceleration in the value composition of capital was due to the effects of different rates of capacity utilization, I adjusted these estimates by the same method used above for the technical composition of capital. (The regression coefficient of the capacity utilization rate was -0.047 with a t-statistic of -5.54). These cyclically adjusted estimates of the value composition of capital are also presented in Table 3.6. The adjusted estimates show a larger increase in the pre-1965 period than in the unadjusted estimates (1.07 per cent), a smaller increase in the post-1965 period (1.45 per cent), and thus a much smaller acceleration in the average annual rate of increase between the two periods. Furthermore, these estimates also show that the acceleration in the value composition of composition of capital did not begin until 1972. From 1965 to 1972 the average annual rate of increase was 0.50 per cent, even lower than the rate of 1.07 per cent in 1947–65. However, there was a sharp acceleration during the remaining years of 1972 to 1977 to a rate of 2.78 per cent.

In order to identify the proximate causes of this sharp acceleration in the value composition of capital in 1972–7, I decomposed the value composition of capital as follows:

$$VCC = \frac{MP \,/\, PL}{RV \,/\, PL} \ \frac{P_c}{P_v} = \frac{TCC}{WR} \ \frac{P_c}{P_v} \tag{3.4}$$

where P_c stands for the price index for the means of production. Thus, according to this decomposition, the value composition of capital varies directly with the technical composition of capital, inversely with the average real wage of productive labor, and directly with the price ratio P_c/P_v.

Estimates of the technical composition of capital and of the average real wage of productive labor have already been presented in Tables 3.5 and 3.3, respectively. Estimates of the price ratio P_c/P_v are presented in Table 3.4.

According to these estimates, the main cause of the acceleration in the value composition of capital in 1972–7 was a 7 per cent increase in the price ratio P_c/P_v, i.e. was a relatively faster increase in the price of the means of production, especially raw materials and other intermediate goods (e.g. oil). The price index for circulating constant capital increased 62 per cent over this brief five-year period, while the price index for fixed constant capital increased 46 per cent and the price index for wage goods increased only 39 per cent. The rate of increase of the price index for circulating constant capital increased sharply during this period, from an annual average rate of 1.5 per cent in 1947–72 to an annual rate of 8.9 per cent in 1972–7. This sharp acceleration in the price of raw materials, etc. was primarily responsible for the rapid increase in the value composition of capital during these years. A small slowdown in real wage growth (from 2.50 per cent in 1947–72 to 2.07 in 1972–7) also contributed to the acceleration in the value composition of capital during these years. It is noteworthy that the value composition of capital did not increase in this period due to an acceleration in the growth rate of the technical composition of capital, which is perhaps what one might expect on the basis of Marx's theory. In fact, the growth rate of the technical composition of capital even declined somewhat from 4.07 per cent in 1947–65 to 3.25 per cent in 1965–72.

These estimates also show that the underlying cause of the secular increase of the value composition of capital is that for the entire period, the technical composition of capital increased at a faster rate than the average real wage of productive labor (3.81 per cent compared to 2.49 per cent). The technical composition of capital increased faster than the real wage throughout the postwar period, usually significantly faster. The closest that real wage growth came to technical composition growth was during the brief 1965–72 period, as a result of slower technical composition growth and slightly faster real wage growth.

3.2.3 The Organic Composition of Capital

The organic composition of capital was defined in Chapter 1 as the money or nominal ratio of the stock of constant capital to the annual flow of new-value (N) (both measured in units of current dollars), i.e. $OCC = C/N$. Estimates of these two magnitudes and the organic composition of capital are shown in Table 3.7. The possible bias in the trend of these estimates of the organic composition of capital is discussed in Appendix C, section C.1.

These estimates show that *the organic composition of capital increased 28 per cent over the entire period*, from 1.49 in 1947 to 1.91 in 1977. In terms of five-year averages, the organic composition of capital increased 24 per cent, from 1.55 in 1947–51 to 1.92 in 1973–7.

Regressing the natural logarithm of the organic composition of capital against time, the coefficient of time is positive (0.0056) and statistically significant at the 1 per cent level (t-statistic = 3.58), thus again indicating a positive trend.

The secular increase in the organic composition of capital is broadly consistent with Marx's hypothesis that the organic composition of capital would tend to increase over time, although once again the approximately 25 per cent increase over three decades is probably less than Marx would have expected. The conclusions reached above concerning the retarding effect of the slower increase of the stock of circulating constant capital on the value composition of capital also apply to the organic composition of capital. The fixed capital component of the organic composition of capital increased 36 per cent, more consistent with Marx's hypothesis, while the circulating capital component *declined* a significant 19 per cent, quite contrary to Marx's hypothesis. Thus the much slower growth of circulating constant capital significantly retarded the increase in the overall organic composition of capital.

It is revealing to compare further the real and price components of the stock of circulating constant capital with the real and price components for final output. Such a comparison indicates that real circulating capital increased at approximately the same rate as real output, but the price index for circulating capital increased approx-

Table 3.7　Organic composition of capital

	C	N	OCC	Index	AOCC	Index
1947	253.5	169.6	1.49	100.0	1.38	100.0
1948	279.5	183.0	1.53	102.2	1.42	102.9
1949	282.5	185.3	1.52	102.0	1.29	93.9
1950	323.6	199.0	1.63	108.8	1.52	110.4
1951	360.7	233.3	1.55	103.4	1.48	107.8
1952	375.2	245.3	1.53	102.4	1.46	106.2
1953	390.2	257.9	1.51	101.2	1.50	109.0
1954	400.0	256.0	1.56	104.5	1.42	102.9
1955	433.3	282.3	1.53	102.7	1.49	108.3
1956	477.5	293.8	1.63	108.8	1.57	113.9
1957	505.4	309.3	1.63	109.3	1.54	111.8
1958	516.7	308.2	1.68	112.2	1.46	105.7
1959	536.5	338.9	1.58	105.9	1.46	106.0
1960	555.6	351.1	1.57	104.9	1.42	103.3
1961	563.0	360.4	1.56	104.6	1.38	99.9
1962	585.2	390.7	1.50	100.2	1.37	99.6
1963	607.1	413.3	1.47	98.3	1.37	99.8
1964	636.4	442.9	1.44	96.2	1.37	99.7
1965	687.6	479.7	1.43	95.9	1.43	103.6
1966	754.9	525.5	1.44	96.1	1.45	105.5
1967	812.9	549.1	1.48	99.1	1.43	104.0
1968	891.6	596.4	1.50	100.0	1.45	105.4
1969	985.1	634.6	1.55	103.9	1.50	109.2
1970	1073.0	654.3	1.64	109.7	1.48	107.6
1971	1171.2	705.5	1.66	111.1	1.47	107.1
1972	1276.4	780.6	1.64	109.4	1.53	111.1
1973	1463.2	864.9	1.69	113.2	1.65	119.7
1974	1807.9	900.6	2.01	134.3	1.90	137.9
1975	1969.1	989.0	1.99	133.2	1.73	125.7
1976	2135.6	1104.7	1.93	129.4	1.75	127.0
1977	2361.6	1235.3	1.91	127.9	1.79	129.7

Average annual rates of change of		OCC	AOCC
	1957–65	−0.23%	0.43%
	1965–77	2.40%	1.87%
	1965–72	1.88%	1.00%
	1972–77	3.12%	3.09%
	1947–77	0.82%	0.87%

Notation and Sources
　C　Constant capital (billions of current dollars) (stock), see Appendix B,
　　　section B.3a, detailed estimates by industry in Appendix A, Table A.2
　N　New-value (billions of current dollars) (flow), see Appendix B, section B.1
OCC　Organic composition of capital (= C/N)
AOCC　Cyclically adjusted organic composition of capital: see text

imately 12 per cent slower than the price index for final output. In other words, the price of raw materials, etc. declined 12 per cent relative to the price of final output over this period (see Appendix A, Table A.4).

This trend in the relative price of raw materials is quite contrary to Marx's expectation that the productivity of labor in the production of raw materials would increase at a slower rate than in the production of final goods, thus resulting in an increase in the relative price of raw materials (see Chapter 1, p. 8). Instead, the "cheapening" of the elements of circulating constant capital was much more significant than Marx expected. As we have seen, this contrary trend in the relative price of raw materials is an important reason why the stock of circulating constant capital increased at a relatively slower rate than fixed capital and thus why the overall organic (and value) composition of capital increased less than Marx probably expected. If the price index for circulating constant capital had simply increased at the same rate as the price index for final output, then, *ceteris paribus*, the organic composition of capital would have increased 35 per cent, compared to the 28 per cent actual increase.

A similar comparison of the real and price components of fixed constant capital reveals that real fixed capital increased approximately 22 per cent faster than real output and the price index for fixed capital increased approximately 20 per cent faster than the price index for final output. These results for fixed capital are much more consistent with Marx's expectation. The "cheapening" of the elements of fixed constant capital was apparently much less effective than for circulating constant capital.

One surprising characteristic of these estimates is the low absolute level of the organic composition of capital, still below 2.0 at the end of the period. In other words, the net stock of constant capital in the late 1970s was still less than twice as great as the annual flow of new-value produced, after more than a century of capital accumulation in the United States. This low level of constant capital is no doubt due in part to a significant devaluation of capital during the Great Depression and during the earlier nineteenth-century depressions. In any case, the low level of the organic composition of capital at this late date suggests that there probably has not been much of a significant long-run tendency for the organic composition of capital to increase over the history of capitalism in the US.

A closer examination of these estimates of the organic composition of capital reveals that they show different trends in three distinct subperiods: a 4 per cent decline in 1947–65 (at an average annual rate of -0.23 per cent); a sharp 14 per cent increase in 1965–72 (at an annual rate of 1.88 per cent); and an even sharper 17 per cent increase in 1972–7 (at an annual rate of 3.12 per cent). The cyclically adjusted estimates of the organic composition of capital, using the same adjustment method as above for the technical composition and the value composition, show the same three distinct subperiods, but with a small increase in the first period, instead of a small decline (a 4 per cent overall increase, at an annual rate of 0.20 per cent), a correspondingly smaller increase in the second period (a 7 per cent increase overall, at an annual rate of 1.00 per cent), and approximately the same sharp increase in the final period. (The regression coefficient of the capacity utilization rate was -0.015, with a t-statistic of -3.51). The cyclically adjusted estimates of the organic composition of capital are also shown in Table 3.7.

Again, in order to identify the proximate causes of these shifts in the trends of the organic composition of capital, I decomposed the organic composition of capital as follows:

$$OCC = \frac{C}{N} = \frac{MP \,/\, PL}{Q \,/\, PL} \frac{P_c}{P_n} = \frac{TCC}{PR} \frac{P_c}{P_n} \tag{3.5}$$

Thus, according to this decomposition, the organic composition of capital varies directly with the technical composition of capital, inversely with the productivity of productive labor, and directly with the price ratio P_c/P_n.

Estimates of the technical composition and of the productivity of productive labor have already been presented in Tables 3.5 and 3.2, respectively. Estimates of the price ratio P_c/P_n are presented in Table 3.4.

According to these estimates, the acceleration in the rate of increase in the organic composition of capital from the first period to the second period was due almost entirely to a significant decline in productivity growth, from 3.36 in 1947–65 to 2.20 in 1965–72. The relative price ratio P_c/P_n also increased very slightly (1 per cent). As noted above, the growth rate of the technical composition of capital declined somewhat after 1965. The positive effect of this decline on the organic composition of capital was offset by the even greater decline of productivity growth.

By contrast, the acceleration in the rate of increase in the third period was due mainly to the 7 per cent increase in the ratio P_c/P_n discussed above in relation to the value composition of capital. A further small decline in productivity growth (from 2.01 to 1.75) also contributed to this acceleration in the organic composition of capital in the third period.

These estimates also show that the underlying cause of the secular increase of the organic composition of capital is that for the entire period the technical composition of capital increased at a faster rate than the productivity of productive labor (3.81 per cent compared to 2.82 per cent). In other words, the rate of increase of the technical composition of capital was greater than the "cheapening" of the means of production, as Marx expected. The gap between these two rates of increase was maintained throughout this period and even increased steadily over the period, due mainly to the slowdown in productivity growth.

Finally, it should be recalled that Marx's hypothesis regarding the trend of the organic composition of capital was concerned solely with the effects of technological change on the composition of capital, or as I have interpreted it, on the ratio of constant capital to new-value. Various other factors which also affect this ratio and which were in effect held constant in Marx's analysis were mentioned in Chapter 1 (pp. 3–4). The most important of these "other factors" in the postwar US economy were: (i) the distribution of capital across industries with unequal compositions of capital; (ii) the turnover time of capital; and (iii) the incidence of multiple shifts. The remainder of this section will analyze in turn the effects of each of these three "other factors" on the value and the organic composition of capital in the postwar US economy, in order to isolate more precisely the effect of technological change on the composition of capital, and thus to test Marx's hypothesis more rigorously.

3.2.4 The Distribution of Capital Across Industries.

We begin by examining the effect of the distribution of capital on the value composition of capital. The effect of the distribution of capital on the organic composition of capital cannot be calculated directly, because it is not possible to estimate new-value for each industry, since the observed estimates of "value added" by industry are affected by the distribution of surplus-value across industries and thus not equal to the new-value produced in each industry. The results from the analysis of the value composition of capital will be used later to estimate the effect of the distribution of capital on the organic composition of capital.

The aggregate value composition of capital may be viewed as a weighted average of the value composition of capital in each industry, with the industry shares of the total variable capital serving as weights. Mathematically,

$$VCC = w_i \times VCC_i \qquad \text{where } w_i = V_i \,/\, V \qquad (3.6)$$

From this equation, we can see that a structural change in the distribution of variable capital (and thus productive labor) from industries with a relatively high value composition to those with a relatively low value composition would have a negative effect on the aggregate value composition, and would slow down the increase in the aggregate value composition.

In order to analyze the effect of the distribution of capital on the aggregate value composition of capital, I first calculated the value composition of capital for each of the eight major industry groups in the private US capitalist economy. These estimates are presented in Table 3.8.

From these estimates we can see that there is considerable variation in the absolute levels of the value composition of capital (VCC) across industries. In 1947, the VCC ranged from highs of 13.0 in Government Enterprises, 7.34 in Agriculture, and 6.23 in Transportation and Public Utilities to lows of 0.78 in Construction and 1.11 in Services. The relative levels of the VCC across industries remained more or less the same during the postwar period. In 1977, the VCC ranged from highs of 14.94 in Agriculture, 13.40 in Government Enterprises, and 9.03 in Transportation, etc. to lows of 1.02 in Construction and 1.62 in Services. The surprisingly high VCC in Agriculture is due in part to the high levels of inventories (or circulating constant capital) in Agriculture, although it is of course also true that agricultural production in the US is highly mechanized and probably the most "capital-intensive" agriculture in the world. The low level of the VCC in Construction and Services is not surprising, since production in these industries is generally very difficult to mechanize and the Service industry has very little circulating constant capital. The wide variation in the VCC across industries suggests that a change in the distribution of capital and labor across industries may have a significant effect on

Table 3.8   Value composition of capital by industry

	MAN	MIN	CON	TPU	SER	WRT	AFF	GOV	TOT
1947	3.08	4.06	0.78	6.23	1.11	2.17	7.34	13.00	3.58
1948	3.06	3.86	0.79	6.43	1.07	2.41	7.54	12.16	3.60
1949	3.19	4.64	0.80	7.02	1.13	2.40	8.24	11.33	3.81
1950	3.24	4.65	0.86	7.29	1.21	2.67	10.03	11.55	3.94
1951	3.11	4.64	0.77	6.96	1.25	2.54	10.55	11.28	3.78
1952	2.99	5.08	0.73	6.92	1.23	2.40	11.07	10.45	3.69
1953	2.80	5.29	0.71	6.88	1.24	2.33	11.42	10.93	3.56
1954	3.08	6.47	0.72	7.40	1.30	2.37	11.78	11.62	3.84
1955	3.05	6.84	0.71	7.48	1.37	2.49	12.41	12.00	3.85
1956	3.20	6.90	0.69	7.68	1.44	2.48	12.41	12.94	3.96
1957	3.30	7.36	0.72	7.91	1.48	2.47	12.40	13.06	4.08
1958	3.56	8.79	0.77	8.37	1.52	2.49	12.06	12.59	4.33
1959	3.33	8.82	0.74	8.19	1.52	2.45	11.81	12.10	4.14
1960	3.36	8.73	0.73	8.14	1.57	2.39	11.69	11.70	4.11
1961	3.48	9.33	0.73	8.17	1.60	2.38	11.23	11.73	4.18
1962	3.34	9.56	0.71	8.01	1.62	2.37	11.35	11.62	4.07
1963	3.31	9.24	0.71	7.78	1.62	2.36	11.14	11.09	3.99
1964	3.27	9.47	0.71	7.57	1.68	2.36	11.06	10.88	3.92
1965	3.29	9.58	0.72	7.46	1.70	2.39	11.50	10.89	3.92
1966	3.34	10.11	0.70	7.44	1.69	2.45	11.83	10.97	3.91
1967	3.50	10.34	0.75	7.62	1.65	2.44	12.48	11.16	4.03
1968	3.52	10.45	0.71	7.65	1.66	2.46	12.56	11.25	4.02
1969	3.63	10.16	0.68	7.65	1.65	2.50	12.62	11.44	4.07
1970	3.96	9.92	0.71	7.89	1.68	2.54	12.62	11.26	4.29
1971	4.23	10.09	0.70	8.17	1.73	2.68	13.65	11.96	4.50
1972	4.06	9.49	0.69	7.86	1.65	2.68	14.69	11.75	4.37
1973	4.10	9.21	0.73	7.73	1.65	2.77	15.25	11.98	4.39
1974	4.96	10.03	0.88	8.99	1.81	3.07	15.52	13.73	5.13
1975	5.19	9.20	1.03	9.71	1.79	3.03	15.75	13.46	5.39
1976	4.86	9.18	1.02	9.31	1.69	2.99	14.76	13.06	5.15
1977	4.71	9.29	1.02	9.03	1.62	2.99	14.94	13.40	5.03

Sources: See Appendix B, section B.3b.

the aggregate *VCC*. It is interesting to note that the *VCC* in Manufacturing was about average for the total private economy throughout the postwar period.

From these estimates we can also see that the *VCC* increased in all industries over this period, although the percentage change differed somewhat across industries, from highs of 128 per cent in Mining (2.8 per cent per year) and 104 per cent in Agriculture (2.4 per cent per year) to lows of 30 per cent in Construction (0.8 per cent per year) and

4 per cent in Government Enterprises. Thus the "primary" industries of Mining and Agriculture were more consistent with Marx's hypothesis of a rapidly rising VCC.

The distribution of variable capital across industries in the postwar US economy is shown in Table A.1 of Appendix A. According to these estimates, there was a modest but significant shift in the distribution of variable capital from industries with a high or average VCC to industries with a low VCC. The most significant changes were in the Services industry, which increased its percentage of the total variable capital from 7 to 12 per cent, and the Construction industry, which increased its percentage of the total variable capital from 8 to 10 per cent. Overall industries with a significantly lower than average VCC (including also Trade) increased their percentage of the total variable capital from 28 to 36 per cent.

In order to estimate the effect of this change in the distribution of variable capital on the aggregate VCC, I calculated what the VCC would have been in 1977 if the distribution of variable capital had remained the same as in 1947, by using equation 3.6 above, but using the 1947 shares of variable capital as the weights for each industry, which were multiplied by the VCC in 1977 for each industry. The result of this calculation is that if the distribution of variable capital had remained constant, the aggregate VCC in 1977 would have been 5.34, compared to the actual level of 5.03. Based on this estimate of the aggregate VCC in 1977, the aggregate VCC would have increased 49 per cent from 1947 to 1977, compared to the actual 41 per cent increase. According to these estimates, the actual change in the distribution of variable capital *by itself* caused an 8 per cent *decline* in the aggregate VCC.

Using this hypothetical estimate of the VCC in 1977, we can derive a similar hypothetical estimate of the OCC in 1977. The hypothetical estimates of the VCC imply that constant capital in 1977 would have been \$2505.5 billion which in turn implies that the OCC in 1977 would have been 2.03, compared to the actual level of 1.91, and that the OCC would have increased 36 per cent from 1947 to 1977, compared to the actual 28 per cent increase. According to these hypothetical estimates, the actual change in the distribution of capital and labor across industries *by itself* also caused an 8 per cent *decline* in the aggregate OCC.[10]

Thus we conclude that the structural change in the distribution of capital and labor across industries had a significant negative effect on the aggregate VCC and OCC in the postwar US economy, and that *technological change by itself* had more of a positive effect on the aggregate *VCC* and *OCC* than it appears on the basis of the aggregate estimates alone. These results, of course, lend further support to Marx's hypothesis of a rising organic composition of capital.

3.2.5 The Turnover Time of Capital

Marx defined the turnover time of capital as the length of time required to recover the advanced circulating capital, (C.II, chapter 7). It is equal to the sum of the time of production and the time of circulation. If the turnover time is measured in the unit of one year, then the inverse of the turnover time (T) is the number of turnovers of the circulating capital per year (n); i.e. $n = 1/T$.

A reduction of the turnover time of capital, *ceteris paribus*, will reduce the stock of circulating constant capital required to maintain a given level of production throughout the year. Such a reduction in the stock of circulating constant capital will in turn reduce the total stock of constant capital and thereby increase the rate of profit.

A rough estimate of the turnover time of capital can be obtained by the ratio of the stock of circulating constant capital (CC_s) to the annual flow of circulating constant capital (CC_f); i.e. $T = CC_s / CC_f$. Estimates of these variables are shown in Table 3.9. (Estimates are calculated for six years only because Wolff's estimates of the flow of circulating constant capital are used and these are only for these six years.) These estimates show that the turnover time of capital did in fact decline significantly in the postwar US economy, from 0.31 in 1947 to 0.23 in 1976 (a 26 per cent decline overall). Or inversely, the number of turnovers per year increased from 3.3 in 1947 to 4.3 in 1976.

In order to estimate the effect of this decline in the turnover time of capital on the value and the organic composition of capital, I calculated hypothetical estimates of these variables, based on the counterfactual assumption that the turnover time of capital remained constant. These hypothetical estimates show that the value composition of capital would have increased 54 per cent over this period, compared to the actual 44 per cent increase, and the organic composition would have increased 39 per cent, compared to the actual 29 per cent increase. Thus these hypothetical estimates suggest that the actual decline in the turnover time of capital *by itself* reduced both the value and the organic composition of capital by 10 per cent, and thus reinforces the conclusion of the previous section that technological change by itself had an even greater negative effect on the

Table 3.9   Turnover of circulating constant capital

	CC_s	CC_f	T	n
1947	82.6	270.1	0.31	3.27
1958	127.3	526.7	0.24	4.14
1963	150.4	655.6	0.23	4.36
1967	199.4	855.5	0.23	4.29
1972	288.7	1151.5	0.25	3.99
1976	473.6	2045.0	0.23	4.32

Notation and Sources

CC_s Stock of circulating constant capital (billions of current dollars), Appendix A, Table A.3

CC_f Flow of circulating constant capital (billions of current dollars), Wolff (1986), supplemented by private correspondence

T Turnover time ($= CC_s / CC_f$)

n Number of turnovers per year ($= 1/T$)

composition of capital than it appears on the basis of the estimates by themselves.

3.2.6   The Incidence of Multiple Shifts

Many productive facilities may be utilized for more than one shift per day. An increased use of multiple shifts, *ceteris paribus*, reduces the composition of capital. With the addition of second and third shifts, the amount of fixed constant capital remains approximately the same, but the amounts of productive labor employed, variable capital invested, and new-value produced all increase, thus reducing the value and the organic composition of capital.

Foss (1984) presents estimates of the average "work week" of fixed capital (plant and equipment) by major industry group from 1929 to 1976. An increasing use of multiple shifts obviously increases the average "work week" of fixed capital. According to Foss's estimates, the most significant changes in the "work week" of fixed capital during the postwar period were an 11 per cent increase in Manufacturing and a 20 per cent increase in Mining. Other industries showed little or no change. According to Foss, the employment of workers on late shifts accounted for almost *90 per cent* of the total increase of production workers from 1952 to 1979 (ibid., p. 4). Such a predominance of expansion by the addition of multiple shifts must have had a significant negative effect of the value and the organic composition of capital.

In order to estimate the effect of this increased incidence of multiple shifts on the value and organic composition of capital, I used Foss's estimates to calculate hypothetical estimates of the value and organic composition of capital in each industry, based on the counterfactual assumptions that the average "work week" of fixed capital remained constant over the postwar period and that the same output was produced instead by a proportional increase of plant and equipment, requiring a proportional increase of fixed constant capital, rather than by longer hours of utilization of the actual plant and equipment. For example, instead of an 11 per cent increase in the "work week" of fixed capital in Manufacturing, it was assumed that the fixed constant capital in Manufacturing was 11 per cent greater in 1977 than the actual amount, and the total constant capital in Manufacturing was recalculated accordingly. These hypothetical estimates of constant capital for each industry were then aggregated and used to calculate hypothetical estimates of the value and the organic composition of capital.

This shows that if the "work week" of fixed capital had remained constant in the postwar period, the value composition of capital would have increased 48 per cent, compared to the actual 44 per cent increase, and the organic composition of capital would have increased 33 per cent, compared to the actual 29 per cent increase. These hypothetical estimates suggest the actual increase in the incidence of multiple shifts *by itself* reduced the value and the organic composition of capital by 4 per cent, and thus that technological change by itself had an even greater positive effect on the composition of capital than we initially concluded.

Combining these results with the results of the previous two sections, the three "other factors" discussed appear to have had the combined effect of reducing the value and the organic composition of capital by 23 per cent from 1947 to 1976. On the basis of these results, it appears that technological change by itself increased the value composition of capital in the postwar US economy by 67 per cent and the organic composition of capital by 52 per cent. These results of course, lend stronger empirical support to Marx's hypothesis of a rising organic composition of capital.

3.3 RATE OF PROFIT

The rate of profit was defined in Chapter 1 as the ratio of the annual flow of surplus-value to the stock of constant capital, i.e. $RP = S / C$.

Annual estimates of these variables are presented in Table 3.10. The rate of profit is shown graphically in Figure 3.1 in terms of index numbers, along with the rate of surplus-value and the value composition of capital (estimates of the rate of profit and the value composition of capital are cyclically adjusted as before). The possible bias in the trend of these estimates of the rate of profit is discussed briefly below and more fully in Appendix C, section C.1.

We have already seen that the value composition of capital increased faster than the rate of surplus-value in the postwar US economy. It follows that the rate of profit must have declined. *The estimates of the rate of profit do in fact show an 18 per cent decline* over this period, from 0.39 in 1947 to 0.32 in 1977. In terms of five-year moving averages, the rate of profit declined 16 per cent, from 0.38 in 1947–51 to 0.32 in 1973–7. Regressing the natural logarithm of the rate of profit against time, the coefficient of time is negative (-0.0030) and statistically significant at the 5 per cent level (t-statistic = -1.61), thus indicating a weak negative trend.

These results are, of course, consistent with Marx's expectations of a falling rate of profit. The rate of profit declined, and for the reason Marx suggested: because the composition of capital increased faster than the rate of surplus-value.

On the other hand, these results are clearly not consistent with the neo-Ricardian "profit squeeze" interpretation of Marx's theory, according to which a *decline* in the rate of surplus-value is supposed to squeeze profits and cause the rate of profit to fall. These estimates show that the rate of surplus-value did not decline; thus the secular version of the "profit squeeze" theory is not valid for the postwar US economy.

These results also provide empirical evidence related to the debate over Okishio's Theorem, discussed in Chapter 1. There we saw that, according to Foley, for economies characterized by both rising real wages and a rising rate of surplus-value, it cannot be determined *a priori* whether technological change will increase or decrease the rate of profit. We have seen in this chapter that the postwar US economy exhibited these characteristics of the "intermediate zone" in the debate over the Okishio Theorem. Now we see that the rate of profit declined significantly in the postwar US economy. Thus these results suggest that it is at least *possible* for technological change in economies falling within this intermediate zone to cause the rate of profit to decline.

However, once again the modest decline in the rate of profit is probably less than would be expected on the basis of Marx's theory.

Table 3.10   Rate of profit

	S	C	RP	Index	ARP	Index
1947	98.9	253.8	0.39	100.0	0.43	100.0
1948	105.3	279.5	0.38	96.6	0.41	95.9
1949	111.1	282.5	0.39	100.8	0.47	110.2
1950	116.8	323.6	0.36	92.5	0.39	90.8
1951	137.8	360.7	0.38	98.0	0.40	93.4
1952	143.6	375.2	0.38	98.1	0.40	94.1
1953	148.4	390.2	0.38	97.5	0.38	89.8
1954	151.8	400.0	0.38	97.3	0.42	98.8
1955	169.9	433.3	0.39	100.5	0.40	94.6
1956	173.3	477.5	0.36	93.1	0.38	88.3
1957	185.5	505.4	0.37	94.1	0.39	91.4
1958	189.0	516.7	0.37	93.8	0.42	98.9
1959	209.2	536.5	0.39	100.0	0.42	99.1
1960	217.2	550.6	0.39	101.1	0.44	101.9
1961	225.8	563.0	0.40	102.8	0.46	106.7
1962	246.7	585.2	0.42	108.1	0.46	107.7
1963	261.1	607.1	0.43	110.2	0.46	107.6
1964	280.6	636.4	0.44	113.1	0.46	118.0
1965	304.1	687.6	0.44	113.4	0.44	104.0
1966	332.5	754.9	0.44	112.9	0.44	102.0
1967	347.5	812.9	0.43	109.6	0.44	103.4
1968	374.5	891.6	0.42	107.7	0.43	101.3
1969	392.4	985.1	0.40	102.1	0.41	96.2
1970	403.9	1073.0	0.38	96.5	0.42	97.7
1971	445.3	1171.2	0.38	97.5	0.43	99.9
1972	488.3	1276.4	0.38	98.1	0.41	95.6
1973	531.4	1463.2	0.36	93.1	0.37	87.2
1974	548.1	1807.9	0.30	77.7	0.32	74.9
1975	623.6	1969.1	0.32	81.2	0.36	84.6
1976	689.7	2135.6	0.32	82.8	0.36	83.2
1977	766.1	2361.6	0.32	83.2	0.35	81.1

Average annual rates of change of	RP	ARP
1947–65	0.70	0.32
1965–77	−2.58	−1.85
1965–72	−2.07	−1.19
1972–77	−3.30	−2.78
1947–77	−0.61	−0.55

Notation and Sources
   S Surplus-value (billions of current dollars) (= N − V) (flow), Table 3.1
   C Constant capital (billions of current dollars) (stock), see Appendix B,
       section B.3a, detailed estimates by industry in Appendix A, Table A.2
 RP Rate of profit (= S/C)
ARP Cyclically adjusted rate of profit: see text

Figure 3.1   The rate of profit and its determinants

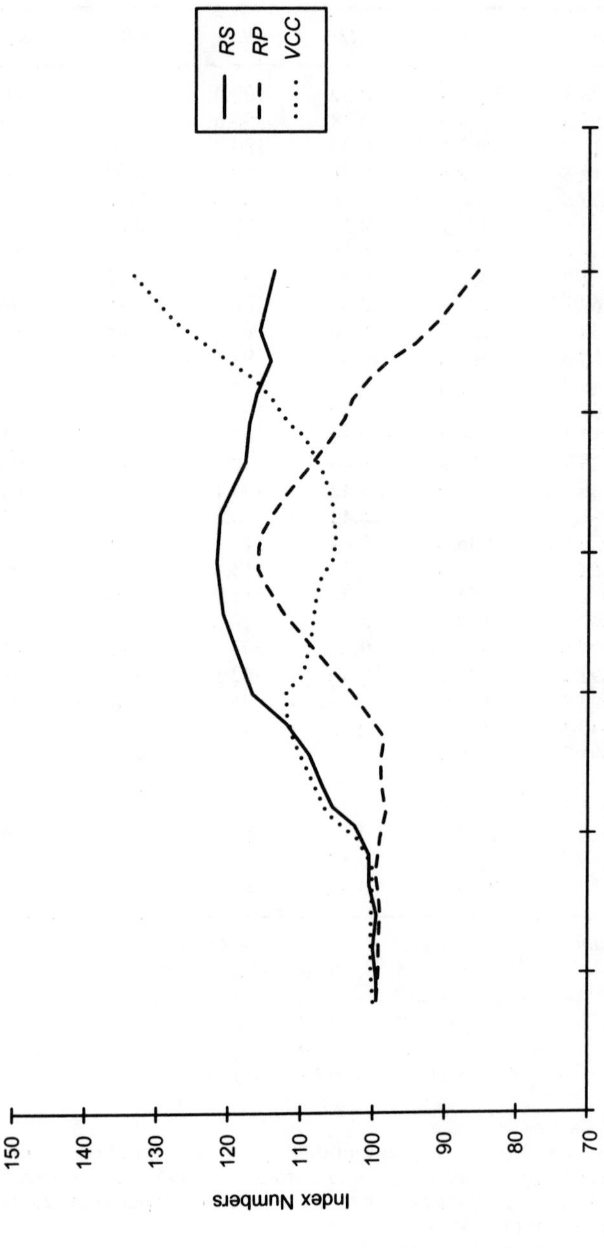

One possible statistical explanation for this less-than-expected decline in the rate of profit is that the actual decline may be underestimated by my estimates. The possibility of bias in the trends of my estimates of the rate of profit and the other Marxian variables is discussed in Appendix C, section C.1. It is concluded there that my estimates of the rate of profit probably have a small upward bias in their trend, i.e. they probably underestimate the actual decline in the rate of profit, such that the "true" rate of profit probably declined 20–25 per cent, rather than the observed 16–18 per cent decline.

Furthermore, as discussed in Chapter 1, Marx's theory is about the effects of changes in technology on the rate of profit, with other factors which also affect the rate of profit held constant. In the previous section, the effects of the three most important of these other influences on the rate of profit were analyzed: the distribution of capital across industries, the turnover of capital, and the incidence of multiple shifts. It was concluded that all three of these "other factors" had a significant negative effect on the composition of capital in the postwar US economy. It follows that these three "other factors" had a significant positive effect on the rate of profit during this period. In other words, if these three "other factors" had remained constant, the rate of profit would have declined by 28 per cent, significantly greater than the actual 18 per cent decline. Thus the negative effect of technological change on the rate of profit was probably greater than the estimates by themselves suggest. This conclusion is, of course, more consistent with Marx's hypothesis of a falling rate of profit.[11]

The most striking feature of the trend in the rate of profit in the postwar US economy through 1977 is the very significant shift in the trend in the mid-1960s. In the pre-1965 period, the rate of profit increased a significant 14 per cent, as the rate of surplus-value increased and the composition of capital remained essentially constant. These trends are very contrary to Marx's predictions. In sharp contrast, in the post-1965 period, the rate of profit declined 26 per cent, both because the rate of surplus-value stopped increasing and because the composition of capital increased significantly. These trends are, of course, quite consistent with Marx's hypotheses.

We have seen above that the most important proximate cause of these significant shifts in the trends of the rate of surplus-value and the composition of capital, and thus in the rate of profit, was the significant slowdown in the productivity growth of productive labor between the two periods. This slowdown was the sole cause of the leveling off of the rate of surplus-value and was the main cause of the increase in the composition of capital in the post-1965 period. Another important cause of this increase was the 7 per cent increase in the price of the means of production relative to the price of final output.

To summarize the results of this empirical test: it appears that the trends of the Marxian variables for the postwar US economy are largely consistent with Marx's hypothesis that technological change would have a negative effect on the rate of profit. The estimates of the rate of profit derived here declined 15–20 per cent over the period of study, and for the reason which Marx argued: because the composition of capital increased faster than the rate of surplus-value. Furthermore, these estimates of the rate of profit probably underestimate the decline in the rate of profit by 5–10 percentage points. Finally, the "other factors" which also influence the rate of profit probably had a significant positive effect on the rate of profit, which implies that technological change by itself had an even greater negative effect on the rate of profit than the estimates show, perhaps as much as an additional 10 percentage points. Thus it seems reasonable to conclude that technological change had a significant negative effect on the rate of profit in the postwar US economy, as suggested by Marx's theory.

3.4   COMPARISON WITH WEISSKOPF'S ESTIMATES

The estimates of the Marxian variables presented above will now be compared with the previous estimates of these variables presented by Weisskopf and Wolff. This comparison will enable us to determine the effects of different interpretations of the conceptual issues discussed in Chapter 2 on the trends of the estimates of the Marxian variables in the postwar US economy. This section compares my estimates with those of Weisskopf and the next section will compare my estimates with those of Wolff.

We saw in Chapter 2 that Weisskopf's estimates of the three Marxian ratios are based on definitions of constant capital, variable capital, and surplus-value which differ from the definitions adopted in this book in two major respects:

1. Weisskopf's estimates of constant capital include the value of tenant-occupied housing.

2. Weisskopf's estimates do not distinguish between productive labor and unproductive labor. Thus his estimates of constant capital and variable capital include capital invested in the non-production activities of circulation and supervision, and his estimates of surplus-value do not include the annual costs of non-production activities.

In addition, Weisskopf's estimates are different from mine in the minor procedural respect that his apply to the Non-Financial Corporate Business (NFCB) sector of the economy and my estimates apply to the Business sector as a whole.

The effect of each of the above conceptual and procedural differences on the estimates of the Marxian variables was estimated by the following method: for each variable, I began with Weisskopf's estimates and then derived alternative series from Weisskopf's estimates by eliminating each of the above conceptual and procedural differences one at a time. The difference in the trends of two successive series then serves as a measure of the effect of the last difference eliminated on the trend of the given variable.[12] The results of this analysis are summarized in Table 3.11.

Table 3.11   Reconciliation of Moseley's and Weisskopf's estimates, 1949–75 (percentage points)

	Rate of Surplus-Value	*Organic Composition of Capital*	*Rate of Profit*
Difference in trends	0.47	0.19	0.20
Conceptual differences			
1. Residential capital	0.00	0.15	−0.04
2. Productive labor	0.45	−0.11	0.23
Sectoral difference	0.02	0.09	0.01

Method: See text.

The most significant difference between the trends of Weisskopf's estimates of the Marxian variables and my estimates is the widely divergent trends in the two estimates of *the rate of surplus-value*. Weisskopf uses the profit share of income as his proxy for the rate of surplus-value. Weisskopf's estimates of the profit share declined 31 per cent over his period of study, from 0.22 in 1949 to 0.15 in 1975 (see Table 3.12) while my estimates of the rate of surplus-value increased 14 per cent over this period. These two estimates are shown graphically in Figure 3.2, with both estimates first converted into index numbers and then converted into five-year moving averages to smooth out cyclical fluctuations.

Table 3.12   Alternative estimates of the rate of surplus-value

	Moseley	Weisskopf	Wolff
1947	1.40		0.96
1948	1.35		
1949	1.50	0.22	
1950	1.42	0.24	
1951	1.44	0.24	
1952	1.41	0.21	
1953	1.35	0.20	
1954	1.46	0.19	
1955	1.51	0.22	
1956	1.44	0.20	
1957	1.50	0.19	
1958	1.59	0.17	1.01
1959	1.61	0.20	
1960	1.62	0.19	
1961	1.68	0.18	
1962	1.71	0.20	
1963	1.71	0.20	1.09
1964	1.73	0.22	
1965	1.73	0.23	
1966	1.72	0.22	
1967	1.72	0.21	1.08
1968	1.69	0.20	
1969	1.62	0.18	
1970	1.61	0.15	
1971	1.71	0.16	
1972	1.67	0.17	0.77
1973	1.59	0.17	
1974	1.55	0.15	
1975	1.71	0.15	
1976	1.66		0.75
1977	1.63		

Sources: Moseley, Table 3.1; Weisskopf (1979); Wolff (1986).

83

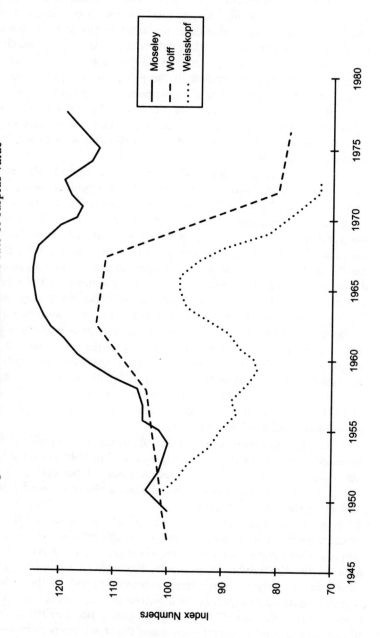

Figure 3.2 Alternative estimates of the rate of surplus-value

These two sets of estimates are not directly comparable because the denominator in the profit share is total income rather than variable capital (or wages) only. However, the ratio of profit to wages has essentially the same trend as the profit share. The ratio of profit to wages in the NFCB sector declined 33 per cent over this period, slightly greater than the decline in the profit share. Thus there is a very significant overall difference of 47 percentage points between the trend of the profit–wages ratio and the trend of my estimates of the rate of surplus-value. This ratio of profit to wages will be used as the basis for the further reconciliation of my estimates with Weisskopf's estimates, which follows.[13]

Since the conceptual issue of whether constant capital includes the value of tenant-occupied housing does not affect profit or wages, the only differences between the ratio of profit to wages in the NFCB sector and my estimates of the rate of surplus-value are the sectoral difference and the different treatments of unproductive labor. We can see From Table 3.11 that the sectoral difference has very little effect on the trend of the ratio of profit to wages, so that the very significant difference between the trends of these two estimates of the rate of surplus-value is due almost entirely to the different interpretations of Marx's distinction between productive labor and unproductive labor.

The trends in the two estimates of *the composition of capital* are also significantly different, but not as divergent as the two trends in the rate of surplus-value. Weisskopf defines the composition of capital as the ratio of capital to potential output.[14] This ratio is the most analogous to my estimates of the organic composition of capital, which I will use as the basis for comparison with Weisskopf's estimates of the composition of capital.

Weisskopf's estimates of the ratio of capital to potential output increased 12 per cent over his period, from 1.67 in 1949 to 1.87 in 1975 (see Table 3.13), while my estimates increased 31 per cent over this period. These two estimates are shown graphically in Figure 3.3, with both estimates converted as before.

These two estimates of the composition of capital are not directly comparable because the denominator in Weisskopf's ratio is potential output rather than actual output. However, since there was no secular trend in the capacity utilization rate, the ratio of capital to actual output has exactly the same trend over this period as the ratio of capital to potential output, i.e. both increased 12 per cent. Thus there is an overall difference of 19 percentage points between the trend of this ratio of capital to actual output and the trend of my estimates of

Table 3.13   Alternative estimates of the organic composition of capital

	Moseley	Weisskopf
1947	1.49	
1948	1.53	
1949	1.52	1.67
1950	1.63	1.58
1951	1.55	1.52
1952	1.53	1.59
1953	1.51	1.57
1954	1.56	1.67
1955	1.53	1.55
1956	1.63	1.61
1957	1.63	1.67
1958	1.68	1.81
1959	1.58	1.65
1960	1.57	1.65
1961	1.56	1.40
1962	1.50	1.56
1963	1.47	1.52
1964	1.44	1.47
1965	1.43	1.43
1966	1.44	1.41
1967	1.48	1.49
1968	1.50	1.49
1969	1.55	1.52
1970	1.64	1.63
1971	1.66	1.65
1972	1.64	1.59
1973	1.69	1.59
1974	2.01	1.75
1975	1.99	1.87
1976	1.93	
1977	1.91	

Sources: Moseley, table 3.7; Weisskopf (1979).

the organic composition of capital. This ratio of capital to actual output will be used as the basis for the remaining reconciliation with Weisskopf's estimates.[15]

We can see from Table 3.11 that the sectoral difference has a fairly significant effect on the estimates of the composition of capital, and that this effect is to raise the percentage increase in the composition of capital by 9 percentage points. Thus estimates of Weisskopf's capital–

86

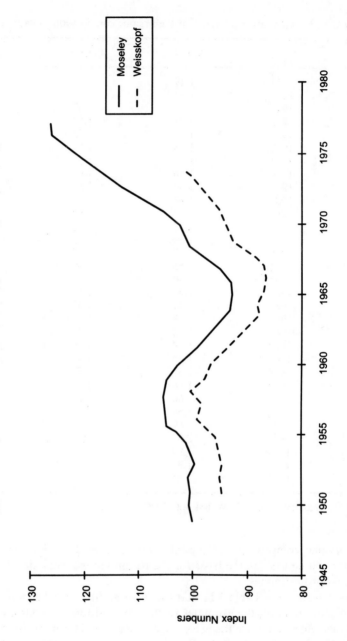

Figure 3.3 Alternative estimates of the organic composition of capital

output ratio for the Business sector increased 21 per cent, almost as much as the 31 per cent increase in my estimates of the organic composition of capital. The two conceptual differences have somewhat offsetting effects. Omitting residential capital from Weisskopf's capital–output ratio raises the increase in this ratio by 15 percentage points, and distinguishing between productive and unproductive labor lowers it by 11 percentage points.

Finally, both estimates of *the rate of profit* declined, but the decline in Weisskopf's estimates was slightly more than twice as large as the decline in my estimates. Weisskopf's estimates declined 38 per cent over his period, from 0.13 in 1949 to 0.08 in 1975 (see Table 3.14), while my estimates declined 18 per cent over his period. Thus there is an overall difference of 20 percentage points between the trends of these two estimates of the rate of profit. These two estimates are shown graphically in Figure 3.4 in terms of index numbers.

We can see from Table 3.11 that the issue of productive and unproductive labor has by far the most significant effect on the trend in the rate of profit. The sectoral difference has almost no effect on the trend in the rate of profit, and excluding residential capital has the effect of increasing the decline in the rate of profit by 4 percentage points. Thus excluding unproductive labor both offsets this effect of residential capital and accounts for all the difference between the trends of Weisskopf's estimates and my estimates.

To summarize this reconciliation between Weisskopf's estimates and my estimates of the Marxian variables, the most important difference between these estimates is the opposite trends in the two estimates of the rate of surplus-value. This divergence is due entirely to the different interpretations of productive and unproductive labor. The two estimates of the composition of capital both increased, with my estimates increasing more than twice as much as Weisskopf's estimates, but most of this difference is eliminated when Weisskopf's ratio is derived for the Business sector. The two conceptual differences between Weisskopf and myself have offsetting effects on the composition of capital. Finally, the two estimates of the rate of profit both declined, with Weisskopf's estimates declining slightly more than twice as much as mine. This difference is due entirely to the different interpretations of productive and unproductive labor.

The main conclusion of this comparison with Weisskopf's estimates is that the conceptual issue which is primarily responsible for the different trends in the two sets of estimates of the Marxian variables is the different interpretations of Marx's distinction between productive and unproductive labor. This conclusion is especially true of the estimates of the rate of surplus-value and the rate of profit.

Table 3.14   Alternative estimates of the rate of profit

	Moseley	Weisskopf	Wolff
1947	0.39		0.15
1948	0.38		
1949	0.39	0.13	
1950	0.36	0.15	
1951	0.38	0.16	
1952	0.38	0.13	
1953	0.38	0.12	
1954	0.38	0.12	
1955	0.39	0.14	
1956	0.36	0.12	
1957	0.37	0.11	
1958	0.37	0.10	0.15
1959	0.39	0.12	
1960	0.39	0.11	
1961	0.40	0.11	
1962	0.42	0.13	
1963	0.43	0.14	0.16
1964	0.44	0.15	
1965	0.44	0.15	
1966	0.44	0.16	
1967	0.43	0.14	0.17
1968	0.42	0.14	
1969	0.40	0.12	
1970	0.38	0.09	
1971	0.38	0.10	
1972	0.38	0.11	0.14
1973	0.36	0.10	
1974	0.30	0.08	
1975	0.32	0.08	
1976	0.32		0.12
1977	0.32		

Sources: Moseley, table 3.10; Weisskopf (1979); Wolff (1986).

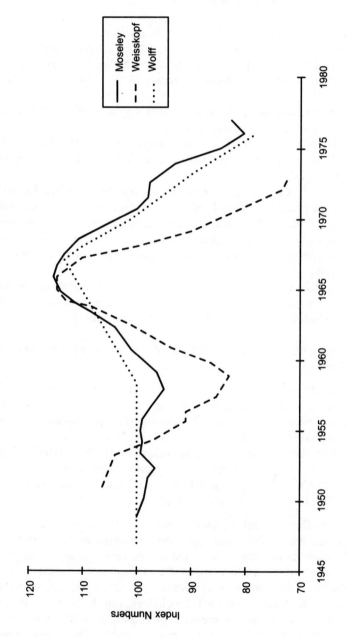

Figure 3.4 Alternative estimates of the rate of profit

3.5   COMPARISON WITH WOLFF'S ESTIMATES

We saw in Chapter 2 that Wolff's estimates are based on definitions of constant capital, variable capital, and surplus-value which differ from the definitions adopted in this book with respect to four of the five conceptual issues discussed. To recapitulate:

1. Wolff's estimates are in units of labor (man-years) rather than in units of money (current prices).
2. Wolff's estimates of constant capital and variable capital include the costs of non-capitalist production, as well as of capitalist production.
3. Wolff's estimates do not distinguish between productive and unproductive labor. Thus his estimates of constant capital and variable capital include capital· invested in the non-production activities of circulation and supervision and his estimates of surplus-value do not include the annual costs of these non-production activities.
4. Wolff's estimates of variable capital do not include the portion of wages paid in taxes to the government; instead these taxes are included in Wolff's estimates of surplus-value.

   In addition, Wolff's estimates differ from my estimates in the following minor procedural respects:

1. Wolff uses the annual flows of circulating constant capital and variable capital as approximations for the stocks of these variables (i.e. Wolff assumes that the turnover time for circulating constant capital is one year).
2. Wolff's estimates of surplus-value (implicitly) include "imputations" for various non-market transactions (primarily the rental value of owner-occupied homes) and also include the value produced by self-employed proprietors.

   The effect of each of these conceptual and procedural differences between Wolff's estimates and my estimates on the trends of the Marxian variables was estimated by the same method used above in the comparison with Weisskopf's estimates. For each variable, I eliminated each of these differences one at a time, calculated a new series at each step, and used the difference in the trends between two successive series as the measure of the effect of the last difference eliminated on the trend of the given variable. The comparison with

Wolff is somewhat more complicated because there are more differences between his estimates and my estimates. The results of this analysis are summarized in Table 3.15.[16]

Table 3.15   Reconciliation of Moseley and Wolff estimates
(percentage points)

	Rate of Surplus-Value	Value Composition of Capital	Rate of Profit
Difference in trends	0.41	0.52	0.02
Conceptual differences			
1. Labor vs. money	0.02	0.11	−0.05
2. Non-capitalist production	0.06	0.26	−0.10
3. Productive labor	0.35	0.21	0.11
4. Taxes on wages	−0.10	−0.03	−0.08
Procedural differences			
1. Circulating capital	0.00	−0.02	0.02
2. Proprietor income and imputations	0.08	0.00	0.12

Method: See text.

The trend in Wolff's estimates of *the rate of surplus-value* is similar to that of Weisskopf's estimates and diverges even more from the trend in my estimates. Wolff's estimates declined 22 per cent over his period of study, from 0.96 in 1947 to 0.75 in 1976 (see Table 3.12), while my estimates increased 19 per cent over this period. Thus there is an overall difference of 41 percentage points in the trends of these two estimates of the rate of surplus-value. These estimates of the rate of surplus-value are shown graphically in Figure 3.2, in terms of index numbers.

We can see from Table 3.15 that the conceptual issue of productive and unproductive labor has the biggest effect by far on the trend of the rate of surplus-value. This issue accounts for almost all the total difference between the trends of Wolff's estimates and my estimates (35 out of 41 percentage points). The other differences have minor and partially offsetting effects on the trend in the rate of surplus-value. Interestingly, the conceptual issue of money vs. labor estimates has almost no effect on the trend of the rate of surplus-value.

The trend of Wolff's estimates of *the composition of capital* diverges from the trend in my estimates almost as much as the two trends of the rate of surplus-value. Wolff defines the composition of capital as the ratio of constant capital to variable capital. Wolff calls this ratio the "organic" composition of capital, but this ratio is analogous to my definition of the "value" composition of capital. Thus I use my estimates of the value composition of capital as the basis for comparison with Wolff's estimates. Wolff's estimates declined 8 per cent over his period of study, from 5.62 in 1947 to 5.16 in 1976 (see Table 3.16), in striking contrast to the 44 per cent increase in my estimates over this period. Thus there is an overall difference of 52 percentage points in the trends of these two estimates of the composition of capital. These two estimates are shown graphically in Figure 3.5.

We can see from Table 3.15 that two conceptual issues account for almost all the total difference between the trends of the two sets of estimates: the issue of non-capitalist production and the issue of productive and unproductive labor, with the latter issue having the largest effect. The issue of money vs. labor has a greater effect on the trend of the composition of capital than on the rate of surplus-value, but this effect is still small. The other differences have very little effect on the trend in the composition of capital.

Since the divergent trends in the estimates of the rate of surplus-value and the composition of capital have roughly opposite effects on the rate of profit, the trends of the two estimates of *the rate of profit* were very similar. Wolff's estimates declined 20 per cent over his period, from 0.15 in 1947 to 0.12 in 1976 (see Table 3.14), while my estimates declined 18 per cent over this period. Thus there is an overall difference of only 2 percentage points in these two estimates of the rate of profit. These two estimates are shown graphically in Figure 3.4.

We can see from Table 3.15 that several conceptual issues have significant effects on the trend in the rate of profit. Excluding unproductive labor has a positive effect on the rate of profit, i.e. reduces the decline in the rate of profit, because the positive effect on the rate of surplus-value is greater than the positive effect on the composition of capital. Excluding proprietor value and imputations also has a significant positive effect on the rate of profit. On the other hand, eliminating the differences on the issues of labor vs. money, non-capitalist production, and taxes on wages all have negative effects on the trend in the rate of profit.

The main conclusion of this comparison with Wolff's estimates is similar to the conclusion with Weisskopf's estimates: the conceptual

Table 3.16   Alternative estimates of the value composition of capital

	Moseley	Wolff
1947	3.58	5.62
1948	3.60	
1949	3.81	
1950	3.94	
1951	3.78	
1952	3.69	
1953	3.56	
1954	3.84	
1955	3.85	
1956	3.96	
1957	4.08	
1958	4.33	5.98
1959	4.14	
1960	4.11	
1961	4.18	
1962	4.07	
1963	3.99	5.67
1964	3.92	
1965	3.92	
1966	3.91	
1967	4.03	5.38
1968	4.02	
1969	4.07	
1970	4.29	
1971	4.50	
1972	4.37	4.68
1973	4.39	
1974	5.13	
1975	5.39	
1976	5.15	5.16
1977	5.03	

Sources: Moseley, Table 3.6; Wolff (1986).

issue which has the most significant effect on the trends of the Marxian variables and which accounts for most of the difference between the trends of my estimates and Wolff's estimates is the issue of productive and unproductive labor. This issue accounts for almost all of the difference in the trends of the two estimates of the rate of surplus-value, for almost half the difference in the trends of the two estimates of the composition of capital, and for more than all the difference in the trends of the two estimates of the rate of profit.

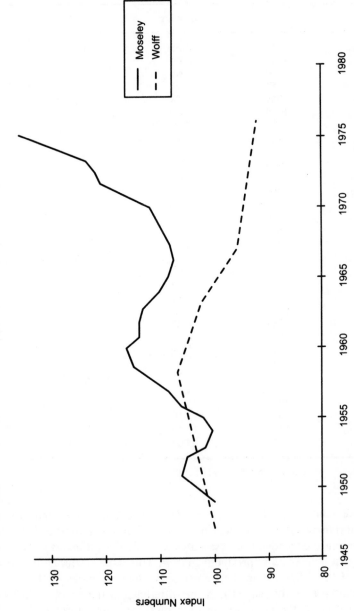

Figure 3.5 Alternative estimates of the value composition of capital

One further conclusion of interest which emerges from this comparison with Wolff's estimates is that the conceptual issue of whether the Marxian variables should be estimated in units of prices or in units of labor-time has very little effect on the trends in the Marxian ratios, at least as Wolff measures the quantities of labor (which ignores unequal skills and unequal intensities, see Chapter 2, pp. 30–1). Thus, even if one adopts the interpretation that estimates of the Marxian variables should be in units of labor-time, estimates of these variables in units of prices appear to be a good approximation of the former. Estimates in units of prices have the advantages of being much easier to derive and being available every year.

Thus it follows from these these comparisons with Weisskopf's and Wolff's estimates that the conclusions one reaches concerning the trends of the Marxian variables in the postwar US economy and concerning the causes of the decline in the rate of profit depends almost entirely on one's interpretation of Marx's distinction between productive and unproductive labor. If this distinction is taken into account, as I have argued it should be in an empirical test of Marx's theory, then in the postwar US economy the rate of surplus-value increased, rather than declined; the composition of capital increased, rather than remained constant; and the rate of profit declined because the composition of capital increased faster than the rate of surplus-value, not because the rate of surplus-value declined.[17]

3.6 ESTIMATES OF THE MARXIAN VARIABLES, 1977–87

Previous sections of this chapter have been concerned with estimates of the key Marxian variables for the long-wave period of expansion from 1947 to 1977. This last section will examine the estimates of these variables for the more recent period of stagnation from 1977 to 1987 (the latest year for which enough data are available to derive the estimates). Estimates of the rate of surplus-value, the value and the organic composition of capital, and the rate of profit for this recent decade are presented in Table 3.17. Estimates of the underlying determinants of these variables – the technical composition of capital, the productivity of labor, the average real wage, and the relative price ratios - are presented in Table 3.18. These estimates are not cyclically adjusted because the capacity utilization rate was approximately equal at the beginning and the end of this decade.[18]

Table 3.17   Estimates of the key Marxian variables, 1975–1987

	RS	VCC	OCC	RP
1975	1.71	5.39	1.99	0.32
1976	1.66	5.15	1.93	0.32
1977	1.63	5.03	1.91	0.32
1978	1.70	5.26	1.95	0.32
1979	1.64	5.32	2.02	0.31
1980	1.70	5.66	2.10	0.30
1981	1.81	5.76	2.05	0.31
1982	1.89	5.92	2.05	0.32
1983	1.93	5.76	1.96	0.34
1984	2.08	5.58	1.81	0.37
1985	2.15	5.47	1.74	0.39
1986	2.23	5.50	1.70	0.41
1987	2.22	5.48	1.70	0.41
Five-year averages				
1975–79	1.67	5.23	1.97	0.32
1983–87	2.12	5.56	1.78	0.39

Notation and Sources
   RS   Rate of surplus-value, see Table 3.1
  VCC   Value composition of capital, see Table 3.6
  OCC   Organic composition of capital, see Table 3.7
   RP   Rate of profit, see Table 3.10

The *rate of surplus-value increased very sharply* during this recent decade, from 1.63 in 1977 to 2.22 in 1987, or measured in terms of five-year averages, from 1.67 in 1973–7 to 2.12 in 1983–7. Thus the rate of surplus-value increased over 25 per cent during this decade, which is greater than the 16 per cent increase during the entire previous thirty-year period.

As we have seen, the underlying determinants of the rate of surplus-value are the productivity of productive labor, the average real wage of productive labor, and the price ratio P_n/P_v. According to the estimates presented in Table 3.18, productivity growth and the ratio P_n/P_v changed very little over this decade. However, real wage growth declined sharply to essentially zero (the *level* of real wages even declined slightly). Thus the underlying cause of the rapid increase in the rate of surplus-value was this cessation of real wage growth. There was no acceleration (or rebound) of productivity growth which would have increased the rate of surplus-value even more sharply. In fact,

Table 3.18   Determinants of the key Marxian variables, 1977–1987

	TCC	PR	WR	P_n/P_v	P_c/P_v	P_c/P_n
1977	22.17	12.45	4.73	1.00	1.08	1.08
1978	22.92	12.70	4.72	1.00	1.09	1.08
1979	22.73	12.30	4.67	1.00	1.10 1.10	
1980	24.01	12.45	4.60	1.00	1.09 1.10	
1981	24.84	12.93	4.63	1.01	1.08 1.07	
1982	26.13	13.24	4.60	1.00	1.04 1.04	
1983	26.81	13.63	4.64	1.00	1.00 1.00	
1984	26.41	14.13	4.59	1.00	0.97 0.97	
1985	27.74	14.47	4.54	0.99	0.92 0.93	
1986	26.98	14.80	4.53	0.99	0.92 0.93	
1987	28.10	14.99	4.53	0.97	0.89 0.91	
1977–87 (annual rates)	2.37%	1.84%	−0.43%			

Notation and Sources
TCC   Technical composition of capital, see Table 3.5
 PR   Productivity of productive labor, see Table 3.2
 WR   Real wage of productive labor, see Table 3.3
Price ratios, see Table 3.4

productivity growth even declined slightly, from 2.08 per cent in 1965–77 to 1.86 per cent in 1977–87. The cessation of real wage growth was in turn probably due primarily to the higher rates of unemployment which prevailed during this period of stagnation.

By contrast, the *value composition of capital remained almost constant* during this decade, after increasing significantly during the previous thirty years. The underlying determinants of the value composition of capital are the technical composition of capital, the average real wage of productive labor, and the price ratio P_c/P_v. We have seen that real wage growth ceased during this decade and this had a positive effect on the value composition of capital. However, this positive effect was almost entirely offset by the negative effect of a steep decline in the ratio P_c/P_v, from 1.08 in 1977 to 0.91 in 1987, and (to a lesser extent) the negative effect of a slowdown in the growth rate of the technical composition of capital, from an annual rate of 3.47 per cent in 1965–77 to 2.37 per cent in 1977–87. The price index for constant capital (P_c) remained almost constant from 1982 to 1987, while P_v increased almost 20 per cent. It is not surprising that the price index for circulating constant capital (or raw materials) remained essentially constant over this period. The price of raw materials fluctuates more widely than the price of final goods, and during a period of stagnation there is usually a relative decline in the price of raw materials. However, it is surprising that the price index for fixed constant capital (buildings and equipment) also remained essentially constant in the 1980s.

In even greater contrast to the rate of surplus-value, the *organic composition of capital* not only did not increase, but even *declined approximately 10 per cent* over this decade (measured in five-year averages). The main underlying cause of this decline in the organic composition of capital was a sharp decline in the price ratio P_c/P_n, which is approximately equal to the ratio P_c/P_v discussed in the last paragraph. The small slowdown in the growth rate of the technical composition of capital also contributed to the decline in the organic composition of capital. As in the case of the rate of surplus-value, there was no acceleration of productivity growth which would have reduced the organic composition of capital even more.

Finally, since the rate of surplus-value increased sharply and the value composition of capital remained essentially constant, the *rate of profit increased significantly* during this period, from 0.32 in 1977 to 0.41 in 1987, or from 0.32 in 1973–7 to 0.39 in 1983–7 (a 22 per cent increase). Thus by the end of the period, the rate of profit was about the same as in the early postwar period, so that the decline in the rate of profit prior to the mid-1970s was entirely offset by the recovery of the rate of profit since the mid-1970s. This result is perhaps not surprising, given the small decline in the rate of profit during the earlier period. However, this result does seem to contradict Marx's hypothesis that a decline in the rate of profit during a period of expansion would generally not be entirely offset by an increase in the rate of surplus-value *alone* during the ensuing period of stagnation, but would also require significant bankruptcies and the devaluation of capital which would reduce the composition of capital. On the other hand, if one takes into account the "other factors" discussed in the previous section (the distribution of capital, etc.), the prior decline in the rate of profit due to technological change alone was greater and would not have been entirely offset by the recent increase.

If one interprets Marx's theory as applying to long-run secular trends, including both the expansion and stagnation phases of long-wave cycles, then Marx's theory is contradicted by these estimates. According to these estimates, there was no permanent decline in the rate of profit; instead the decline during the expansion phase was fully offset by the increase during the stagnation phase (although the regression coefficient of time for the natural logarithm of the rate of profit was negative (-0.0035), and significant at the 1 per cent level; t-statistic $= -2.5403$).

Examining the underlying determinants of the Marxian variables over the entire postwar period, three factors stand out: (i) The slow-down in productivity growth after the mid-1960s, which had a negative effect on the rate of surplus-value, a positive effect on the organic composition of capital, and thus a negative effect on the rate of profit. This slowdown in productivity growth appears to have been the main underlying cause of the decline in the rate of profit from the mid-1960s to the mid-1970s. (ii) An even greater slowdown in real wage growth after the mid-1970s, which had a strong positive effect on the rate of surplus-value and the rate of profit during this period. (iii) Fluctuations in the relative price of the means of production, especially raw materials. During the early phase of the period of expansion (1947–65) and the recent period of stagnation (1977–87), the relative price of the means of production declined significantly, which had a negative effect on the composition of capital and thus a positive effect on the rate of profit. By contrast, during the later phase of the period of expansion (1965–77), the relative price of the means of production increased sharply, and thus contributed to the increase in the composition of capital and the decline in the rate of profit.

These shifts in trends are shown in Figures 3.6 and 3.7. Figure 3.6 shows the period averages of the "real" determinants of the nominal Marxian variables: the technical composition of capital, the productivity of productive labor and the average real wage of productive labor. The most striking feature of this graph is that all variables show a declining trend over the three periods, which would seem to be pervasive evidence of an economy in decline. The trends in the nominal Marxian variables thus depend on the *relative rates of decline* of the underlying real determinants. The decline in productivity growth was fairly even over the three periods. The decline in real wage growth, by contrast, was concentrated in the most recent decade. Figure 3.7 shows the three relative price ratios at the beginning and end year of each of the three periods. The outstanding feature of this graph is the "hump" in the two ratios P_c/P_v and P_c/P_n in the 1970s and 1980s. The significant increases in these price ratios in the 1970s contributed to the increase in the composition of capital during these years, and the reversals in these price ratios in the 1980s contributed to the absence of an increase in the composition of capital during this most recent decade.

101

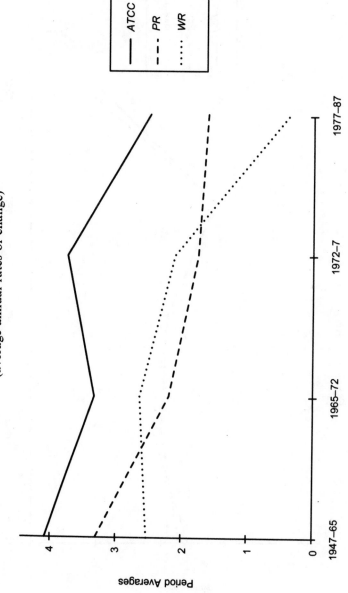

Figure 3.6 Real determinants of the Marxian values, 1947–87 (average annual rates of change)

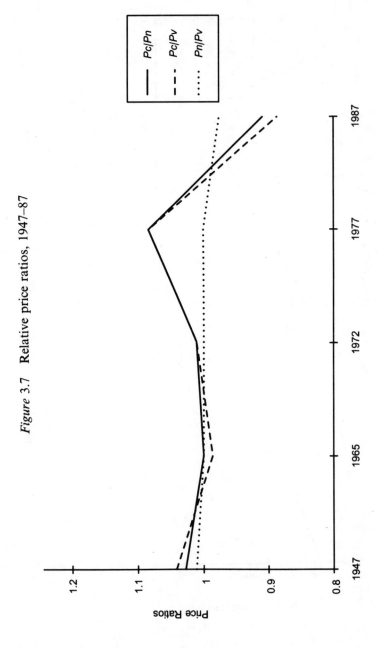

Figure 3.7   Relative price ratios, 1947–87

4 The Decline of the Conventional Rate of Profit

The preceding chapters have been concerned with a rigorous empirical test of Marx's theory of the tendency of the rate of profit to decline as a result of technological change. This test involved the derivation of conceptually rigorous estimates of the Marxian rate of profit and its determinants for the postwar US economy. The main conclusion is that the Marxian rate of profit declined due to an increase in the composition of capital, consistent with the hypothesis of Marx's theory. This conclusion is very different from that reached by Weisskopf and Wolff in their earlier estimates of the Marxian variables. The main reason for these different conclusions is the different treatments of Marx's concepts of productive labor and unproductive labor.

Both Weisskopf (1985) and Wolff (1987b) have responded to my critique of their estimates of the Marxian variables by acknowledging that I am probably correct with respect to a rigorous empirical test of Marx's theory, as he defined his concepts. However, they both argue that for an analysis of the current crisis, it is more important to analyze the rate of profit as it is conventionally defined, rather than the rate of profit as Marx defined it, because the conventional rate of profit is a more direct determinant of capital accumulation than the Marxian rate of profit. I agree that the conventional rate of profit is more important than the Marxian rate of profit in an analysis of the current crisis, but I argue that an empirical test of Marx's theory of the falling rate of profit is none the less an important task in its own right, especially given all the controversy over this theory in recent decades. In any case, an analysis of the conventional rate of profit should not be confused with an empirical test of Marx's theory, as Weisskopf and Wolff appear to do.

Following Weisskopf's and Wolff's suggestion, and recognizing the importance of the conventional rate of profit in an analysis of the current crisis, this chapter is devoted to analyzing the conventional rate of profit. The main difference between the conventional rate of profit and the Marxian rate is that the former does not take into account Marx's distinction between productive labor and unproductive labor (a more complete discussion of these two concepts of the rate of profit is presented below).

In the postwar US economy through the late 1970s, the conventional rate of profit declined even more than the Marxian rate. For the Business sector, the conventional rate of profit declined approximately 40 per cent, compared to the 15–20 per cent decline in the Marxian rate of profit.[1] This significant decline in the conventional rate of profit seems to be an important cause of the economic stagnation of the 1970s and 1980s. It seems plausible that the decline of the rate of profit resulted in a slowdown of investment spending, which in turn contributed to the rise of unemployment of the past decade. At the same time, the decline of the rate of profit probably also contributed to the acceleration in the rate of inflation, as capitalist enterprises attempted to restore their rate of profit by increasing prices at a faster rate. Thus the decline of the rate of profit seems to be at least partially responsible for both the "twin evils" of higher unemployment and higher inflation. It is important to understand the underlying causes of this decline in order to have some idea about the likely trend in the rate of profit in the future and thus about the likelihood of a full recovery from the current economic crisis.[2]

Although the empirical fact of the decline in the rate of profit has been rather thoroughly analyzed (e.g. Lovell, 1978; Leibling, 1980; Feldstein *et al.*, 1983; Holland and Meyers, 1984), there have been very few attempts by mainstream economists to explain the causes of this decline. Lovell concluded his paper with the observation that the decline in the rate of profit is "a major puzzle for future investigations" (ibid., p. 787). Similarly, Feldstein *et al.*, concluded that most of the decline in the rate of profit "remains to be explained" (ibid., p. 154) and that "without understanding why profitability was lower in the 1970's than in the earlier period, it is not possible to say whether this has been a permanent or temporary decline" (ibid., p. 150).

Radical economists, on the other hand, have progressed further in explaining this decline in the rate of profit. The most common type of explanation offered by radical economists is generally referred to as the "profit squeeze" theory. Both Weisskopf (1979) and Wolff (1986) have presented "profit squeeze" type explanations of the decline in the rate of profit. The first section of this chapter briefly reviews the explanations of the decline in the rate of profit presented by Weisskopf and Wolff. Section 4.2 then presents an alternative explanation of this important phenomenon, which is based on Marx's distinction between productive and unproductive labor. Section 4.3 conducts a preliminary empirical test of these competing explanations of the decline in the conventional rate of profit.

4.1 PROFIT SQUEEZE EXPLANATIONS

The distinguishing characteristic of the profit squeeze explanations of the decline in the rate of profit is their emphasis on a roughly proportional decline in the *share* of profit (in total income) as the main proximate cause of the decline in the *rate* of profit.[3] In other words, a change in the distribution of income to the detriment of capitalists is emphasized as the most important cause of this decline.

Profit squeeze explanations may be illustrated by decomposing the conventional rate of profit into the product of the share of profit and the output–capital ratio, as follows:

$$CRP = \frac{P}{K} = \frac{P}{Y} \times \frac{Y}{K} \qquad (4.1)$$

where P refers to profit, K to the capital stock, and Y to total income or output. According to this accounting framework, the rate of profit varies directly with the share of profit and with the output–capital ratio.

According to both Weisskopf's and Wolff's estimates, the output–capital ratio remained essentially constant over the postwar period.[4] Thus, according to these estimates, the decline in the rate of profit was due to a roughly proportional decline in the share of profit.

Further analysis is then usually conducted in terms of the wage share (W/Y), which is equal to one minus the profit share. Wages here refer to the total employee compensation of both productive and unproductive workers. The question then becomes: what were the causes of the significant increase in the wage share in the postwar US economy? Weisskopf and Wolff present different explanations of the increase in the wage share, which will now be briefly reviewed in turn.

4.1.1 Weisskopf: "Rising Strength of Labor"

According to Weisskopf, the fundamental cause of the increase in the wage share in the postwar US economy was the lower rates of unemployment that prevailed in this period, especially in the late 1960s and early 1970s. It is argued that these lower rates of unemployment increased the bargaining power of workers and enabled them to gain a higher share of total income at the expense of capitalists. This "rising strength of labor" variant of the profit squeeze theory is sometimes referred to as the "reserve army" variant, because of its emphasis on lower unemployment as the fundamental cause of the increase of the wage share.[5]

In his analysis, Weisskopf distinguishes between "offensive" and "defensive" strength of labor. This distinction is based on a further decomposition of the nominal wage share into the product of the real wage share and the ratio of the price of wage goods (P_w) to the price of all final goods (P_y), as follows:

$$\frac{W}{Y} = \frac{w}{y} \times \frac{P_w}{P_y} \tag{4.2}$$

where the lower-case letters represent real variables. "Offensive" and "defensive" strengths of labor are then distinguished according to whether an increase in the nominal wage share is due to an increase in the real wage share or to an increase in the relative price ratio, respectively.[6]

Weisskopf's estimates are for the Non-Financial Corporate Business (NFCB) sector of the US economy and for the period 1949–75. His estimates show that the real wage share remained more or less constant over this period (actually declined slightly) and that the relative price ratio P_w/P_y increased 11 per cent. Thus, in Weisskopf's terms, this was a situation of "defensive" strength of labor. Weisskopf argues that the increase in the relative price of wage goods resulted in an increase in the nominal wage share rather than in a reduction in the real wage share because the lower rates of unemployment increased the bargaining power of workers and enabled them to maintain their real wage share in spite of the adverse trend in the price of wage-goods.[7]

4.1.2   Wolff: "Slower Productivity Growth"

Wolff presents a different explanation of the increase in the wage share in the postwar US economy. He argues that the main cause of the increase of the wage share was the slowdown in productivity growth since the mid-1960s, not a rising strength of labor.[8]

Wolff's estimates are for the economy as a whole, including both the entire Business sector and the Government and Household sectors of the economy, rather than for the Non-Financial Corporate Business sector only.[9] Wolff's period of study is from 1947 to 1976 (slightly longer than Weisskopf's period). For the entire economy, the two proximate determinants of the nominal wage share in equation (4.2) had very different trends from in the NFCB sector: the relative price ratio P_w/P_y remained essentially constant and the real wage share increased 10 per cent. Thus according to Wolff's estimates, the proximate cause of the increase in the nominal wage share was a roughly proportional increase in the real wage share.

In order to analyze the proximate causes of this increase in the real wage share, Wolff in effect further decomposes the real wage share into the ratio of the average real wage to the average productivity of labor, by dividing both the total real wage and the total real output by the number of workers employed (L) – including both productive and unproductive workers – as follows:[10]

$$\frac{w}{y} = \frac{w/L}{y/L} \tag{4.3}$$

Thus according to this accounting framework, the trend in the real wage share depends on the relative rates of increase of the average real wage and the average productivity of labor.

According to Wolff's estimates, from 1947 to 1967, these two determinants of the real wage share increased at approximately the same rate (3 per cent), so that the real (and nominal) wage share remained essentially constant. However, from 1967 to 1976, productivity growth declined sharply to less than 1 per cent. Real wage growth also declined, but significantly less so, to approximately 2 per cent. Thus Wolff concludes that the main cause of the increase in the real (and nominal) wage share was this sudden and unexpected slowdown in productivity growth since the mid-1960s. Wolff argues that capitalists responded to this productivity slowdown by reducing labor compensation, but not fast enough or deep enough.

Wolff attributes this slowdown in productivity to a combination of "accidental" causes: the increase in energy prices, the more rapid growth of the labor force, the decline in research and development spending, etc.

Wolff also emphasizes that the "strength of labor" and the rate of unemployment play no role in his explanation of the increase in the wage share. He notes that the fact that average real wage growth actually slowed down slightly, rather than accelerated, after the mid-1960s suggests that the "strength of labor" was not increasing during this period.

4.1.3 Summary

Thus we see that both Weisskopf and Wolff explain the decline in the rate of profit by a decline in the share of profit, but their further explanations of the decline in the share of profit are very different. Weisskopf attributes the decline in the share of profit primarily to the lower rates of unemployment in the postwar US economy, which increased the strength of labor relative to capital in the conflict over the distribution of income. Wolff, on the other hand, attributes the decline in the profit share primarily to a largely accidental slowdown in productivity growth. In Section 4.3 below, we will return to these two variants of the profit squeeze theory and will examine the prediction implied by each concerning the trend in the share and the rate of profit after the mid-1970s.

4.2   MARXIAN EXPLANATION

We turn now to an alternative explanation of the decline in the rate of profit which emphasizes Marx's distinction between productive labor and unproductive labor, discussed in Chapter 2. The first step in this explanation is to formulate a Marxian theory of the conventional rate of profit. Such a theory was not explicitly presented by Marx himself. However, it can easily be derived from his basic concepts and assumptions.[11]

4.2.1   Marxian Theory of the Conventional Rate of Profit

The conventional rate of profit is by definition equal to the ratio of the amount of profit (P) to the total stock of capital invested (K).[12] According to Marx's theory of value discussed in Chapter 2 above, profit, the numerator in the conventional rate of profit, is equal to the difference between the annual flow of surplus-value (S) and the annual flow of unproductive capital (U_f) (mostly the wages of non-production workers, but also the annual depreciation costs of non-production buildings, equipment, and materials):[13]

$$P = S - U_f \qquad (4.4)$$

Similarly, according to Marx's theory, the stock of capital, the denominator in the rate of profit, should be divided into constant capital (C) and the stock of capital invested in non-production structures and equipment (U_s):[14]

$$K = C + U_s \qquad (4.5)$$

Combining equations (4.4) and (4.5), we obtain the following Marxian equation for the conventional rate of profit (CRP):

$$CRP = \frac{P}{K} = \frac{S - U_f}{C + U_s} \qquad (4.6)$$

Finally, following Marx's procedure of relating other variables to variable capital, the "source" of surplus-value, we divide all terms on the right-hand side of the above equation by the annual flow of variable capital and obtain:

$$CRP = \frac{S/V - U_f/V}{C/V + U_s/V} = \frac{RS - UF}{CC + US} \qquad (4.7)$$

From equation (4.7) it can be seen that, according to this Marxian accounting framework, the conventional rate of profit depends not only on the composition of capital (CC)[15] and the rate of surplus value (RS) (the determinants of the Marxian rate of profit), but also on the two ratios of unproductive capital to variable capital ($UF = U_f/V$ and $US = U_s/V$). More precisely, the conventional rate of profit varies inversely with these two ratios of unproductive capital to variable capital.

4.2.2 Estimates of the Marxian Determinants

In order to apply this Marxian theory of the conventional rate of profit to the postwar US economy, annual estimates of these Marxian variables were derived for the period 1947–77 for the total Business sector.[16] These estimates are presented in Table 4.1.

Table 4.1   The conventional rate of profit and its Marxian determinants, 1947–1977

	RS	CC	UF	US	RP
1947	1.40	3.58	0.54	0.30	0.22
1948	1.35	3.60	0.53	0.30	0.21
1949	1.50	3.81	0.59	0.32	0.22
1950	1.42	3.94	0.58	0.32	0.20
1951	1.44	3.78	0.56	0.31	0.22
1952	1.41	3.69	0.57	0.31	0.21
1953	1.35	3.56	0.58	0.30	0.20
1954	1.46	3.84	0.64	0.33	0.20
1955	1.51	3.85	0.65	0.34	0.21
1956	1.44	3.96	0.67	0.36	0.18
1957	1.50	4.08	0.70	0.38	0.18
1958	1.59	4.33	0.75	0.42	0.18
1959	1.61	4.14	0.75	0.41	0.19
1960	1.62	3.11	0.78	0.42	0.19
1961	1.68	4.18	0.81	0.45	0.19
1962	1.71	4.07	0.81	0.45	0.20
1963	1.71	3.99	0.80	0.46	0.21
1964	1.73	3.92	0.81	0.47	0.21
1965	1.73	3.92	0.80	0.48	0.21
1966	1.72	3.91	0.81	0.50	0.21
1967	1.72	4.03	0.84	0.52	0.19
1968	1.69	4.02	0.84	0.53	0.19
1969	1.62	4.07	0.85	0.54	0.17
1970	1.61	4.29	0.89	0.58	0.15
1971	1.71	4.50	0.93	0.62	0.15
1972	1.67	4.37	0.89	0.61	0.16
1973	1.59	4.39	0.87	0.61	0.14
1974	1.55	5.13	0.92	0.69	0.11
1975	1.71	5.39	0.98	0.69	0.12
1976	1.66	5.15	0.95	0.66	0.12
1977	1.63	5.03	0.94	0.66	0.12

Notation and Sources

RS   Rate of surplus-value, see Table 3.1
CC   Value composition of capital, see Table 3.6
UF $= U_f/V$
    U_f Flow of unproductive capital, see Appendix A, Table A.5
    V Variable capital, see Table 3.1
US $= U_s/V = (K-C)/V$
    U_s Stock of unproductive capital
  K   Total stock of fixed and circulating capital
    Fixed capital, from *Fixed Reproducible Tangible Wealth in the US*, US Department of Commerce, table A2
    Circulating capital, from *National Income and Product Accounts*, US Department of Commerce, table 5.10
  C   Constant capital, see Table 3.6
CRP   Conventional rate of profit $= P/K = (S - U_f)/K$
  S   Surplus-value, see Table 3.1

We have already seen in Chapter 3 that the rate of surplus-value increased 17 per cent and the composition of capital increased 41 per cent over this period. We can see from Table 4.1 that the two ratios of unproductive capital to variable capital had even more striking trends: the ratio *UF* increased 72 per cent; and the ratio *US* increased 117 per cent (from a small initial magnitude).[17] Thus, according to the Marxian theory presented here, the proximate causes of the decline in the conventional rate of profit in the postwar US economy were the significant increases in the composition of capital and in the two ratios of unproductive capital to variable capital.

In order to estimate the individual contributions of each of these proximate determinants to the total decline in the rate of profit, I decomposed the total decline into four components, each one of which corresponds to the contribution of one of the four Marxian determinants to the total decline in the rate of profit. The results of this exercise are shown in Table 4.2. These estimates show that the proximate determinant which contributed the most to the decline in the rate of profit was the ratio *UF*. The increase in the ratio *UF* had a substantially greater negative effect on the rate of profit than the increase in the composition of capital, the trend which Marx emphasized in his analysis of the "Marxian" rate of profit. These negative effects were partially offset by the increase in the rate of surplus-value, which had a significant positive effect on the rate of profit.

This Marxian explanation of the decline in the rate of profit is partially compatible with Wolff's "productivity slowdown" explanation discussed above. As we saw in Chapter 3, even if productivity is defined in terms of productive labor only, there was a significant slowdown in productivity growth after 1965, similar to that emphasized by Wolff, although the productivity slowdown for productive labor was less than for all employees.[18] This productivity slowdown had a significant negative effect on the rate of surplus-value and a significant positive effect on the composition of capital, both of which had a negative effect on the conventional rate of profit. However, Marxian theory suggests that this productivity slowdown by itself would have resulted in only a small decline in the rate of profit. The most important cause of this decline was the very significant increase in the flow ratio of unproductive capital to variable capital (*UF*).

This conclusion raises the obvious further question: what were the underlying causes of the very significant increases in the two ratios of unproductive capital to variable capital, especially the ratio *UF*?

Table 4.2   Contributions of the Marxian determinants to the decline of the
conventional rate of profit, 1947–77

RS	0.051
CC	−0.051
UF	−0.085
US	−0.012

Total decline in	*CRP*	−0.099

These contributions were calculated according to the following
method, which is adopted from Wolff (1986):

$$\text{Let } A = RS - UF$$
$$B = CC + US$$

Then:

$$\Delta CRP = \frac{A_2}{B_2} - \frac{A_1}{B_1}$$

From which it can be derived that:

$$\Delta CRP = B^*(\Delta A) - A^*(\Delta B) \tag{4.8}$$

$$\text{where: } A^* = A' / B_1 B_2$$
$$B^* = B' / B_1 B_2$$
$$A' = (A_1 + A_2) / 2$$
$$B' = (B_1 + B_2) / 2$$

The contributions of each of the four Marxian variables to the
overall decline in the rate of profit were calculated from equation
(4.8) by allowing each variable to change one at a time and holding
the other three variables constant.

e.g. the contribution of *RS* is given by

$$B^*(\Delta RS)$$

The numerator in the ratio *UF*, the annual flow of unproductive
capital (U_f), consists almost entirely of the wages of unproductive

labor, which accounted for a consistent 95 per cent of U_f throughout the postwar period (see Table A.5 in Appendix A). Thus in further analysis we can safely ignore the second component of U_f, the annual depreciation costs of unproductive buildings, equipment and materials, and concentrate on the ratio of the wages of unproductive labor (U_w) to variable capital. I call this latter ratio UW ($= U_w/V$). The ratio UW increased 72 per cent over the period of study from 0.52 in 1947 to 0.89 in 1977 (see Table A.5 in Appendix A). Thus, by the end of this period, the wages of unproductive labor employed within capitalist enterprises were almost equal to the wages of productive labor.

The ratio UW can be further decomposed into the product of the ratio of unproductive labor (UL) to productive labor (PL), both measured in terms of numbers of workers,[19] and the ratio of the average annual wage of unproductive labor (AU_w) to the average annual wage of productive labor (AV):

$$UW = \frac{U_w}{V} = \frac{UL}{PL} \times \frac{AU_w}{AV} \tag{4.9}$$

Thus there are two possible causes of the increase in the ratio UW: an increase in the ratio UL/PL and/or an increase in the ratio of relative wages, AU_w/AV.

It turns out that in the postwar US economy, the ratio of relative wages AU_w/AV remained more or less constant at approximately 1.5 (see Table A.6 in Appendix A). Thus the increase in the ratio UW was due entirely to a roughly proportional increase in the ratio of unproductive labor to productive labor (UL/PL).

Estimates of unproductive labor and productive labor in the postwar US economy are presented in Table 4.3 and shown graphically in Figure 4.1. These estimates show that the number of unproductive workers (i.e. workers employed in circulation and supervision activities) increased 143 per cent over this period, from 10.5 million in 1947 to 25.5 million in 1977, while the number of productive workers increased only 34 per cent, from 29.6 million in 1947 to 39.6 million in 1977, thus resulting in an 83 per cent increase in the ratio of unproductive labor to productive labor, from 0.35 in 1947 to 0.64 in 1977. According to the Marxian theory presented here, this very significant increase in the ratio of unproductive labor to productive labor was the most important cause of the decline of the conventional rate of profit in the postwar US economy.

Table 4.3   The ratio of unproductive labor to productive labor

	PL	UL	UL/PL	Index
1947	29.6	10.5	0.35	100.0
1948	30.2	10.8	0.36	101.5
1949	28.7	10.8	0.38	106.8
1950	29.7	11.0	0.37	105.1
1951	31.2	11.7	0.37	105.8
1952	31.4	12.2	0.39	110.2
1953	32.1	12.7	0.40	112.1
1954	30.6	12.9	0.42	119.1
1955	31.4	13.4	0.43	120.3
1956	32.0	14.0	0.44	123.5
1957	31.7	14.3	0.45	127.6
1958	29.9	14.3	0.48	135.1
1959	31.0	14.8	0.48	135.1
1960	31.0	15.3	0.49	139.0
1961	30.5	15.4	0.51	143.0
1962	31.1	15.8	0.51	144.2
1963	31.4	16.2	0.52	146.3
1964	31.8	16.7	0.53	148.6
1965	32.9	17.4	0.53	149.2
1966	34.3	18.3	0.53	150.6
1967	34.5	19.0	0.55	155.6
1968	35.2	19.7	0.56	158.0
1969	36.3	20.6	0.57	160.4
1970	36.0	21.0	0.58	165.1
1971	35.7	21.1	0.59	167.5
1972	37.0	21.8	0.59	166.4
1973	38.8	22.8	0.59	166.4
1974	39.0	23.5	0.60	170.3
1975	36.9	23.5	0.64	180.1
1976	38.3	24.3	0.64	179.8
1977	39.6	25.5	0.64	181.9

Notation and Sources
  PL   Productive labor (millions of workers), see Appendix B, section B.4a
       detailed estimates by industry in Appendix A, Table A.7
  UL   Unproductive labor (millions of workers), see Appendix B, section
       B.4a, detailed estimates by industry in Appendix A, Table A.8

Somewhat surprisingly, in a separate work, Wolff (1987a) also argues that the relative increase of unproductive labor was one of the major causes of the economic stagnation of the 1970s-80s.[20] He contends that the increase of unproductive labor resulted in an

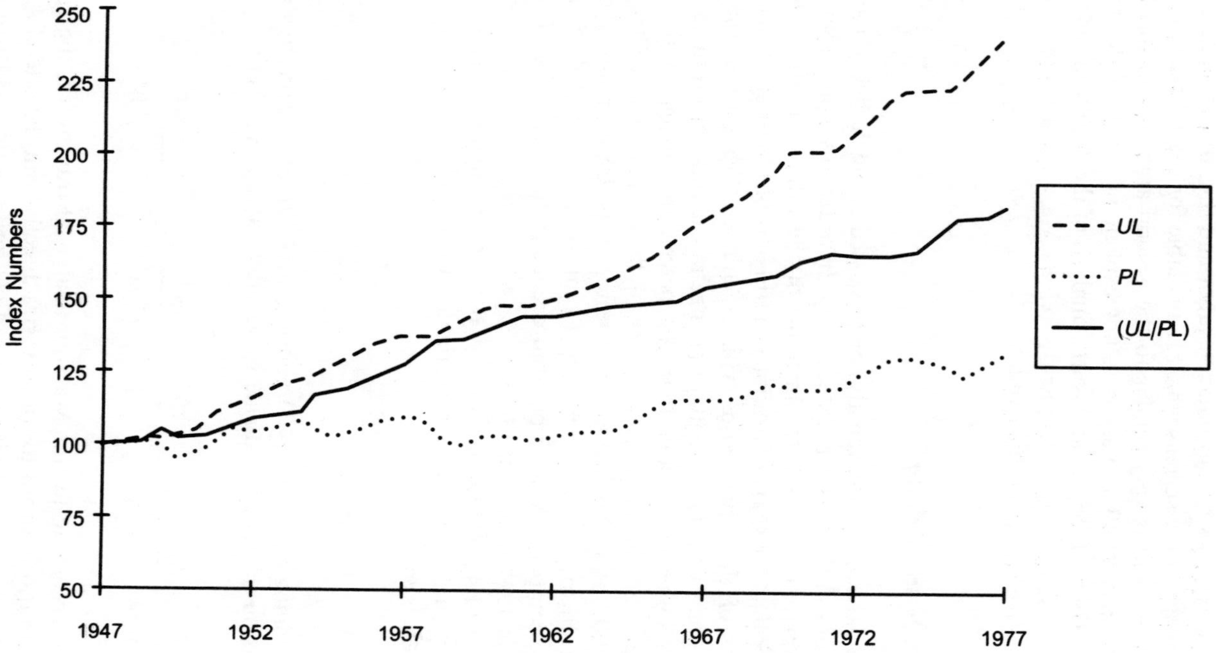

Figure 4.1   The ratio of unproductive labor to productive labor

increase in the percentage of the total surplus which must be used to pay the expenses of unproductive labor and thus in a reduction in the percentage of the surplus which is available for capital accumulation. This argument is very similar to the general argument of this book, except that Wolff's analysis is not explicit in terms of the rate of profit. On the other hand, Wolff's analysis of the decline in the rate of profit, discussed above explicitly, rejects Marx's distinction between productive and unproductive labor.[21]

4.2.3 Share of Profit

A similar explanation can also be presented óf the decline in the *share* of profit in the postwar US economy. In order to simplify somewhat, this analysis is conducted in terms of the ratio of profit to wages, rather than the share of profit (the ratio of profit to total income). The trends of these two ratios will, of course, always be in the same direction (with the percentage change in the ratio of profit to wages being somewhat greater than the percentage change in the profit share), and the underlying causes of these trends will be the same for both ratios. For the Business sector of the US economy, the ratio of profit to wages declined 35 per cent, from 0.56 in 1947 to 0.37 in 1977, compared to a 26 per cent decline in the share of profit, from 0.36 in 1947 to 0.27 in 1977.

According to Marxian theory, the conventional concept of wages (W) should be divided into variable capital and the wages of unproductive labor:

$$W = V + U_w \tag{4.10}$$

Combining equations (4.1) above and (4.10), and again dividing all terms on the right-hand side by variable capital, we obtain:

$$\frac{P}{W} = \frac{S - U_f}{V + U_w} = \frac{S/V - U_f/V}{1 + U_w/V} = \frac{RS - UF}{1 + UW} \tag{4.11}$$

Thus, according to this Marxian analytical framework, the conventional ratio of profit to wages varies directly with the rate of surplus-value and indirectly with the two flow ratios of unproductive capital to variable capital, UF and UW.

We have already seen above that all three of these Marxian determinants of the profit–wages ratio increased significantly in the postwar US economy. Thus, according to this analysis, the proximate causes of the decline in the profit–wages ratio were the increases in the two ratios of unproductive capital to variable capital, *UF* and *UW*.

We have also seen above that the two ratios *UF* and *UW* are virtually identical and that the cause of the significant increase in both these ratios was a roughly proportional increase in the ratio of unproductive labor to productive labor. Thus, even if one accepts the emphasis of the profit squeeze theorists on the decline in the share of profit as the proximate cause of the decline in the rate of profit, Marxian theory suggests that the main cause of the decline in the share of profit was the same cause already identified of the decline in the rate of profit: the very significant increase in the ratio of unproductive labor to productive labor.[22]

Finally, these conclusions raise in turn the further very important question: what were the underlying causes of this very significant increase in the ratio of unproductive labor to productive labor, which had such adverse effects on the rate and the share of profit in the postwar US economy? This question is a complicated and difficult one, and is the subject of the next chapter.

4.3 EMPIRICAL TEST

We have considered above three competing explanations of the decline of the rate of profit in the postwar US economy – the two profit squeeze explanations by Weisskopf and Wolff and the alternative Marxian explanation presented here. All three of these explanations are ex-post explanations based on accounting relations, which are true by definition. All three explanations are consistent with the facts as internally defined by each theory. How can we decide which of these competing explanations is empirically more valid?

One way to begin to discriminate empirically between these competing explanations is to determine the predictions implied by each explanation concerning the trend in the rate of profit and the share of profit after the period of study, and then compare these implied predictions with the actual trends in these variables during the post-period years. This exercise will not provide a conclusive empirical test of these competing explanations, primarily because none of these three explanations implies definite and precise predictions concerning the post-period trends in the rate and the share of profit. But these explanations do seem to imply somewhat different predictions concerning these post-period trends, so some information regarding their relative empirical validity can be gained from this exercise.

According to the profit squeeze accounting framework, the rate of profit depends on the share of profit and the output–capital ratio (see equation 4.1). Weisskopf's and Wolff's explanations of the decline in the rate of profit generally ignored the output–capital ratio (which, according to their estimates, remained essentially constant during their period of study), and thus these explanations imply no prediction about the trend in this ratio, nor therefore in the rate of profit, after the period of study (except perhaps that the output–capital ratio would continue to remain trendless and thus that the trend in the rate of profit would continue to depend almost entirely on the trend in the share of profit). Instead, the most definite predictions which seem to be implied by these profit squeeze explanations concern the post-period trend in the share of profit.

According to Weisskopf, the decline in the share of profit prior to 1975 was due primarily to the lower rates of unemployment during this period, which increased the bargaining power of workers. This explanation seems to imply the prediction that the significantly higher rates of unemployment which have prevailed since 1975 should have resulted, *ceteris paribus*, in a significant increase in the share of profit. Two other variables which also affect the share of profit are held constant in the above *ceteris paribus* assumption: the relative price ratio P_w/P_y and the capacity utilization rate. The relative price ratio P_w/P_y has remained more or less constant since 1975 and thus had no effect on the trend in the share of profit during this period.[23] The rate of capacity utilization was significantly higher in recent years (81.1 per cent in Manufacturing in 1987) than it was in 1975 (72.3 per cent), which should have contributed to an *increase* in the share of profit. The estimates of the share of profit presented below will be adjusted to take this cyclical effect into account. Weisskopf's explanation seems to imply the prediction that these cyclically adjusted estimates of the share of profit should show a significant increase over this period. It is not possible to determine precisely the magnitude of the increase in the share of profit which is predicted by Weisskopf's explanation, but this explanation seems to suggest that a decade of higher rates of unemployment probably should have reversed a large part of the decline in the share of profit prior to 1975.[24]

According to Wolff, the decline in the share of profit was due primarily to the slowdown in productivity growth in the decade prior to 1976, which in turn is attributed to a combination of accidental causes. This explanation does not imply as definite a prediciton concerning the post-period trend in the share of profit as does Weisskopf's explanation. However, the accidental nature of these causes seems to suggest that they should gradually disappear and that the share of profit should return to its earlier higher levels. In fact, most of the accidental trends cited by Wolff (the increase in energy prices, the faster increase in the labor force, etc.) have been largely reversed since 1976. Thus Wolff's theory also seems to imply the prediction of a significant increase in the share of profit since the mid-1970s, though with less certainty than Weisskopf's theory.[25]

Finally, according to the alternative Marxian explanation presented here, the share of profit depends on the rate of surplus-value and the ratio UF (ultimately on the ratio UL/PL). Furthermore, Marx's theory suggests that the higher rates of unemployment which have prevailed in the 1980s should have resulted in a significant increase in the rate of surplus-value. Although Marx's theory provides no prediction regarding the trend of the ratio UF, it seems reasonable to assume that this ratio should continue to increase after the mid-1970s, at roughly the same rate as before. If so, then the negative effect on the profit share of this continued increase in the ratio UF would at least partially offset the positive effect of the increase in the rate of surplus-value. The net effect of these two conflicting influences is difficult to predict with precision, but at least this alternative Marxian theory seems to suggest that the profit share should not have increased very much, if at all, over the last decade. In other words, this Marxian theory implies the prediction, in sharp contrast to Weisskopf's "rising strength of labor" variant of the profit squeeze theory, that the higher rates of unemployment since the mid-1970s should *not* have resulted in a significant increase in the share of profit.

This alternative Marxian theory also suggests a similar prediction regarding the rate of profit. According to this theory, the rate of profit depends on the composition of capital in addition to the rate of surplus-value and the ratio UF, the determinants of the share of profit.[26] Furthermore, Marx's theory suggests that, in a period of stagnation (like the last decade), the composition of capital should not increase very rapidly, as the prices of machinery and raw materials increase less rapidly and some capital is devalued through bankruptcies and write-offs. If the composition of capital increases slower than the ratio *UW*, which is expected, then the rate of profit will increase correspondingly more than the share of profit (compare equations 4.7 and 4.11). However, this alternative Marxian theory seems to suggest that the increase in the rate of profit will not be very large.

These implied predictions will now be compared with the actual trends in the share of profit and the rate of profit from 1975 to 1987 (the latest year for which the necessary data are available at this time) for the Business sector of the US economy (the trends for the Non-Financial Corporate Business sector are not significantly different). Estimates of both the share and the rate of profit are cyclically adjusted, using the same method as in Chapter 3.[27] The unadjusted and adjusted estimates are shown in Table 4.4.

Table 4.4   The rate of profit and the share of profit, 1975–1987

	SP	ASP	RP	ACRP
1975	0.27	0.30	0.12	0.15
1976	0.27	0.29	0.12	0.15
1977	0.27	0.28	0.12	0.14
1978	0.27	0.27	0.12	0.13
1979	0.25	0.26	0.11	0.12
1980	0.24	0.25	0.10	0.12
1981	0.26	0.27	0.11	0.13
1982	0.25	0.28	0.11	0.14
1983	0.25	0.27	0.11	0.14
1984	0.28	0.30	0.14	0.16
1985	0.28	0.29	0.14	0.16
1986	0.28	0.29	0.15	0.16
1987	0.27	0.28	0.14	0.16
1975–79	0.27	0.28	0.12	0.14
1983–87	0.27	0.29	0.14	0.16

Notation and Sources
  SP   Share of profit $= P/N = (S - U_f)/N$
  S   Surplus-value, see Table 3.1
  U_f Flow of unproductive capital, see Appendix A, Table A.5
  N   New-value, see Table 3.1
  ASP   Cyclically adjusted share of profit, see text
  RP   Conventional rate of profit, see Table 4.1
  ARP   Cyclically adjusted conventional rate of profit, see text

Five-year averages of the share of profit show that the unadjusted estimates remained essentially constant over this recent decade and that the adjusted estimates increased a slight one percentage point (from 0.28 to 0.29, or less than 5 per cent). Thus, after more than a decade of higher unemployment and the reversal of many of Wolff's causes of the productivity slowdown, *there has been only a very small increase in the share of profit*. This crucial fact contradicts the predictions implied by both Weisskopf's and Wolff's variants of the profit squeeze theory, especially Weisskopf's "rising strength of labor" variant. By contrast, this absence of a significant increase in the share of profit is more consistent with the alternative Marxian theory presented here. The higher rates of unemployment during the last decade resulted, as expected, in a significant increase in the rate of surplus-value (see Table 4.5). However, the positive effect of this increase in the rate of surplus-value was almost completely offset by the negative effect of a continued increase in the ratio *UF* (see Table 4.5), so that the share of profit remained essentially unchanged. Estimates of the ratio *UL/PL*, the underlying determinant of the ratio UF, are also presented in Table 4.5.

Table 4.5   The Marxian determinants of the conventional rate of profit, 1975–87

	RS	CC	UF	US	UL/PL
1975	1.71	5.39	0.98	0.69	0.64
1976	1.66	5.15	0.95	0.66	0.64
1977	1.63	5.03	0.94	0.66	0.64
1978	1.70	5.26	0.98	0.70	0.65
1979	1.64	5.32	1.00	0.67	0.66
1980	1.70	5.66	1.06	0.72	0.68
1981	1.81	5.76	1.09	0.74	0.70
1982	1.89	5.92	1.16	0.78	0.72
1983	1.93	5.76	1.20	0.80	0.73
1984	2.08	5.58	1.22	0.80	0.73
1985	2.15	5.47	1.26	0.79	0.75
1986	2.23	5.50	1.32	0.80	0.77
1987	2.22	5.48	1.33	0.79	0.78

Notation and Sources
    RS   Rate of surplus-value, see Table 3.1
    CC   Value composition of capital, see Table 3.6
    UF   = U_f/V, see Table 4.1
    US   = U_s/V, see Table 4.1
UL/PL   see Table 4.3

Five-year averages of the rate of profit show that both the unadjusted and the adjusted estimates increased two percentage points (or about 15 per cent). Thus the rate of profit in the mid-1980s remained 30–40 per cent below its early postwar levels. This absence of a significant increase in the rate of profit after 1975 is consistent with the prediction implied by the alternative Marxian explanation of the decline in the rate of profit prior to 1975. Similar to the profit share, the positive effect of the increase in the rate of surplus-value on the profit rate was offset by continued increases in the the ratio UF and in the composition of capital (see Table 4.5). Since the composition of capital increased slower than the ratio UF, the rate of profit did increase slightly more than the share of profit.

Thus, although the above is not a conclusive test of these three competing explanations of the declines in the share and the rate of profit in the postwar US economy, the evidence of the past decade weighs in favor of the alternative Marxian explanation presented here, based on Marx's distinction between productive labor and unproductive labor.

4.4   CONCLUSION

This chapter has argued that the most important cause of the decline of the rate of profit in the postwar US economy was the very significant increase in the relative proportion of unproductive labor during this period. It has argued further that this Marxian explanation of the decline of the rate of profit is more consistent than Weisskopf's and Wolff's "profit squeeze" explanations with the absence of a significant increase in the share and rate of profit since the mid-1970s. A more complete empirical test of these competing explanations requires further detailed analysis and the passage of more time.

If the rate of profit remains at its current depressed level in the years ahead, this would provide additional empirical support for the Marxian explanation presented here. At the same time, such a depressed rate of profit would continue to exert upward pressure on both the rate of unemployment and the rate of inflation and would also increase the likelihood of a severe economic depression within the next decade. This possibility will be discussed further in Chapter 6.

5 Causes of the Increase of Unproductive Labor

The previous two chapters have identified a very important phenomenon in the postwar US economy: the almost doubling of the ratio of unproductive labor to productive labor. This very significant increase in the relative proportion of unproductive labor accounts for almost all the differences in the trends of my estimates and the prior estimates of the rate of surplus-value and the composition of capital and, according to Marx's theory, is the most important cause of the decline in the conventional rate of profit. This chapter presents a preliminary analysis of the underlying causes of this important phenomenon. The results are by no means conclusive; indeed, a thorough analysis of this question would require a book in itself. The purpose of this chapter is simply to identify promising hypotheses for further research. We will also discuss whether the possible causes identified are inherent or accidental features of capitalist economies.

Marx himself did not analyze the likely trend over time in the relative proportions of unproductive and productive labor. This trend plays no role in Marx's theory of the "laws of motion of capitalism", including the tendency of the rate of profit to fall. As we have seen, this tendency was derived by Marx solely in terms of productive capital and labor. Thus, an explanation of the relative increase of unproductive capital and labor would be, in effect, an extension of Marx's basic theoretical framework to account for new phenomena neither experienced nor foreseen by Marx.

One possible international cause of the relative increase of unproductive labor in the postwar US economy, especially since the late 1960s, was the phenomenon of "runaway shops", i.e. the shift of production operations overseas (usually to low-wage developing countries) by US corporations and the re-export of the products to the US. However the number of production workers in these "runaway shops" was very small in comparison to the total number of production workers in the US; the former was certainly less than 1 million workers (concentrated in a few labor-intensive industries, such as textiles and electronics), compared to the 40 million production workers in the US in 1977. Even under the extreme assumptions that 1 million foreign production workers should be added to our estimates of productive labor for 1977 and *no* corresponding foreign non-production workers added to our estimates of unproductive labor, the resulting hypothetical ratio of unproductive labor to productive labor is only slightly less than the actual ratio for 1977 (0.63 compared to 0.64), so that the phenomenon of "runaway shops" can explain only a very small portion of the total relative increase of unproductive labor in the postwar US economy. We must look within the US economy for the causes of this increase, which may or may not be inherent to all capitalist economies.

5.1   DETAILED ESTIMATES OF UNPRODUCTIVE LABOR

In this section, detailed estimates of the specific types of unproductive labor will be examined in order to determine their relative empirical significance in the postwar US economy. As a first step in this analysis, the estimates of unproductive and productive labor presented in Chapter 4 were revised somewhat in order to reduce several conceptual problems in the original estimates. These conceptual estimates are discussed in Appendix B, section B.5, along with the sources and methods used to address these problems. The main source of additional data employed is the decennial *Census of the Population*. Thus these revised estimates are derived only for the four census years from 1950 to 1980.

These revised estimates are presented in Table 5.1, along with the original estimates for these census years (revised detailed estimates by industry are presented in Appendix A, Tables A.9 and A.10). It can be seen that these revisions had the overall effect of reducing the increase of the ratio of unproductive labor to productive labor over the period 1950–80 from 83 to 70 per cent. Although this relative increase of unproductive labor is somewhat smaller, it is still very large, and the conclusions reached in previous chapters regarding the trends of the Marxian variables and the negative effect of this increase of unproductive labor on the conventional rate of profit are not significantly altered.

These revised estimates of unproductive labor were then divided into the two main types: circulation labor and supervisory labor. These estimates are presented in Table 5.2. The data categories used to estimate these main types of unproductive labor are described in

Table 5.1   Revised estimates of the ratio of unproductive labor to productive labor, 1950–80

	Revised estimates				Original estimates	
	PL*	*UL**	*UL*/PL**	*Index*	*UL/PL*	*Index*
1950	28.0	12.8	0.46	100	0.37	100
1960	29.5	16.8	0.57	124	0.49	126
1970	34.6	22.3	0.64	143	0.58	150
1980	40.3	31.4	0.78	170	0.68	183

Notation and Sources
  PL*   Productive labor (millions of workers), see Appendix B, section B.5a, detailed estimates by industry in Appendix A, Table A.9
  UL*   Unproductive labor (millions of workers),see Appendix B, section B.5a, detailed estimates by industry in Appendix A, Table A.10
Original estimates, see Table 4.3

the notes to this table. According to these estimates, circulation labor accounted for over 80 per cent of the total unproductive labor during this period, with this percentage declining slightly from 85 to 83 per cent. Thus, of the two main types of unproductive labor, circulation labor was considerably more empirically significant in the postwar US economy.

Circulation labor may in turn be divided into two subtypes: commercial and financial labor. Commercial labor is defined as labor employed in functions related to the buying and selling of currently produced output. Financial labor is defined as labor employed in the remaining circulation functions, such as banking, insurance, real estate, etc.

Estimates of these two subtypes of circulation labor are also presented in Table 5.2. The data categories used to estimate these subtypes of circulation labor are also described in the notes to the table. According to these estimates, commercial labor accounted for approximately 80 per cent of the total circulation labor (with this percentage declining slightly from 83 to 80 per cent). Thus commercial labor accounted for almost two-thirds of the total unproductive labor in the postwar US economy (and for approximately the same fraction of the total increase of unproductive labor during this period). These estimates suggest that the most important task in an analysis of the

Table 5.2   Detailed estimates of main types of unproductive labor
(millions of workers)

	COM	FIN	CRC	SUP	UL*	COM CRC	CRC UL
1950	8.9	1.9	·10.8	2.0	12.8	.83	.85
1960	11.6	2.6	14.2	2.6	16.8	.81	.84
1970	14.8	3.6	18.5	3.8	22.3	.80	.83
1980	21.0	5.2	26.1	5.3	31.4	.80	.83
Increase 1950–80	12.0	3.3	15.3	3.3	18.6		
% total increase of UL	65%	18%	82%	18%			

Notation
COM   Commercial labor: unproductive labor in Wholesale and Retail
        Trade; sales workers in "productive industries" (i.e. all industries
        except Wholesale and Retail Trade and Finance, Insurance and Real
        Estate); 75% of clerical workers in "productive industries"; total
        labor in Business Services.
  FIN   Financial labor: total labor in finance, insurance, and real estate.
  CRC   Circulation labor: commercial labor plus financial labor.
  SUP   Supervisory labor: total unproductive labor minus circulation labor.
  UL*   Revised estimates of total unproductive labor.

Sources
Productive labor by industry: Appendix A, Table A.9.
Unproductive labor by industry: Appendix A, Table A.10.

causes of the relative increase of unproductive labor in the postwar
US economy is to explain the increase of the category of commercial
labor.
    These detailed estimates of unproductive labor are admittedly very
rough; no doubt further refinement could be done. However, I do not
think this additional effort would significantly change the conclusions
just stated concerning the relative magnitudes of the specific types of
unproductive labor.
    It should also be pointed out that the above estimates of unproduc-
tive and productive labor and of the specific types of unproductive
labor are all in terms of numbers of *workers*. I also derived similar

estimates of these variables in terms of numbers of labor *hours*. These estimates in terms of hours show approximately the same trends and proportions as the estimates in terms of workers just discussed. The estimates in terms of hours are presented in Table A.11 of Appendix A.

The remaining sections of this chapter will examine the possible causes of the increase of each of these three types of unproductive labor, beginning with commercial labor, the empirically most significant type.

5.2   COMMERCIAL LABOR

Commercial labor increased 134 per cent from 1950 to 1980, while productive labor increased only 44 per cent, thus resulting in a 63 per cent increase in the ratio of commercial trade labor to productive labor, from 0.32 in 1950 to 0.52 in 1980. Why did the amount of labor required to perform the commercial functions of buying and selling, accounting, advertising, etc. increase so much more rapidly than the amount of labor required for production?

To begin with, part of this increase is due to the fact that my estimates of commercial labor include only wage earners, i.e. do not include self-employed persons and unpaid family members who also perform commercial functions. During the postwar period, there was a significant transformation of these two categories of non-wage earners (mainly self-employed persons) into wage earners. Therefore, part of the increase in my estimates is due to this structural transformation, rather than to a true increase in the total amount of commercial labor relative to productive labor.

In order to assess how much of the increase in my ratio of commercial labor to productive labor is due to this structural transformation, I re-estimated commercial labor, including these two categories of non-wage earners engaged in commercial activities. Using this broader definition of commercial labor, the ratio of commercial labor to productive labor increased 44 per cent, instead of the 63 per cent increase in my estimates of wage earners only. Thus, this structural transformation within the commercial sector of the economy accounted for less than one-third of the increase in my estimates of the ratio of commercial labor to productive labor. Most of the increase in this ratio remains to be explained.

Aside from this structural transformation, the ratio of commercial labor to production labor depends on the following two proximate causes: (i) the relative rates of productivity growth of production labor and commercial labor; and (ii) the quantity of "services" provided with each unit of output sold, such as credit, advertising and promotion, warranties and adjustments, free trials, etc. The dependence of the ratio of commercial labor to production labor on these two proximate causes can be shown by the following formal model:[1]

1. Let S represent the quantity of services per unit of output sold. Then it is assumed that the output of commercial labor (Q_C) is equal to the product of S and the quantity of goods produced by production labor and sold by trade labor (Q_P), i.e.

$$Q_C = (Q_P)(S) \tag{5.1}$$

2. Next the productivity of production labor ($= Q_P / L_P$) can be expanded as follows:

$$\frac{Q_P}{L_P} = \frac{(Q_P)}{(Q_C)} \frac{(Q_C)}{(L_C)} \frac{(L_C)}{(L_P)} \tag{5.2}$$

3. Now let A_P represent the productivity of production labor, A_C represent the productivity of commercial labor ($= Q_C/L_C$), and X_C represent the ratio of commercial labor to production labor ($= L_C/ L_P$). Since from equation (5.1), $(Q_P)/(Q_C) = 1/S$, equation (5.2) can be rewritten as:

$$A_P = (1/S)(A_C)(X_C) \tag{5.3}$$

which can be rearranged as:

$$X_C = (A_P/A_C) S \tag{5.4}$$

It can be seen from this equation, that there are two possible causes of an increase in the ratio X_C: (i) slower productivity growth of commercial labor compared to production labor; i.e. slower reduction in the labor required to provide a given quantity of services with each sales commodity sold, compared to the labor required to produce each commodity; and/or (ii) an increase in the services provided per unit of output sold. The latter cause corresponds to what Baran and Sweezy

(1966) have called the "sales effort", which they attribute to the "realization problem".

It is very difficult to determine the relative empirical significance of these two possible causes of an increase in the ratio X_C, primarily because it is very difficult to measure the variable S, the quantity of services provided with each commodity sold. The difficulty of measuring S also makes it difficult to measure Q_T and A_T.

The most common measure of output in the Wholesale and Retail Trade sector of the US economy (which is similar to, but not exactly the same as, the output of commercial labor, as defined above, which also includes trade labor in the non-trade sectors) is provided by the Bureau of Economic Analysis. This measure is derived by deflating total sales by the price of the output sold. Thus this measure essentially assumes that the quantity of services per unit of output sold (S) remains constant and measures the output of the commercial sector (Q_C) by the quantity of goods sold in that sector, which is approximately equal to the quantity of goods produced in the manufacturing sector (analogous to Q_P as defined above). Thus, using this measure of output of commercial labor (with suitable adjustments for the minor conceptual differences) would lead to the conclusion that the increase in the ratio X_C is due solely to the slower increase of productivity of commercial labor compared to production labor. But this conclusion follows directly from the assumption of constant S. Therefore, this measure of output of commercial labor is of no use in the determination of the relative significance of the two possible causes of the increase of the ratio X_C.[2]

An alternative approach is to attempt to measure the most important individual sales services in the US economy and to determine whether one or more of these important services increased significantly over the postwar period. Although this approach will not result in an aggregate measure of S, it should yield some insights into the direction and magnitude of any change in S.

The most likely source of a significant increase in the "sales effort" in the postwar US economy was an increase in the percentage of consumer sales financed by credit. Credit sales require the additional labor of investigation, record-keeping, collection, etc. (all of which increase with the length of the term of the credit).

The ratio of consumer installment credit extended to total consumer sales did in fact increase significantly (almost doubled) during this period: from around 11 per cent in 1948–52 to approximately 19 per cent in 1978–82 (see Table 5.3). This increase in the percentage of

consumer sales financed by credit was made possible by a number of
innovations by lenders of consumer credit during this period, such as
longer maturities, lower down payments, "revolving" credit in department stores, "all-purpose" bank credit cards, the extension of credit
to non-durable goods and services, increased consumer loans by
commercial banks, etc. In addition, the longer maturities require
more labor for a given amount of credit extended. Thus there appears
to have been a significant increase in the credit-related "sales effort"
in the postwar US economy.

Table 5.3   Consumer installment credit (billions of dollars)

	1950	1960	1970	1980
1. Credit extended	21.6	49.8	112.2	342.6
2. Consumer spending	192.1	330.7	640.0	1732.6
3. (1)/(2)	11.2%	15.1%	17.5%	19.8%
4. Credit held by financial institutions	17.1	41.3	90.7	288.6
5. Percentage of total installment credit (4)/(1)	79.2%	82.9%	80.8%	84.2%

Source: Federal Reserve Board, *Federal Reserve Bulletin*

However, most of this increase of consumer credit was held by
financial institutions (commercial banks, finance companies, credit
unions, etc.) rather than by retail or manufacturing companies. The
percentage of total consumer installment credit held by financial
institutions increased from 79 per cent in 1950 to 84 per cent in
1980 (see Table 5.3). Thus, almost all the additional labor required
to process the increased consumer credit was employed in the Finance
industry, which is classified above as financial labor, not as commercial labor. In other words, the increase in the credit-related "sales
effort" may have been a cause of the increase of financial labor during
this period, but was only a minor cause of the increase of commercial
labor, the most important category, which is now being analyzed.[3]
    For the first half of the twentieth century, Barger (1955) comes to
an even stronger conclusion regarding the amount of credit extended
by commercial enterprises; he concludes that there was probably a

"*decline* in the relative amount of service furnished by merchants to the public in the form of credit sales" (ibid., p. 35, emphasis added). Barger attributed this decline mainly to the transfer of the financing of consumer credit from the merchant to outside financial institutions, a trend which was pioneered by the automobile industry and which, as we have seen, continued in the postwar period.

Another possible source of an increase in the "sales effort" is an increase of advertising. However, advertising cost was only a very small percentage of consumer sales and remained fairly constant over the postwar period (2–3 per cent) (source: Internal Revenue Service, *Corporate Income Tax Returns*). Furthermore, employment in advertising agencies in 1980 was less than 1 per cent of the total commercial labor (approximately 150 000 out of 21 million) and this percentage has even declined slightly since the 1950s (source: Bureau of Labor Statistics, *Employment and Earnings*). Thus, there does not seem to have been a significant increase in the advertising-related "sales effort" in the postwar period.

A third possible source of an increase in the "sales effort" is an increase in the proportion of sales transactions in which payment is made by check rather than cash. Check transactions require more time to fill out the check, to record identifying information, to process the check, etc. According to one estimate, in 1975 almost one-third of all payments in sales transactions were made by check.[4] Although no similar estimate exists for early in the postwar period, it seems likely that this proportion was much lower than one-third early in the period. Another indication of the relative increase of check transactions is that the number of checks processed by banks increased approximately 6 per cent per year, which is considerably faster than the number of sales transactions (for further discussion of the increase in the number of checks, see section 5.3 below). There thus seems to have been a significant increase in the check-related "sales effort" in the postwar US economy, which in turn required additional commercial labor.

A final possible source of an increase in the "sales effort" in the postwar US economy is a lengthening of the hours during which retail stores remain open, e.g. open more at night (including all night in some cases) and on weekends. Open hours have been increased in order to provide "more convenient shopping" for consumers. Foss (1984) presents aggregate estimates of the average weekly hours of retail stores from 1929 to 1976. According to Foss's estimates, retail store hours increased 15 per cent from 1950 to 1976 (57.4 to 65.9 hours) (ibid., p. 87). Thus there does seem to have been a significant increase in the hours-related "sales effort" in the postwar US economy, which required additional commercial labor to keep retail stores open longer.

On the other hand, working in the opposite direction, the spread of "self-service" sales (vending machines, gasoline stations, discount stores, etc.) had the effect of reducing the commercial labor required for each commodity sold. The magnitude of this opposite effect is difficult to measure, but it did to some extent offset any increase in the "sales effort" from the other sources discussed above.

My tentative conclusion from the above analysis is that there was no more than a minor increase in the quantity of sales services performed by commercial labor in the postwar US economy, i.e. that the variable S in equation (5.4) did not increase very much. The main sources of a growth in the "sales effort" performed by commercial labor seems to have been an increase both in store hours and in the proportion of check transactions. However, these were at least partially offset by the trend toward "self-service" for some commodities. Oi (1987) concludes that the quantity of sales services of retail stores *declined* in the postwar period, especially credit and delivery services.[5]

By process of elimination, it follows from equation (5.4) that the more important cause by far of the relative increase of commercial labor in the postwar US economy was its slower productivity growth, compared to production labor. As a result, a greater percentage of the total labor force had to be employed as commercial labor in order to sell the more rapidly increasing output of productive labor. Barger (1955, chapter 3) came to a similar conclusion for his earlier period of study. More definite conclusions would require direct estimates of the labor employed in the various aspects of the "sales effort", which are very difficult, and perhaps impossible, to derive.[6]

The underlying cause of the slower productivity growth of commercial labor would seem to be that it is inherently more difficult to mechanize buying and selling than it is to mechanize production, because buying and selling in most cases must remain to a large extent a person-to-person transaction. For example, in the automobile industry, continual mechanization has greatly increased the productivity of production workers, but the sale of each automobile requires highly personalized service which has made it difficult to increase the number of cars sold per salesperson (or at least seems to require such service in modern capitalist economies).

Barger (1955) attributed the relative increase of "distribution" labor in an earlier period to this same cause: the slower increase in output sold per labor-hour in distribution compared to the increase in output produced per labor-hour in production. Barger's explanation of the differential is that "technology changed far less rapidly in Retail and Wholesale Trade than it did in Manufacturing, Mining, and Agriculture" (ibid., p. 10).

Wolff (1987a, pp. 13-18) also argues that the main cause of the relative increase of employment in Wholesale and Retail Trade in the postwar period was the slower productivity growth of this sector. However, later in this book (ibid., pp. 172–9) he argues that the main cause of the relative increase of unproductive labor in general was a "realization problem", which suggests an increase in the "sales effort", rather than slower productivity growth. Wolff presents evidence to support the "slower productivity growth" explanation, but none to support the "realization problem" explanation.

Marx argued, and the history of capitalism seems to demonstrate, that technological change of production is an inherent feature of capitalist economies. If, as seems to be the case, technological change of exchange is much more difficult than technological change of production, then the slower productivity growth of commercial labor and the consequent increase in the relative employment of commercial labor would also seem to be inherent tendencies of capitalist economies. In fact, the relative proportion of commercial labor does seem to have increased in all capitalist economies since the mid-nineteenth century (for the US, see Barger, 1955; for the rest of the world, see Melman, 1951). Further, on the basis of Marx's assumption that commercial labor produces no value, the relative increase of commercial labor causes the conventional rate of profit to decline. Thus this analysis suggests another way in which technological change causes a decline of the rate of profit, besides increasing the composition of capital: the relatively slower pace of technological change of exchange increases the relative proportion of commercial labor. This additional inherent cause of the decline of the conventional rate of profit has hitherto received very little attention, but it seems to have been very important in the postwar US economy.

5.3 FINANCIAL LABOR

The second type of circulation labor is financial labor, or labor employed in the Finance, Insurance, and Real Estate industry. Financial labor increased 173 per cent from 1950 to 1980, while productive labor increased only 44 per cent, so that the ratio of financial labor to productive labor increased 91 per cent, from 0.07 in 1950 to 0.13 in 1980.

Similar to commercial labor analyzed above, the ratio of financial labor to production labor depends on the following two proximate causes: (i) the rate of output growth of financial labor (checks, loans, insurance policies, real estate sales and rentals, etc.) compared to the output of production labor; and (ii) the rate of productivity growth of financial labor compared to production labor.

The dependence of the ratio of financial labor to production labor on these two proximate causes can be shown by the following formal model, similar to the model employed above in the analysis of commercial labor:

1. The productivity of production labor ($= Q_P/L_P$) may be expanded as follows:

$$\frac{Q_P}{L_P} = \frac{Q_P}{Q_F} \frac{Q_F}{L_F} \frac{L_F}{L_P} \tag{5.5}$$

2. Using similar notation to that employed above, let A_P represent the productivity of production labor, A_F the productivity of financial labor ($= Q_F/L_F$), and X_F the ratio of financial labor to production labor ($= L_F/L_P$). Then equation (5.5) can be rewritten as:

$$A_P = (Q_P/Q_F) \ (A_F) \ (X_F) \tag{5.6}$$

which can be rearranged as:

$$X_F = (Q_F/Q_P) \ (A_P/A_F). \tag{5.7}$$

It can be seen from this equation that there are two possible causes of an increase in the ratio X_F: (i) faster output growth of financial labor compared to production labor; and (ii) slower productivity growth of financial labor compared to production labor.

Financial labor is actually a very heterogeneous category, which consists of labor in the following three subindustries: (i) Finance (banks, other credit agencies, and security and commodity brokers); (ii) Insurance (carriers and agents); and (iii) Real Estate (operators and agents). The output of each of these three subindustries is, of course, very different in nature.

Empirically, the most significant of these three subindustries is the Finance subindustry, which accounted for 54 per cent of the total increase of finance labor from 1950 to 1980 (see Table 5.4). The Insurance subindustry is the second most significant subindustry, accounting for 29 per cent of the total increase of finance labor during this period. These three subindustries will be discussed in the order of their empirical significance.

Table 5.4   Financial labor (millions of workers)

	Finance	Insurance	Real estate	Total financial	Banks
1950	632	742	509	1883	424
1960	1067	1048	545	2660	671
1970	1675	1308	713	3696	1050
1980	2499	1747	1101	5347	1576
Increase 1950–80	1867	1005	592	3464	1152
% of increase of total	54%	29%	17%		33%

Source: Bureau of Labor Statistics, Bulletin 1311–12, *Employment, Hours, and Earnings*

5.3.1   Finance

In the Finance subindustry, banks accounted for 62 per cent of the total increase of labor employed (see Table 5.4). In addition, the data available for the output of commercial banks is much more complete than for the remainder of the Finance subindustry. Therefore, this analysis of the Finance subindustry will focus on commercial banks.

The US Bureau of Economic Analysis' estimates of the output of commercial banks is one of the most problematic and controversial in national income accounting. The BEA estimates assume that the output of banks consists only of services rendered to depositors (checking, bookkeeping, etc.) and does not include lending services to borrowers (US Department of Commerce, 1954, pp. 46–7). Since there are generally no explicit charges for these services, the BEA estimates assume that there are implicit non-monetary charges (equal to the net interest received by banks) and the current dollar measure of the output of banks consists almost entirely of these imputed charges. The current dollar measure is then deflated by a combination of an imputed rate of interest and the Consumer Price Index to obtain the constant dollar measure of the output of banks.

The BEA estimates of output of commercial banks have been criticized by many researchers (e.g. Speagle and Silverman, 1953; Warburton 1958). It is beyond the scope of the present investigation to examine these estimates and the criticisms of them in detail. For what they are worth, the BEA estimates yield the following results: for the period 1950–80, the output of banks increased at an average annual rate of 4.2 per cent, compared to a 3.3 per cent rate of increase of the output of production labor. At the same time, according to these estimates, there was essentially no increase in the productivity of labor in banks (even a small decline), since the number of workers in banks increased at almost the same rate (4.4 per cent) as the BEA estimates of the output of banks. Thus, these BEA estimates suggest that the relative increase of banking labor compared to production labor in the postwar US economy was the result of a combination of both the proximate causes identified above: faster output growth of banks and slower productivity growth of bank labor, with the latter the more significant of the two causes. However, these results should not be considered as definitive because of the questionable nature of the BEA estimates of the output of banks on which they are based.

More reliable estimates of the output of commercial banks have been presented by other researchers (Speagle and Kohn, 1958; and Brand and Duke, 1982).[7] These take into account not only the checking services to depositors, but also the lending services to borrowers. Even more importantly, these measures are based on more direct physical measures of these banking services (such as the number of checks processed, the number of loans processed, etc.), rather than on imputed service charges. For different subperiods within the postwar period (Speagle and Kohn for 1945–55, and Brand and Duke for 1967–80), both these studies conclude that the output of banks increased between 5 and 6 per cent per year, considerably faster than the BEA estimates. A growth rate of 5.5 per cent of banking output implies that the productivity of bank labor increased approximately 1.0 per cent per year, closer than the BEA estimates to the 2.1 per cent rate of productivity increase for production labor. Thus, these more reliable estimates suggest that the main proximate cause of the relative increase of bank labor was the faster output growth of banks, rather than slower productivity growth of bank labor.

A more complicated picture emerges from a detailed examination of the individual component indexes for checks and loans. Both sets of estimates cited in the previous paragraph show that the number of checks increased between 6.5 and 7 per cent per year and that the number of loans increased around 3.5 per cent per year. Further, Brand and Duke's estimates show that the number of bank workers employed in these two functions increased at approximately the same rate (between 4 and 4.5 per cent) between 1967 and 1980. If this latter trend is extrapolated back into the early postwar period, then these estimates together suggest different conclusions concerning the causes of these two types of bank labor: (i) the relative increase of bank labor employed in the processing of checks was due entirely to its faster output growth; the productivity of this type of bank labor increased at approximately the same rate as the productivity of productive labor. (ii) On the other hand, the relative increase of the other main type of bank labor, that employed in the processing of loans, was due entirely to its slower productivity growth (in fact its productivity appears to have even declined slightly); the output of this second type of bank labor increased at approximately the same rate as the output of productive labor. However, this latter conclusion seems to be contradicted by the estimates presented in the previous section of an increase in the percentage of sales financed by credit, most of which is provided by financial institutions.

These estimates are very rough and certainly should be refined further, but they are consistent with our intuition. The processing of checks is fairly easily automated and in fact has been automated to a considerable extent over the postwar period; thus we would expect relatively rapid productivity growth in this activity. On the other hand, the processing of loans remains a largely labor-intensive activity, due to its specialized nature and the need to maintain close contact with borrowers; thus we would not expect much productivity growth in this activity.

The most likely underlying cause of the rapid increase in the number of bank checks in the postwar period was the spread of personal checking accounts and the increasing use of personal checks as a means of payment in sales transactions, discussed above in relation to commercial labor. As a result of this trend, the number of checks processed increased at a faster rate than the quantity of output produced and sold.[8]

It is an interesting question whether the increasing use of personal checks in the postwar US economy is an inherent tendency of capitalist economies, or is instead due to accidental causes which may turn out to be temporary. The increasing use of personal checks is usually attributed to such factors as: (i) increasing incomes, which increases the dollar value of purchases and creates a greater security risk if payments are made in cash; and (ii) greater need for consumers to keep records of purchases for taxes, warranties, and other legal purposes. Increasing incomes and greater security risks seem to be inherent tendencies of capitalist economies. On the other hand, the US system of personal taxes, with its many deductions and loopholes does not seem to be an inherent feature of capitalist economies. In addition, electronic fund transfers offer a less labor intensive alternative to checks that could serve the same purposes of security and records.

5.3.2   Insurance and Real Estate

For the other two subindustries that employ financial labor, Insurance and Real Estate, the BEA estimates of output are similarly flawed. BEA estimates of the output of the Insurance subindustry consist mainly of imputed charges for the saving services of life insurance companies, and for the Real Estate subindustry consist mainly of imputed rent of owner-occupied houses. For what they are worth, these estimates show that for the period 1950–80, the output of the Insurance subindustry increased at approximately the same rate as the output of production labor, while the output of the Real Estate subindustry increased considerably faster than that of production labor (4.7 per cent compared to 3.3 per cent). Thus, these estimates suggest that the main proximate cause of the relative increase of Insurance labor was slower productivity growth and that the main proximate cause of the relative increase of Real Estate labor was faster output growth. However, I have no confidence in these conclusions because of the questionable nature of the BEA estimates on which they are based.

Contrary to the case of commercial banking, I know of no attempts to derive direct physical aggregate measures of the output of the Finance and Real Estate industries. For the Insurance industry, such measures would presumably include the number of policies of different types (life, health, casualty, etc.). For the Real Estate industry, the measures of output would presumably include the number of real estate rentals and the number of real estate sales (in contrast to the BEA estimates, which assume that real estate companies are involved only in rental operations). In the absence of more reliable estimates of output, it is not possible to draw even tentative conclusions concerning the relative significance of the two proximate causes identified above for the relative increase of the labor in these two subindustries.

My hypothesis at this point for both of these industries is that the main proximate cause at work was slower productivity growth. The reason for this hypothesis is that labor in both these industries is essentially involved in sales transactions, similar to commercial labor. Labor in the Insurance industry sells insurance (or keeps accounts of these sales); similarly, labor in the Real Estate industry sells or rents real estate. These sales transactions would seem to be inherently more difficult to mechanize than production operations, similar to the sales transactions of current output performed by commercial labor, discussed above.

5.4 SUPERVISORY LABOR

5.4.1 Causes of Increase

We turn now to the third type of unproductive labor: supervisory labor employed in the "productive" industries of the economy, such as Manufacturing, Services, etc. Supervisory labor is employed in the design and/or implementation of one of the following methods of capitalist control over production workers and the labor process: direct supervision, performance records and reports, rules and procedures, incentive pay schemes, etc. The ratio of supervisory labor to productive labor in productive industries increased 86 per cent from 0.07 in 1950 to 0.13 in 1980. This section will discuss some of the possible causes of this significant relative increase of supervisory labor in the postwar US economy.

Following Marx (especially C.I, Part 4) and Braverman (1974), we hypothesize that the degree of capitalist control over workers depends on the following "other factors", in addition to the amount of supervisory labor (with the nature of the relation, whether positive or negative, in parentheses): the level of skills of workers (negative), the rate of unemployment (positive), the size of firms (negative), the prevalence of unions (negative), and the divisions among workers (positive). If these "other factors" change in a way that reduces capitalist control, then the amount of supervisory labor would have to be increased if a given degree of capitalist control is to be maintained. In this sense, such changes in these "other factors" may be considered as causes of the increase of supervisory labor, i.e. they require an increase in supervisory labor in order to maintain a given degree of capitalist control. This response by capitalists to these various changes may not be immediate, but may instead occur after some time lag. The following pages present a preliminary assessment of the extent to which these "other factors" changed in the postwar US economy.

One important change which has occurred during the twentieth century, especially in Manufacturing, is a significant increase in the size of firms. In 1977, 66 per cent of employees in Manufacturing were in firms of more than 1000 employees and 45 per cent were in firms of more than 10 000 employees. These percentages had increased since 1958, the earliest year for which these data are available, from 56 and 33 per cent, respectively (source: Bureau of the Census, *Enterprise Statistics*). Another indication of the increasing size of firms in Manufacturing in the postwar period is that the percentage of production workers employed in multi-unit firms increased from 56 per cent in 1947 to 74 per cent in 1977 (source: Bureau of the Census, *Census of Manufacturing*, "Type of Organization"). Presumably, if earlier data were available, they would show much lower percentages in large and multi-unit firms in the early twentieth century. It could be argued that some of the increase of supervisory labor in Manufacturing in the postwar period was a delayed reaction to the increasing size of firms in the decades preceding this period.

Edwards (1979) argues that as the size of firms increased in the twentieth century, the older and simpler forms of control, based on the personal and direct authority of the owners and managers, no longer sufficed to maintain an adequate intensity of labor. In response to this problem, Edwards argues, many large firms instituted a new system of "bureaucratic control" in the postwar period. Bureaucratic control consisted primarily of elaborate and detailed systems of record-keeping, the primary purpose of which was to monitor closely the work performance of each employee. This new form of control required that more and more labor be devoted to the creation and processing of these performance records. Other aspects of bureaucratic control, which also required an increase of supervisory labor, are detailed rules and procedures to govern all tasks which workers must perform, finely graded "job ladders" to maintain the sense of job mobility, and an extension of incentive pay schemes. Edwards also notes that there was a significant increase of direct supervision in the postwar period to administer these new forms of bureaucratic control.

It is interesting that some neo-classical economists have also argued that larger firms have more "control problems" than smaller firms, although these are usually attributed to such causes as "communication loss" or "subgoal pursuit" by middle managers (utility maximization rather than profit maximization), rather than to the class conflict between managers and workers. It has been suggested that these "diseconomies of management" are an important reason why the long-run average cost curve of firms eventually slopes upward, thus establishing an upper limit to the size of firms and the power of monopolies, and making possible a competitive equilibrium in industries. For example, Williamson (1967) argued that the cumulative effects of communication losses over successive levels of hierarchy "are fundamentally responsible for limitations to firm size".

In a later work, Williamson (1970) argued, following Chandler (1962), that many corporations had largely solved the control problems that result from increasing size by the development of the "multi-divisional" form of corporate organization. This multi-divisional form created quasi-autonomous operating divisions (organized along product or geographical lines), each with its own functional departments (production, sales, finance, etc.), and freed top management to concentrate on long-run strategic planning, assisted by an elite staff of specialists. Thus this "solution" to the control problems of large corporations greatly expanded the ranks of managers and significantly increased the ratio of managers to production workers. The most striking evidence of this effect is the rapid increase of employment in "central administrative offices", which grew more than twice as fast as production workers in Manufacturing in the postwar period (source: US Bureau of the Census, *Enterprise Statistics*).

However, the increased size of firms was much less significant in other industries besides Manufacturing. In these other industries, other factors besides increased size must have been primarily responsible for the relative increase in supervisory labor.

Another important development, related to the larger size of firms, was the rise of unions beginning in the 1930s and continuing through the 1950s. The percentage of employees in the total economy who were union members increased from 7 to 25 per cent over this period;

in the industrial sectors, this percentage increased from 11 to 33 per cent; and in Manufacturing, the center of most of the union organizing efforts, this percentage increased from about 20 per cent to about 65 per cent. After the 1950s, these percentages declined somewhat, but unions none the less remained a much more powerful force than in the early twentieth century. The existence of unions constrained the arbitrary power of capitalists over wages, working conditions, job assignments, firings, promotions, etc. and probably contributed to the institution of bureaucratic control described above. Clark (1984) argues that attempts by managers to increase their control over production in the twentieth century were in large part responses to the growth of unions and other forms of workers' collective action.

Another important change in the "other" determinants of capitalist control, which may have precipitated an increase of supervisory labor, was the lower rates of unemployment which prevailed in the postwar period, compared to earlier historical periods. Marx argued in *Capital* that unemployment "completes the despotism of capital" (C.I, chapter 25). In these terms, the lower rates of unemployment in the postwar period reduced the despotism of capital and presumably enabled workers to resist capitalist control more effectively. As a result, more supervisory labor was required in order to maintain a given degree of capitalist control. Weisskopf (1985) suggests that the lower rates of unemployment in the postwar period was an important cause of the increase of supervisory labor.

All three of the "other" determinants of capitalist control discussed thus far seem to have changed in ways (*ceteris paribus*) that reduced capitalist control and thus generated a need for an increase of supervisory labor. The two remaining "other" determinants, the skills of workers and the intra-class divisions among workers, are harder to measure and evaluate. However, it does not appear likely that these two remaining factors changed in ways that reduced capitalist control and thus requiring an increase of supervisory labor. If anything, these two factors probably had the opposite effects.

Marx argued that technological change in capitalism would in general reduce the level of skills required by production workers (C.I, Part 4). Braverman (1974) has argued that Marx's prediction has essentially come true for the US economy (the subtitle of Braverman's book is "the degradation of work in the 20th century"). However, critics of Braverman have argued that the average level of skills of production workers has not declined significantly in the US economy since the early twentieth century (e.g. Elger, 1979; Attewell, 1987). More research is needed in order to determine how significant the changes have been in the level of skills in the US economy. My tentative conclusion is that the level of skills has declined somewhat, but probably not enough to have had a significant effect on capitalist control or on the amount of supervisory labor required. If there was a significant decline in the average level of skills, then less supervisory labor was needed to maintain capitalist control.

There are two main divisions within the working class in the US: between white and black workers and between male and female workers. Gordon, Edwards and Reich (1982) argue that these divisions in the working class increased significantly in the postwar period, due primarily to a strategy followed by capitalists of creating "segmented" labor markets (segmented in a double sense: between "primary" and "secondary" sectors and between "independent" and "subordinate" jobs within the primary sector). Their index of income inequality by labor market segment increased from 1930 to 1970 by approximately 50 per cent (ibid., p. 232). Bowles, Gordon and Weisskopf (1983) have provided a similar measure of the divisions among workers as the ratio of white male earnings to a composite of black and white female earnings. This measure increased approximately 50 per cent from 1948 to 1979 (ibid., p. 130). Although these measures are rough approximations and may overstate the increase of divisions among workers, it seems highly unlikely that these divisions declined in the postwar period and thus improbable that the increase of supervisory labor was due to a decline in divisions among workers.

In summary, the most likely possible causes of the increase of supervisory labor in the postwar US economy are: the increased size of firms, the rise of unions, and lower rates of unemployment. The first two of these causes apply primarily to Manufacturing.

It is very difficult to test statistically the relative significance of these possible causes. The main reason for this difficulty is that no data exist for individual *firms* which distinguish between production workers and non-production workers. The data for production and non-production workers used in this study are all classified either by *establishment* (individual plants) or by *industry*. This lack of data makes it impossible to attempt to correlate the ratio of non-production workers to production workers with the size of firms or the existence of unions (the rate of unemployment is, of course, a macroeconomic variable that applies to all firms simultaneously).

Thus an important task for further research along these lines is to develop a data base of the ratio of non-production to production workers for individual firms.[9]

The discussion of supervisory labor thus far has been based on the assumption that managers increased supervisory labor in the postwar period in order to maintain a given degree of control in the face of adverse changes in the "other" determinants of capitalist control. A further possible cause of the relative increase of supervisory labor in the postwar US economy is that managers attempted not only to *maintain* a given degree of control, but also to *increase* their control. The aim of the greater control over labor would be, not just to maintain a given intensity of labor, but to increase the level of intensity, and thus to increase productivity and profits.

Over the broad sweep of the last century or more, it does appear that capitalists have attempted to increase their control over production workers, and have largely succeeded in doing so (although not without many struggles). Up until the late nineteenth century, skilled workers in many industries exercised considerable control over the organization and pace of their own work. In subsequent decades, many firms mounted a multi-faceted offensive against this worker control. This offensive included the destruction of unions, the division of labor and deskilling, technological change, "scientific management," etc. (see e.g. Braverman, 1974; Stone, 1974; Work Relations Group, 1978; Zimbalist (ed.), 1979; Clawson, 1980). It seems likely that in the postwar period, capitalists have continued these attempts to increase their control over workers and the labor process.

It is very difficult, if not impossible, to distinguish empirically between attempts by managers to increase their control and attempts to maintain a given degree of control, made necessary by adverse changes in external factors. The main reason for this difficulty is the inability to measure the degree of capitalist control, except perhaps indirectly by the methods of control discussed above (direct supervision, detailed instructions, performance reports, etc.). However, these methods could be undertaken either to maintain or to increase the degree of capitalist control.

Of all the various possible causes of the increase of supervisory labor discussed above, which ones seem to be inherent tendencies of capitalist economies and which ones seem instead to be more or less unique to the postwar US economy, or at least to the postwar period? The first two of the possible causes identified above would seem to be inherent tendencies of capitalist economies. The increased size of firms seems to result from the very process of capital accumulation, as well as from the competitive nature of capitalism (C.I, chapter 25). The emergence of unions results from the class conflict between capitalists and workers over wages, working conditions, the intensity of labor, etc. (although the strength of unions in a particular period depends on the rate of unemployment and other factors). On the other hand, the lower rates of unemployment of the postwar period does not seem to be an inherent tendency, but instead appears to have been a temporary phenomenon, due in large part to expansionary government fiscal and monetary policies. However, the limits of such expansionary government policies seemed to have been reached in the 1970s, and rates of unemployment in the US (and elsewhere) have been much higher since then.

We also saw above that another possible cause of the increase of supervisory labor was attempts by capitalists to increase their control over workers. It is an interesting question whether or not such attempts, assuming they occurred, are inherent in capitalist economies. On the one hand, one could argue that the imperatives of capital accumulation and the class struggle would require that capitalists would always seek to increase their control over workers. On the other hand, the Japanese economy may present an actual counter-example of such an inherent tendency. There is much anecdotal evidence that Japanese firms typically have a much lower ratio of managers and supervisors to production workers than US firms, and this ratio has not increased significantly in the postwar period. Further comparative studies of the proportion of supervisory labor in Japan and in other major capitalist countries should shed additional light on this question.

Finally, part of the labor I have counted as supervisory labor was probably devoted to the control of inventories, rather than the control of labor. The main purpose of these efforts to control inventories was to minimize the risk of losses in the event of future recessions. For example, Chandler (1962) argues that the multi-divisional form of corporate organisation was developed by DuPont and General Motors in the 1920s in response to the severe depression of 1920–1. Such efforts to control inventories and reduce risk have increased in the postwar period. This labor should really be counted as circulation labor, since its function is related to the market, anarchic nature of capitalism, not to the control of labor. The risk or uncertainty which this labor is intended to minimize is obviously an inherent feature of capitalist economies.

5.4.2 Effects of Increase

We turn now to a separate question related to supervisory labor: instead of the *causes* of the increase of supervisory labor, we now reconsider the *effects* of this increase on the conventional rate of profit. Thus far we have assumed that since supervisory labor does not directly produce value and surplus-value, an increase of supervision labor reduces the rate of profit. We now consider the possible indirect effects of the increase of supervisory labor on the rate of profit, through its effects on the intensity of labor and the rate of surplus-value.

If it is assumed that the managers of firms are pure profit maximizers, then the attempts discussed above to maintain or increase their control would be undertaken only if the expected benefits in the form of higher output and/or lower costs were greater than the increased costs of supervision, i.e. only if these actions were expected to increase the rate of profit. Furthermore, if these attempts turned out to be as successful as intended, then it follows that these actions would result in a higher rate of profit than would have occurred without these attempts. In terms of the Marxian variables, these attempts by managers to maintain or increase their control would result in a higher rate of surplus-value due to a higher intensity of labor than would otherwise have been the case.

To the extent that these dynamics actually occurred in the postwar US economy, it would not be correct to say that the increase of supervisory labor caused a decline in the rate of profit, as we did in Chapter 4. Rather, in this case, the increase of supervisory labor acted as a "countertendency" to the decline of the rate of profit, i.e. it prevented an even greater decline which would have resulted from a smaller increase in the rate of surplus-value (and perhaps even a decline in the rate of surplus-value). In this case, the causes of the decline of the rate of profit in the postwar US economy would be more in line with Marx's theory of the falling rate of profit. In the absence of the increase of supervisory labor, the rate of profit would have declined even more than it actually did, due to the cause emphasized by Marx: a greater increase in the composition of capital than in the rate of surplus-value. However, this qualification of our earlier conclusions applies only to supervisory labor, which is only approximately 20 per cent of the total unproductive labor. The more significant increase of circulation labor would still be a direct cause of the decline of the rate of profit; but the contribution of the increase of unproductive labor to the decline of the rate of profit would be somewhat less and the contribution of the increase of the composition of capital would be somewhat greater than in our prior analysis in Chapter 4 (see below for a more precise estimate of these revised contributions).[10]

On the other hand, there is a large literature which suggests that managers of firms are not always pure profit maximizers. Radical economists have argued that managers attempt to monopolize decision-making power in their own hands, even if this top-down control may be less profitable (e.g. Braverman, 1974; Marglin, 1974; Gordon, 1976; Hodgson, 1982–3; Drago, 1984–5). Mainstream economists (beginning with Berle and Means, 1932) have argued that with the separation of ownership and management, managers attempt to maximize their own utility, and their utility functions include other arguments besides profits. It has been argued specifically that one of the areas in which non-owner managers do not always maximize profits is the size of their own staffs (Williamson, 1963).[11] This form of "empire-building", it is argued, is often undertaken to increase the power and prestige of top managers, independent of its effect on profits (or rather subject only to the constraint of a minimum level of profits). These actions would, of course, have to be justified by managers in terms of profit maximization, but such justifications may serve to hide these other motivations. This non-profit maximizing behavior is generally considered to be possible because of less than perfectly competitive markets.

Melman (1983) argues that even though managers may be profit maximizers, profit maximization does not necessarily imply cost minimization. Specifically, Melman argues that in the "defense industry" in the US, cost minimization has been largely replaced by cost maximization. This important shift has been made possible and is consistent with profit maximization because of the "cost-plus" nature of Pentagon contracts. One area in which costs have been allowed to accelerate, without regard to cost minimization, is precisely the administrative bureaucracy of line and staff managers. Melman cites evidence of very high ratios of administrative labor to production labor in military contractors (ibid., p. 90).

A complicating factor here is that for most of supervisory labor it is very difficult to forecast and measure reliably the effects of an increase of supervisory labor on output and costs (Mack, 1959). Thus managers base their decisions in this area on largely subjective evaluations, which may be heavily influenced by the (perhaps unconscious) motives of power and "empire-building". Even though managers consciously aim to maximize profits, their decisions with respect to supervisory labor may deviate significantly from this norm.

To the extent that the growth of supervisory labor in the postwar US economy was for reasons other than profit maximization, then this increase would be a direct cause of the decline of the rate of profit, as stated in Chapter 4, and the qualification to our earlier conclusions stated above would not apply.

Furthermore, even if managers increased supervisory labor solely to maximize profits, there is the possibility that these attempts may turn out to be unsuccessful. The increase of supervisory labor may fail to increase the intensity of labor due to the resistance of workers (Work Relations Group, 1978). There is very little reliable evidence, one way or the other, concerning the effects of an increase of supervisory labor on the intensity of labor or on output or productivity. Melman (1983, chapter 4) cites several studies of individual industries (mainly Ph.D. dissertations by his students at Columbia University) as evidence that an increase of "administrative" labor has generally *not* resulted in higher output and profits. Dumas (1986) largely follows Melman on this point, but acknowledges that "this question is far from closed, and further empirical investigation would certainly be worthwhile" (ibid., p. 69).

On the other hand, there is a considerable literature which suggests that increased worker control (the inverse of capitalist control) in individual firms usually *raises* the productivity of labor (for a review of this literature, see Blumberg, 1968). Presumably, an increase in the productivity of labor results in an increase in the rate of profit for these firms. This evidence suggests that attempts by capitalists to increase their control (i.e. reduce worker control) would have the opposite effects. Drago (1984–5) makes precisely this argument: that increased managerial control in the postwar US economy was one of the important causes of the decline of the rate of profit during this period.

Another indication that, whatever the intention of managers, the effect of the significant increase of supervisory labor in the postwar period was *not* to increase profits, is the actions of managers themselves in recent years. An increasingly prevalent trend in the 1980s has been the reduction of the number of levels of hierarchy and the number of staff specialists ("downsizing" or "delayering") (Tomasko, 1987; Sanderson and Schein, 1986).[12] A related recent trend is the establishment of "work teams" which often reduces the layers of supervisors and managers. Thus it appears that many corporate managers have come to the conclusion that the earlier increases of supervisory labor did not pay off in higher profits and that one way to increase profits at the present time is to *reduce* supervisory labor, not to increase it.

To the extent that these attempts to maintain or increase managerial control (even for the purpose of profit maximization) were not successful, then the increase of supervisory labor would again be a direct cause of the decline of the rate of profit, as stated in Chapter 4.

The empirical determination of which of these various possible effects of the relative increase of supervisory labor actually occurred in the postwar US economy is an extremely difficult task. Perhaps a reasonable "middle-ground" assumption at this point is that on balance the increase of supervisory labor had little or no net effect on the rate of profit, i.e. the cases in which the increase of supervisory labor was for the purpose of profit maximization and was successful were offset by the cases in which the increase of supervisory labor was for purposes other than profit maximization or were unsuccessful. In other words, the direct negative effect of the actual increase of supervisory labor on the rate of profit was approximately offset by the indirect positive effect of this increased supervisory labor. In this case, the results of the analysis of the contributions of the four Marxian determinants to the total decline of the conventional rate of profit presented in Chapter 4 would have to be modified. The positive contribution of the rate of surplus-value and the negative contributions of the ratios UF and US would be smaller, and the negative contribution of the composition of capital would be larger.

Table 5.5 presents the revised contributions of the four Marxian determinants to the total decline in the conventional rate of profit, based on the assumption that the increase of supervisory labor had no net effect on the rate of profit.[13] We can see that, under this assumption, the negative contribution of the ratio UF is still larger than the negative contribution of the composition of capital, but only 40 per cent larger, rather than twice as large as in the original analysis.

It was mentioned at the end of the previous subsection that part of the labor I have counted as supervisory labor should really be counted as circulation labor, since its main function is to minimize the risk of inventory losses, not to control labor. The effects of the increase of this type of labor on the rate of profit would be somewhat different from that of supervisory labor. If this type of labor succeeded in reducing the stock of constant capital which must be invested in inventories, then it would have a positive indirect effect on the rate of

Table 5.5   Revised contributions of the Marxian determinants to the decline
of the conventional rate of profit, 1947–77

	Revised	Original
RS	0.028	0.051
CC	–0.054	–0.051
UF	–0.065	–0.085
US	–0.010	–0.012
Total decline in CRP	–0.099	

Method: See Table 4.2.

profit by reducing the composition of capital (rather than by increasing the rate of surplus-value, as in the case of supervisory labor). The
net effect on the rate of profit of an increase of this type of labor
would then depend on the relative magnitudes of this indirect positive
effect and the direct negative effect of the increase in the ratio *UF*.
This modification would increase the negative contribution of the
composition of capital and reduce the negative contribution of the
ratio *UF* to the decline in the rate of profit. Under reasonable
assumptions regarding the magnitude of these effects, it is not likely
that the estimated contributions would change very much as a result
of this qualification. On the other hand, since the main function of
this type of labor was to minimize the risk of future losses, there may
not be a reduction of inventory costs and thus no indirect positive
effect on the rate of profit. In this case, the additional costs of control
are a kind of insurance premium: they lower current profits, but also
reduce future risks.

5.5   CONCLUSIONS

The main conclusions of this long and wide-ranging chapter are:

(1)   The quantitatively most significant type of unproductive labor in
postwar US economy was commercial labor, which accounted for
almost two-thirds of the total increase of unproductive labor. The
other two types of unproductive labor, financial labor and supervisory

labor, each accounted for approximately half the remaining increase of unproductive labor.

(2)   The main cause of the relative increase of commercial labor appears to have been the slower productivity growth of commercial labor compared to productive labor.

(3)   The main cause of the relative increase of financial labor appears to have been the faster output growth of banks, compared to the output of productive labor, which appears to have been due primarily to the spread of personal checking.

(4)   The most likely causes of the relative increase of supervisory labor were: the increased size of firms, the increase of union membership, the lower rates of unemployment in the postwar period, and the attempts by managers to increase their control over production workers.

(5)   Of these causes of the relative increase of unproductive labor, the slower productivity growth of commercial labor, the increased size of firms, and the increase of union membership seem to be inherent tendencies of capitalist economies.

(6)   A reconsideration of the effects of the increase of supervisory labor on the rate of profit suggested that the contributions of the four Marxian determinants to the total decline in the conventional rate of profit, previously estimated in Chapter 4, should probably be revised as follows: the negative contribution of the ratio UF (and hence of the ratio of unproductive labor to productive labor) is probably still greater than the negative contribution of the composition of capital, but is probably considerably less than twice as great as was concluded in Chapter 4. This conclusion is more consistent with Marx's emphasis on a rising composition of capital in his theory of the falling rate of profit.

Obviously, much more research needs to be done on all these points in order to test these hypotheses further and to understand more completely the underlying causes of the very significant increase in the relative proportion of unproductive labor in the postwar US economy, and the effects of this increase on the rate of profit.

Chapter 6 will discuss the implications of these conclusions for the likely future trend in the ratio of unproductive labor to productive labor and in the conventional rate of profit and thus for the likelihood of a full recovery from the economic crisis of the 1970s and 1980s.

6 Conclusion

This final chapter will first review the main conclusions of the preceding chapters. Suggestions for further research along these lines will then be presented. In the final two sections, the implications of these conclusions will be briefly reviewed, both for the likely future trend of the conventional rate of profit and for the likely effectiveness of government policies to raise the rate of profit. These last two sections are more speculative than the rest of the book.

6.1 MAIN CONCLUSIONS

Chapter 3 presented an empirical test of Marx's theory of the falling rate of profit. According to the estimates presented, the trends of the Marxian variables for the postwar long-wave period of expansion were largely consistent with Marx's hypothesis that the rate of profit would tend to decline due to technological change. The Marxian rate of profit declined for the reason suggested by Marx's theory: because the composition of capital increased faster than the rate of surplus-value. This conclusion is strengthened by a consideration of the effects of "other factors" (the distribution of capital, the turnover of capital, and multiple shifts) on the rate of profit. These "other factors" all had significant positive effects on the rate of profit, which implies that technological change by itself had an even greater negative effect on the rate of profit than my estimates show. On the other hand, these results are clearly not consistent with the "profit squeeze" interpretation of Marx's theory, because the rate of surplus-value did not decline, but instead increased modestly.

These conclusions concerning the trends of the rate of surplus-value and the composition of capital are essentially the opposite of the prior conclusions reached by Weisskopf and Wolff. The main reason for the divergent trends between my estimates of these variables and Weisskopf's and Wolff's prior estimates is that these prior estimates fail to take into account Marx's distinction between productive labor and unproductive labor.

Chapter 4 was concerned with an analysis of the causes of the decline in the conventional rate of profit in the postwar US economy. It was concluded that the main cause of this decline was a very significant increase in the ratio of unproductive labor to productive labor. According to Marx's theory, this relative increase of unproductive labor required that a greater portion of the surplus-value produced by productive labor had to be used to pay the costs of unproductive labor, thus leaving a smaller portion of surplus-value as the profit of capitalists. The second most important cause of the decline in the conventional rate of profit was the increase in the composition of capital, the trend which Marx emphasized in his analysis of the falling rate of profit. This alternative Marxian explanation of the decline in the conventional rate of profit receives stronger empirical support than the competing "profit squeeze" explanations presented by Weisskopf and Wolff from the very important fact that the rate of profit has not increased significantly since the mid-1970s. According to this explanation, a recovery in the conventional rate of profit has been inhibited by the continued increase in the ratio of unproductive labor to productive labor.

Chapter 5 presented a preliminary analysis of the underlying causes of the very significant increase in the relative proportion of unproductive labor in the postwar US economy. The quantitatively most significant type of unproductive labor by far was commercial labor, which accounted for almost two-thirds of the total increase of unproductive labor. The main cause of the relative increase of commercial labor appears to have been the slower productivity growth of commercial labor compared to productive labor, which required that a greater portion of the total labor had to be employed as commercial labor in order to sell the more rapidly increasing output of productive labor. The two other types of unproductive labor, financial labor and supervisory labor, each accounted for approximately half of the remaining increase of unproductive labor. The main cause of the relative increase of financial labor appears to have been the spread of personal checking as a means of making payments. The relative increase of supervisory labor appears to have been due to more diverse causes: the increased size of firms, the increase of union membership, and the attempts by managers to increase their control over production workers.

6.2 FURTHER RESEARCH

This section will suggest various ways in which the research presented in this book can and should be extended. The most obvious and perhaps most important extension of this study would be to derive similar estimates of all the Marxian variables for other capitalist nations, both advanced and less developed. This research should build upon similar estimates of the rate of surplus-value in France by Delaunay (1989), estimates of the rate of surplus-value in five European countries by Gouverneur (1983), and estimates of all three Marxian ratios in the UK by Freeman (1988). Such estimates would enable us to determine whether the trends of the Marxian variables in these other countries for the postwar period were similar to the trends in the US. Did the Marxian rate of profit in these other countries decline because the composition of capital increased faster than the rate of surplus-value? If so, then the conclusions reached here concerning the empirical test of Marx's theory of the falling rate of profit would appear to apply also to the world capitalist economy, the level of aggregation to which Marx's theory most rigorously applies. Further, did the ratio of unproductive labor to productive labor increase as significantly as in the US and were the relative rates of increase of the specific types of unproductive labor similar to the US? If so, then it would appear that the trends of these variables observed in the US economy are inherent tendencies of capitalist economies, at least for the postwar period.

Another obvious extension would be to derive similar estimates of all the Marxian variables for earlier historical periods, both for the US economy and for other economies. The major obstacle to this line of research is the scarcity of data from which to derive such estimates, especially data which distinguish between productive and unproductive labor. For the US, such research should build upon the pioneering estimates of Gillman (1958) and Mage (1963), especially the latter. Both of these earlier studies make the crucial distinction between productive and unproductive labor. However, both are flawed in other respects. Gillman's estimates are only for the Manufacturing sector of the economy and thus are of only limited use. Mage's estimates are for the non-agricultural private economy and thus are more rigorously correct than Gillman's in this respect. However, Mage's estimates are flawed in two other respects: (i) taxes on profit and wages are not included either as variable capital or as surplus-value, and (ii) the wages of unproductive labor are included as constant capital rather than as surplus-value. In spite of these flaws, the detailed estimates provided by Mage could be used as the basis from which to derive alternative estimates based on the definitions adopted in this book. The results of this research would enable us to determine the long-run secular trends of the Marxian variables, at least in the US economy, since the beginning of the twentieth century. Most importantly: did the Marxian rate of profit decline in the long-wave period of expansion in the decades prior to the Great Depression? If so, was this decline due to an increase in the composition of capital or to a reduction in the rate of surplus-value? Further, did the conventional rate of profit also decline during this period of expansion? Did the ratio of unproductive to productive labor increase as rapidly as in the postwar period? What happened to all these variables during the Great Depression and World War II? A thorough re-examination of this earlier period would be a valuable contribution to Marxian empirical research.

In Chapter 4, a preliminary empirical test of the three competing explanations of the decline of the conventional rate of profit presented by Weisskopf, Wolff, and myself was conducted. Further research could devise more discriminating empirical tests which would enable us to determine with greater certainty the relative empirical validity of these competing explanations. It will probably be difficult to devise such tests. However, the attempt to do so should provide additional insights, not only about the relative strengths and weaknesses of the competing explanations of the decline in the rate of profit, but also concerning the general methodological question of how to discriminate between competing explanations of the same phenomena, which has recently received much attention (e.g. Blaug, 1980; Caldwell, 1982; McCloskey, 1985). Most of the discussion of this latter question thus far has been at a very abstract level. It seems that this methodological discussion would benefit from an application of this question to a concrete research topic, such as the decline of the rate of profit.

Chapter 5 presented a preliminary analysis of the causes of the relative increase of unproductive labor in the postwar US economy. Additional research could examine all the suggested hypotheses. Most important would be to determine the causes of the slower productivity growth of commercial labor, the largest group of unproductive labor. A greater understanding of the causes of this increase would give us a better idea of whether it is likely to continue in the future, and thus is likely to continue to exert downward pressure on the conventional rate of profit. It would also be important to determine the relative significance of the several possible causes suggested of the increase of supervisory labor. Toward this end, another task, mentioned in Chapter 5, would be to develop a micro data base of individual firms which would include data on the relative proportions of unproductive and productive labor within firms and would also include data on the possible causes of the increase of supervisory labor, such as the size of firms, the existence of unions, etc. Finally, further research could attempt to determine more precisely the effect of an increase of supervisory labor on the conventional rate of profit.

Another type of extension would be to examine in detail the employment of unproductive labor within individual firms, preferably large multinational firms. Such a "case-study" approach should be able to determine with greater precision the specific occupations which have increased the most rapidly, and the causes of these additions of unproductive labor. It might also be able to shed some light on the question raised in Chapter 2 concerning the proportion of the labor of managers and supervisors which is devoted to productive functions. This information could perhaps be used to revise the estimates presented here of productive labor and variable capital.

6.3   FUTURE TRENDS

It was argued in Chapter 4 that an important cause of the economic stagnation of the 1970s and 1980s was the significant decline in the conventional rate of profit during the preceding long-wave period of expansion. If this argument is valid, then an important precondition for a full and lasting recovery from the current stagnation is a significant increase in the conventional rate of profit to its earlier higher levels. This section will discuss the implications of the conclusions reached in Chapter 4 concerning the causes of the decline of the conventional rate of profit for the likely future trend of this rate of profit, and thus for the likelihood of a full recovery from the current stagnation.

According to the Marxian theory presented in Chapter 4, the conventional rate of profit depends on the rate of surplus-value, the composition of capital, and the ratio of unproductive labor to productive labor. What are the likely trends of these Marxian determinants of the conventional rate of profit over the next decade or so?

The rate of surplus-value will probably continue to increase in the decade ahead, due to continued high unemployment, but perhaps not as rapidly as in the previous decade. Real wage growth of productive workers has already been cut to zero; further cuts would mean absolute declines in real wages. Future productivity growth is more difficult to predict, but in the current conditions of stagnation, it does not seem likely that productivity growth will accelerate significantly. The higher rates of unemployment may result in some increase in the intensity of labor and thus in a short-run increase of productivity growth, but is unlikely to have a significant longer-run effect (the intensity of labor cannot continue to be increased).

If the current stagnation continues, i.e. in the absence of either more rapid capital accumulation or a deep depression, the composition of capital is not likely to increase very much, similar to the past decade.[1] On the other hand, the composition of capital may increase somewhat faster, because further reductions in the relative price of the means of production (P_c/P_n) are not likely to continue.

Chapter 5 discussed the possible causes of the three types of unproductive labor: commercial, financial, and supervisory labor. It was seen that the main cause of the relative increase of commercial labor was the slower productivity growth of commercial labor, which appears to be an inherent tendency of capitalist economies. Thus it appears that commercial labor, the largest and most significant type of unproductive labor, will continue to increase relative to productive labor in the decade ahead.

It was also concluded in Chapter 5 that the main cause of the relative increase of financial labor appears to have been the spread of personal checking as a means of making purchases. Although it may be argued that an increasing need for an alternative to cash as a means of payment is an inherent tendency of capitalist economies, it seems possible and perhaps even likely that technological innovations, such as electronic fund transfers, will provide a cashless alternative which requires much less labor to process than checks. Thus the relative increase of financial labor may slow down in the coming decade.

Finally, the main causes of the relative growth of supervisory labor appear to have been the larger size of firms, the expansion of union membership, lower rates of unemployment, and perhaps the attempt by managers to enhance their control over production workers. The size of firms will probably continue to increase, which should require more supervisors in the decade ahead. On the other hand, the growth of union membership and the lower rates of unemployment have both been significantly reversed in the last decade, which should require fewer supervisors in the decade ahead. Furthermore, as mentioned in Chapter 5, some firms have concluded that the larger administrative bureaucracies built up in the postwar period have not contributed to profitability and have begun to reduce these bureaucracies. In addition, various types of "worker participation" arrangements are becoming more popular, which may reduce the relative proportion of supervisory labor. All in all, it appears that the ratio of supervisory to productive labor is likely to continue to increase, but less rapidly than in the previous decades.

Thus, of the three types of unproductive labor, commercial labor is the most likely to continue to expand significantly in the 1990s. However, since commercial labor is the largest type of unproductive labor, the overall ratio of unproductive to productive labor will probably continue to increase, although at a slower rate than in the previous four decades. The continued increase in the ratio of unproductive to productive labor will in turn continue to have a negative effect on the conventional rate of profit.

Thus, according to Marx's theory, the trend of the conventional rate of profit over the next decade or so will depend on the relative weights of two offsetting influences: the positive effect a higher rate of surplus-value and the negative effect of a higher ratio of unproductive labor to productive labor. It is difficult to predict with precision what the net effect of these two opposing influences will be. However, it seems reasonable to conclude, similar to our conclusion in Chapter 4 for the 1980s, that the Marxian theory presented here implies the important prediction that the conventional rate of profit will *not* increase significantly in the 1990s. Without such an increase, the current period of stagnation is likely to continue.

This implied prediction of Marxian theory may be contrasted with those of the two "profit squeeze" theories presented by Weisskopf (1979) and Wolff (1986). As we saw in Chapter 4, Weisskopf's "rising strength of labor" version of the "profit squeeze" theory implies the prediction that the higher rates of unemployment that are likely to persist in the years ahead should continue to reduce the strength of labor, which in turn should increase the rate of profit significantly. Wolff's "slower productivity growth" version of the "profit squeeze" theory implies a less definite prediction, but it seems to suggest that the chances of a significant increase in the rate of profit are fairly good, certainly much better than that implied by the Marxian theory presented here. Thus both the "profit squeeze" theories imply more optimistic predictions than alternative Marxian theory presented here, regarding the future trend of the conventional rate of profit and thus concerning the likelihood of a full recovery from the current stagnation.

Further analysis of the likely course of events over the next decade would require a consideration of additional factors, besides the rate of profit. Most importantly, the causes and effects of the growing level of debt of all kinds (business, government, consumer, and international) would have to be analyzed. Such an analysis is beyond the scope of this book. I will simply state my tentative hypothesis at this point: the combination of lower rates of profit and higher levels of debt reinforces the likelihood of another deep depression in the 1990s. This combination has already brought more and more capitalist enterprises to the brink of bankruptcy and beyond. The next recession, or the one after that, could be the one to set off an avalanche of bankruptcies and a deepening depression. As long as the rate of profit remains low and the levels of debt continue to grow, the chances of another Great Depression will continue to grow.

6.4 LIMITS OF GOVERNMENT POLICIES

As discussed in the previous section, the Marxian theory presented here suggests that the main precondition for a full and lasting recovery from the current stagnation is a significant increase in the rate of profit. This conclusion implies that the effectiveness of expansionary government policies (e.g. fiscal and monetary policies) intended to stimulate recovery depends primarily on the effect of these policies on the rate of profit. This final section briefly discusses the likely effects of government policies on the Marxian determinants of the conventional rate of profit and thus on the rate of profit itself. The discussion is based on the pioneering work of Paul Mattick, who was the first to extend Marx's theory in a rigorous way to the question of the effectiveness of government economic policies.[2]

In the first place, it does not seem likely that government policies can have much of an impact on the rate of surplus-value. In order to do so, these policies would have to affect real wages and/or the productivity of productive labor. Expansionary policies intended to reduce unemployment might have a positive effect on the real wage and thus a negative effect on the rate of surplus-value. On the other hand, the inflationary consequences of these policies might have opposite effects on the real wage and the rate of surplus-value. Government policies appear to have little impact on the productivity of labor.[3]

Likewise, it seems improbable that government policies can have much of an effect on the composition of capital. The value and organic composition of capital depend on the technical composition of capital and the productivity of labor, both of which seem to be largely unaffected by government policies. If anything, expansionary policies enable some firms to avoid bankruptcy and thus inhibit the primary way in which the composition of capital has been reduced during previous depressions (which admittedly is a quite painful way to raise the rate of profit).

The ineffectiveness of government policies also seems to apply to the ratio of unproductive to productive labor, the final Marxian determinant of the conventional rate of profit. It does not seem likely that government policies can have much of an impact on the causes of the relative increase of unproductive labor identified in Chapter 5: the slower productivity growth of commercial labor, the spread of personal checking, and the various causes of the increase of supervisory labor (the increased size of firms, the increase of union membership, lower unemployment, attempts by managers to increase their control, etc.). Most importantly, if the argument presented in Chapter 5 is valid, that the slower productivity growth of commercial labor is due to the inherent difficulties of mechanizing exchange activities, then it is unlikely that government policies will be able to accelerate significantly the pace of technological change in exchange activities.

Thus it appears that there is not much government policies can do to increase the rate of profit and so satisfy the most important precondition for a lasting recovery from the current stagnation. The inability of government policies markedly to increase the rate of profit leaves the economy vulnerable to the danger of another great depression, as discussed in the previous section. Mattick argued that the next depression could be even worse than the Great Depression of the 1930s, because the Keynesian "solution" to depressions has already been tried and failed. If another Great Depression does indeed occur in the 1990s, this would provide additional empirical support for the Marxian theory presented in this book.

Appendix A
Detailed Estimates

Table A.1   Variable capital by industry
(billions of dollars)

	MAN	MIN	CON	TPU	SER	WRT	AFF	GOV	Total
1947	33.1	2.5	5.5	11.0	4.8	9.3	3.0	1.6	70.8
1948	36.0	2.9	6.6	11.8	5.5	9.7	3.3	1.9	77.7
1949	33.3	2.5	6.6	11.5	5.4	9.7	3.1	2.1	74.2
1950	38.5	2.8	7.4	12.2	5.6	10.3	3.1	2.2	82.2
1951	45.7	3.2	9.2	13.9	6.2	11.5	3.3	2.5	95.5
1952	48.8	3.2	10.0	14.8	6.7	12.2	3.2	2.9	101.7
1953	54.1	3.3	10.4	15.7	7.1	12.9	3.1	2.9	109.5
1954	49.6	2.9	10.5	15.1	7.2	12.9	3.0	2.9	104.2
1955	54.6	3.1	11.3	16.0	7.7	13.6	2.9	3.1	112.4
1956	58.0	3.5	12.5	17.2	8.4	14.6	3.0	3.2	120.4
1957	59.1	3.5	12.8	17.9	8.9	15.2	3.1	3.4	123.9
1958	55.0	3.0	12.4	17.5	9.1	15.3	3.3	3.7	119.2
1959	61.0	3.2	13.5	18.5	9.8	16.4	3.4	4.0	129.7
1960	62.3	3.2	13.9	19.0	10.2	17.4	3.5	4.3	133.9
1961	61.4	3.1	14.1	19.1	10.9	17.7	3.7	4.5	134.6
1962	66.8	3.1	15.0	19.9	11.7	18.7	3.8	4.8	143.9
1963	70.3	3.2	16.0	20.9	12.6	20.0	4.0	5.3	152.3
1964	74.8	3.3	17.5	22.2	13.4	21.3	4.1	5.7	162.3
1965	81.5	3.5	19.0	23.7	14.6	23.0	4.3	6.1	175.6
1966	90.7	3.6	21.1	25.3	16.3	24.9	4.4	6.6	192.9
1967	93.7	3.7	21.7	26.6	17.8	26.6	4.4	7.0	201.6
1968	102.6	3.9	24.7	29.0	19.9	29.3	4.7	7.7	221.8
1969	110.2	4.3	28.0	31.9	22.3	32.0	5.1	8.4	242.2
1970	109.0	4.6	29.1	34.3	24.0	34.2	5.4	9.6	250.4
1971	110.2	4.8	31.5	36.4	25.5	36.1	5.5	10.2	260.2
1972	124.1	5.4	35.3	41.0	29.5	39.9	5.8	11.4	292.3
1973	141.9	6.1	40.8	46.6	33.9	44.8	6.8	12.6	333.6
1974	144.3	7.4	42.7	50.0	37.5	48.8	7.7	14.1	352.5
1975	147.1	9.3	39.9	52.2	41.2	51.9	8.2	15.7	365.4
1976	170.3	10.5	43.0	58.9	47.0	58.4	9.4	17.3	415.0
1977	194.1	12.4	48.3	66.2	54.1	65.3	10.2	18.6	469.2
1978	217.4	13.4	57.2	73.0	54.9	72.7	11.4	19.6	519.6
1979	242.1	16.3	66.7	82.1	62.6	80.9	13.0	21.5	585.2
1980	249.0	19.1	68.5	87.8	71.1	86.6	14.9	23.8	620.8
1981	268.0	23.4	71.6	96.0	80.7	94.6	16.0	26.6	676.9
1982	256.9	23.8	71.3	100.6	87.3	98.8	16.4	27.3	682.4
1983	267.1	19.8	80.5	103.8	98.7	103.5	15.8	29.3	718.4
1984	296.5	21.2	77.4	110.4	109.8	114.2	16.6	31.8	778.1
1985	303.9	20.9	88.8	115.3	108.5	123.8	17.3	34.4	812.9
1986	307.8	17.8	95.2	118.2	116.1	130.1	18.1	35.8	839.1
1987	320.9	16.4	97.3	125.4	132.1	139.6	19.7	38.9	890.1

Sources: See Appendix B, section B.2.

Table A.2   Constant capital by industry
(billions of dollars)

	MAN	MIN	CON	TPU	SER	WRT	AFF	GOV	Total
1947	102.1	10.2	4.3	68.6	5.3	20.2	22.0	20.8	253.5
1948	110.0	11.2	5.2	75.8	5.9	23.3	24.9	23.1	279.5
1949	106.1	11.6	5.3	80.8	6.1	23.3	25.5	23.8	282.5
1950	124.6	13.0	6.4	88.9	6.8	27.5	31.1	25.4	323.6
1951	142.1	14.9	7.1	96.7	7.7	29.2	34.8	28.2	360.7
1952	146.0	16.3	7.3	102.5	8.3	29.2	35.4	30.3	375.2
1953	151.4	17.5	7.4	108.0	8.8	30.1	35.4	31.7	390.2
1954	153.0	18.8	7.6	111.7	9.4	30.6	35.3	33.7	400.0
1955	166.6	21.2	8.1	119.7	10.6	33.8	36.0	37.2	433.3
1956	185.7	24.2	8.7	132.1	12.1	36.1	37.2	41.4	477.5
1957	195.3	25.8	9.3	141.5	13.2	37.6	38.4	44.4	505.4
1958	196.1	26.4	9.5	146.4	13.9	38.1	39.8	46.6	516.7
1959	203.2	28.2	10.0	151.5	14.9	40.2	40.1	48.4	536.5
1960	209.2	27.9	10.2	154.6	16.0	41.5	40.9	50.3	550.6
1961	213.7	28.9	10.3	156.1	17.4	42.2	41.6	52.8	563.0
1962	223.4	29.6	10.6	159.4	18.9	44.3	43.1	55.8	585.2
1963	232.6	29.6	11.3	162.7	20.4	47.1	44.5	58.8	607.1
1964	244.8	31.3	12.4	167.9	22.4	50.2	45.3	62.0	636.4
1965	268.1	33.5	13.6	176.7	24.8	55.0	49.4	66.4	687.6
1966	302.5	36.4	14.8	188.2	27.6	61.0	52.0	72.4	754.9
1967	328.4	38.3	16.3	202.6	29.3	65.0	54.9	78.1	812.9
1968	360.9	40.8	17.5	221.7	33.0	72.0	59.0	86.6	891.6
1969	400.5	43.7	19.0	244.2	36.8	80.0	64.4	96.1	985.1
1970	432.7	45.6	20.5	270.5	40.4	87.0	68.2	108.1	1073.0
1971	465.6	48.4	22.1	297.2	44.1	96.7	75.1	122.0	1171.2
1972	504.1	51.2	24.4	322.1	48.7	106.8	85.2	133.9	1276.4
1973	582.2	56.2	30.0	360.2	55.9	124.1	103.7	151.0	1463.2
1974	716.0	74.2	37.5	449.5	67.9	149.8	119.5	193.6	1807.9
1975	763.8	85.5	41.3	507.0	73.5	157.4	129.2	211.4	1969.1
1976	828.1	96.4	44.0	548.4	79.2	174.9	138.8	225.9	2135.6
1977	914.9	115.2	49.2	597.7	87.6	195.5	152.4	249.3	2361.6
1978	1060.2	140.6	60.0	664.6	101.1	230.8	180.6	296.6	2734.5
1979	1218.3	165.3	66.9	747.5	110.9	260.4	202.2	340.8	3112.2
1980	1381.0	200.1	71.3	847.9	124.5	290.7	223.7	374.9	3514.3
1981	1553.6	263.7	78.2	939.5	140.7	319.9	237.9	402.4	3900.9
1982	1557.1	289.0	76.0	986.8	147.6	328.2	237.7	412.6	4035.0
1983	1603.6	263.6	74.4	1017.7	159.9	350.3	240.8	424.4	4134.7
1984	1697.6	263.8	76.8	1059.7	174.9	387.4	240.9	442.6	4343.7
1985	1737.5	270.0	78.6	1084.8	179.0	396.6	247.0	453.1	4446.6
1986	1803.8	280.3	81.6	1126.0	185.8	411.6	256.0	470.3	4615.4
1987	1906.0	296.2	86.2	1189.8	196.4	435.0	270.5	497.0	4877.1

Sources: See Appendix B, section B.3b.

Table A.3   Fixed and circulating constant capital
(billions of dollars)

	FC	CC	C
1947	170.9	82.6	253.5
1948	192.3	87.2	279.6
1949	203.8	78.7	282.5
1950	225.6	98.0	323.7
1951	250.2	110.5	360.7
1952	266.0	109.2	375.2
1953	280.1	110.1	390.2
1954	292.4	107.6	400.0
1955	318.5	114.8	433.3
1956	353.5	124.0	477.5
1957	377.8	127.6	505.4
1958	389.4	127.3	516.7
1959	404.5	132.0	536.5
1960	414.6	136.0	550.6
1961	425.1	137.9	563.0
1962	440.6	144.6	585.2
1963	456.7	150.4	607.1
1964	480.2	156.2	636.4
1965	517.1	170.5	687.6
1966	567.5	187.4	754.9
1967	613.5	199.4	812.9
1968	678.1	213.5	891.6
1969	750.5	234.6	985.1
1970	829.0	244.0	1073.0
1971	910.4	260.8	1171.2
1972	987.7	288.7	1276.4
1973	105.5	357.7	1463.2
1974	373.5	434.4	1807.9
1975	529.7	439.4	1969.1
1976	662.0	473.6	2135.6
1977	842.1	519.5	2361.6
1978	132.2	602.3	2734.5
1979	407.2	705.0	3112.2
1980	2738.3	776.0	3514.3
1981	3074.4	826.6	3901.0
1982	3228.4	806.7	4035.1
1983	3316.3	818.4	4134.7
1984	3466.1	877.6	4343.7
1985	3583.1	863.5	4446.6
1986	3752.3	863.1	4615.4
1987	3935.6	941.5	4877.1

Notation
FC   Fixed constant capital
CC   Circulating constant capital
C   Total constant capital

Sources: See Appendix B, section B.3a.

Appendix A

Table A.4   Real and price components of fixed and circulating constant capital

	RFC	RCC	RC	P_{fc}	P_{cc}	P_c
	(billions of 1972 dollars)					
1947	364.4	116.1	462.6	46.9	71.2	54.8
1948	373.5	121.6	483.6	51.5	71.7	57.8
1949	384.6	117.2	496.2	53.0	67.2	56.9
1950	414.0	127.7	528.5	54.5	76.7	61.2
1951	423.3	141.4	555.4	59.1	78.2	64.9
1952	442.7	145.7	582.5	60.1	75.0	64.4
1953	457.6	147.2	599.9	61.2	74.8	65.0
1954	473.8	145.0	614.7	61.7	74.2	65.1
1955	506.4	152.8	655.2	62.9	75.1	66.1
1956	525.2	158.6	680.9	67.3	78.2	70.1
1957	532.1	160.1	690.4	71.0	79.7	43.2
1958	549.3	158.3	705.5	70.9	80.4	73.2
1959	560.3	165.3	724.3	72.2	79.9	74.1
1960	571.9	168.8	739.1	72.5	80.6	74.5
1961	590.5	171.8	760.6	72.0	80.3	74.0
1962	607.7	179.7	785.8	72.5	80.5	74.5
1963	624.8	187.2	810.7	73.1	80.3	74.9
1964	650.7	194.3	843.4	73.8	80.4	75.4
1965	692.2	206.1	896.6	74.7	82.7	76.9
1966	737.9	222.9	959.4	76.9	84.1	78.7
1967	771.7	235.1	1006.0	79.5	84.8	80.8
1968	818.9	244.1	1062.5	82.8	87.5	83.9
1969	865.6	255.1	1120.0	86.7	92.0	88.0
1970	908.0	258.9	1166.6	91.3	94.2	92.0
1971	946.4	267.0	1213.3	96.2	97.7	96.5
1972	987.7	277.2	1264.6	100.0	104.2	100.9
1973	1065.1	294.4	1353.2	103.8	121.5	108.1
1974	1190.2	306.0	1484.5	115.4	142.0	121.8
1975	1157.1	299.2	1453.5	132.2	146.9	135.5
1976	1199.2	307.0	1503.2	138.6	154.3	142.1
1977	1259.1	320.3	1576.5	146.3	162.2	149.8
1978	1356.4	336.3	1687.7	157.2	179.1	162.0
1979	1409.4	343.6	1742.7	170.8	205.2	178.6
1980	1470.6	338.6	1795.8	186.2	229.2	195.7
1981	1520.5	347.6	1859.9	202.2	237.8	209.7
1982	1541.0	340.1	1876.4	209.5	237.1	215.0
1983	1606.7	336.5	1934.9	206.4	243.2	213.7
1984	1669.6	361.3	2022.8	207.6	242.9	214.7
1985	1747.5	357.3	2111.3	207.2	241.7	212.4
1986	1771.0	363.7	2140.1	212.4	237.3	216.1
1987	1849.0	378.6	2233.6	212.9	248.7	218.4

Sources:
RFC Real fixed constant capital ($= FC/P_{fc}$), FC
      FC Fixed constant capital, see Table A.3
RCC Real circulating constant capital, US National Income and Product
      Accounts, Table 5.11
RC Real total constant capital ($= C/P_c$)
     C Constant capital, see Table A.3
P_{fc} Price index for fixed constant capital, US National Income and
      Product Accounts, Table 7.4
P_{cc} Price index for circulating constant capital ($= CC/RCC$)
      CC Circulating constant capital, see Table A.3
P_c Price index for total constant capital ($= w_1 \times P_{fc} + w_2 \times P_{cc}$)
     where $w_1 = FC/C$ and $w_2 = CC/C$ for each year

Table A.5 The flow of unproductive capital
(billions of dollars)

	U_f	U_w	U_d	U_w/U_f	U_w/V	Index
1947	38.4	36.5	1.9	0.95	0.52	100.0
1948	42.8	40.6	2.2	0.95	0.52	101.2
1949	44.0	41.7	2.3	0.95	0.56	109.1
1950	47.5	45.0	2.4	0.95	0.55	106.3
1951	53.8	51.0	2.8	0.95	0.53	103.6
1952	58.4	55.5	3.0	0.95	0.55	105.9
1953	63.3	60.2	3.1	0.95	0.55	106.6
1954	66.7	63.5	3.2	0.95	0.61	118.3
1955	72.5	69.1	3.4	0.95	0.61	119.3
1956	80.4	76.5	3.8	0.95	0.64	123.3
1957	87.1	82.8	4.2	0.95	0.67	129.8
1958	89.7	85.3	4.4	0.95	0.72	138.9
1959	97.9	93.3	4.6	0.95	0.72	139.5
1960	104.9	99.9	5.0	0.95	0.75	144.8
1961	109.2	103.9	5.3	0.95	0.77	149.8
1962	116.7	111.1	5.6	0.95	0.77	149.7
1963	121.9	115.7	6.1	0.95	0.76	147.5
1964	131.4	124.7	6.7	0.95	0.77	149.1
1965	141.1	133.8	7.3	0.95	0.76	147.8
1966	156.4	148.2	8.2	0.95	0.77	149.1
1967	170.0	160.9	9.2	0.95	0.80	154.8
1968	186.4	176.1	10.4	0.94	0.79	154.0
1969	206.5	195.6	10.9	0.95	0.81	156.6
1970	223.6	212.1	11.6	0.95	0.85	164.3
1971	242.2	229.5	12.7	0.95	0.88	171.1
1972	261.6	247.7	13.9	0.95	0.85	164.4
1973	291.0	275.8	15.1	0.95	0.83	160.4
1974	323.3	305.6	17.7	0.95	0.87	168.2
1975	356.3	336.7	19.6	0.94	0.92	178.8
1976	394.5	373.4	21.1	0.95	0.90	174.6

Continued over

	U_f	U_w	U_d	U_w/U_f	U_w/V	Index
1977	438.7	415.3	23.5	0.95	0.89	171.7
1978	510.4	483.4	26.9	0.95	0.93	180.6
1979	582.5	551.2	31.2	0.95	0.94	182.8
1980	656.3	620.7	35.5	0.95	1.00	194.0
1981	735.2	694.4	40.7	0.94	1.03	199.1
1982	794.0	747.9	46.0	0.94	1.10	212.8
1983	860.2	811.2	49.0	0.94	1.13	219.1
1984	948.9	895.7	53.2	0.94	1.15	223.4
1985	1026.1	967.9	58.1	0.94	1.19	231.0
1986	1105.6	1043.5	62.1	0.94	1.24	241.3
1987	1197.3	1131.4	65.9	0.94	1.27	244.2

Notation and Sources
U_w Wages of unproductive labor ($= W - V$)
  W Total wages, US National Income and Product Accounts, Table 6.5
  V Variable capital, see Appendix B, section B.2
U_d Depreciation of unproductive fixed capital, see Appendix B, section B.1 (6)
U_f Flow of unproductive capital ($= U_w + U_d$)
V Variable capital, see Appendix B, section B.2

Table A.6 Relative average wages of productive labor and unproductive labor

	V	PL	AV	U_w	UL	AU_w	AU_w/AV
1947	70.8	29.6	2390	36.5	10.5	3484	1.46
1948	77.7	30.2	2577	40.6	10.8	3747	1.45
1949	74.2	28.7	2588	41.7	10.8	3852	1.49
1950	82.2	29.7	2767	45.0	11.0	4077	1.47
1951	95.5	31.2	3057	51.0	11.7	4362	1.43
1952	101.7	31.4	3238	55.5	12.2	4532	1.40
1953	109.5	32.1	3409	60.2	12.7	4724	1.39
1954	104.2	30.6	3405	63.5	12.9	4931	1.45
1955	112.4	31.4	3576	69.1	13.4	5168	1.44
1956	120.4	32.0	3759	76.5	14.0	5470	1.46
1957	123.9	31.7	3902	82.8	14.3	5783	1.48
1958	119.2	29.9	3981	85.3	14.3	5963	1.50
1959	129.7	31.0	4181	93.3	14.8	6292	1.51
1960	133.9	31.0	4313	99.9	15.3	6548	1.52
1961	134.6	30.5	4419	103.9	15.4	6745	1.53
1962	143.9	31.1	4631	111.1	15.8	7009	1.51
1963	152.3	31.4	4857	115.7	16.2	7138	1.47
1964	162.3	31.8	5099	124.7	16.7	7458	1.46
1965	175.6	32.9	5330	133.8	17.4	7696	1.44
1966	192.9	34.3	5629	148.2	18.3	8121	1.44

	V	PL	AV	U_w	UL	AU_w	AU_w/AV
1967	201.6	34.5	5844	160.9	19.0	8476	1.45
1968	221.8	35.2	6295	176.1	19.7	8946	1.42
1969	242.2	36.3	6675	195.6	20.6	9503	1.42
1970	250.4	36.0	6964	212.1	21.0	10101	1.45
1971	260.2	35.7	7290	229.5	21.1	10857	1.49
1972	292.3	37.0	7897	247.7	21.8	11372	1.44
1973	333.6	38.8	8608	275.8	22.8	12094	1.41
1974	352.5	39.0	9040	305.6	23.5	13014	1.44
1975	365.4	36.9	9905	336.7	23.5	14327	1.45
1976	415.0	38.3	10848	373.4	24.3	15350	1.41
1977	469.2	39.6	11854	415.3	25.5	16313	1.38
1978	519.6	41.3	12593	483.5	26.9	18003	1.43
1979	585.1	43.2	13542	551.3	28.4	19405	1.43
1980	620.7	42.7	14541	620.8	29.0	21390	1.47
1981	676.7	42.7	15840	694.4 ·	29.7	23395	1.48
1982	682.1	41.4	16489	747.9	29.7	25222	1.53
1983	718.4	41.4	17344	811.2	30.1	26976	1.56
1984	778.1	43.7	17809	895.7	31.7	28621	1.58
1985	812.9	44.6	18226	967.9	33.5	28928	1.59
1986	839.1	45.3	18544	1043.5	34.7	30110	1.62
1987	890.1	45.9	19383	1121.4	35.5	31599	1.63

Notation and Sources

V Variable capital (billions of dollars), see Appendix B, section B.2

PL Productive labor (millions of workers), see Appendix B, section B.4a

AV Average wages of productive labor ($= V / PL$)

U_w Wages of unproductive labor (billions of dollars), see Appendix A, Table A.5

UL Unproductive labor (millions of workers), see Appendix B, section B.4a

AU Average wages of unproductive labor ($= U_w / UL$)

Table A.7 Productive labor by industry
(thousands of workers)

	MAN	MIN	CON	TPU	SER	WRT	AFF	GOV	Total
1947	12990	871	1786	3728	3031	4121	2427	657	29611
1948	12910	906	1954	3752	3107	4315	2505	717	30165
1949	11790	839	1949	3579	3049	4298	2418	755	28677
1950	12523	816	2101	3606	3066	4371	2495	750	29728
1951	13368	840	2343	3782	3176	4546	2414	780	31249
1952	13359	801	2360	3796	3239	4667	2333	852	31407
1953	14055	765	2341	3836	3260	4755	2271	847	32130
1954	12817	686	2316	3640	3271	4728	2295	846	30598
1955	13288	680	2477	3689	3381	4838	2227	850	31429
1956	13436	702	2653	3775	3512	4967	2133	856	32033
1957	13189	695	2577	3771	3574	4962	2106	875	31749
1958	11997	611	2420	3532	3488	4868	2144	885	29945
1959	12603	590	2577	3561	3605	5044	2124	931	31035
1960	12586	570	2497	3555	3617	5158	2088	972	31043
1961	12083	532	2426	3460	3731	5117	2110	996	30455
1962	12488	512	2500	3456	3846	5200	2061	1016	31079
1963	12555	498	2562	3447	3940	5280	2027	1041	31350
1964	12781	497	2637	3490	4059	5435	1861	1060	31820
1965	13434	494	2749	3561	4182	5679	1756	1089	32944
1966	14296	487	2818	3638	4346	5910	1642	1137	34275
1967	14308	469	2741	3718	4476	6061	1547	1168	34487
1968	14514	461	2822	3757	4699	6271	1512	1200	35236
1969	14767	472	3012	3863	4912	6547	1488	1225	36287
1970	14044	473	2990	3914	5094	6688	1492	1260	35955
1971	13544	455	3071	3872	5198	6808	1473	1266	35687
1972	14045	475	3257	3943	5501	7068	1474	1246	37009
1973	14834	486	3405	4034	5843	7358	1524	1268	38751
1974	14638	530	3294	4079	6074	7500	1569	1312	38996
1975	13043	571	2808	3894	6120	7512	1615	1332	36895
1976	13638	592	2814	3918	6411	7825	1746	1307	38251
1977	14110	615	3004	3993	6727	8149	1688	1292	39578
1978	14610	628	3336	4087	7054	8548	1683	1310	41256
1979	15085	721	3581	4304	7559	8909	1714	1336	43209
1980	14214	762	3421	4293	7973	8906	1770	1351	42689
1981	14020	841	3261	4283	8331	8979	1675	1334	42724
1982	12790	831	3004	4194	8531	8914	1782	1323	41368
1983	12697	723	3036	4060	8914	8957	1719	1313	41419
1984	13456	714	3356	4259	9379	9510	1700	1316	43690
1985	13214	688	3652	4387	9378	10110	1708	1463	44600
1986	13023	554	3890	4371	9821	10349	1721	1522	45252
1987	13021	530	3924	4458	10201	10435	1790	1563	45922

Sources: See Appendix B, section B.4a

Table A.8   Unproductive labor by industry
(thousands of workers)

	MAN	MIN	CON	TPU	SER	WRT	GOV	FIN	Total
1947	2555	84	223	438	531	4835	77	1728	10470
1948	2672	88	244	437	542	4958	83	1800	10824
1949	2651	91	245	422	541	4967	89	1828	10834
1950	2718	85	263	428	560	5015	89	1888	11046
1951	3025	89	294	444	594	5197	92	1956	11691
1952	3273	97	308	452	638	5338	102	2035	12242
1953	3494	101	318	454	670	5492	100	2111	12740
1954	3497	105	330	444	696	5507	103	2200	12882
1955	3594	112	362	452	750	5698	104	2298	13370
1956	3807	120	386	469	824	5892	106	2389	13993
1957	3985	133	385	470	881	5925	109	2438	14326
1958	3948	140	397	444	906	5882	111	2481	14309
1959	4072	142	427	450	985	6084	118	2549	14826
1960	4210	142	429	449	1044	6234	123	2629	15259
1961	4243	140	433	443	1109	6220	127	2688	15403
1962	4365	138	448	450	1196	6366	132	2754	15849
1963	4440	137	448	456	1268	6498	138	2830	16215
1964	4493	137	460	461	1396	6726	140	2911	16724
1965	4628	138	483	475	1497	7037	145	2977	17381
1966	4918	140	499	520	1621	7335	163	3058	18254
1967	5139	144	507	550	1734	7546	173	3185	18977
1968	5267	145	528	561	1835	7828	179	3337	19681
1969	5400	147	563	579	2035	8158	184	3512	20577
1970	5323	150	598	601	2132	8353	194	3645	20995
1971	5079	154	633	604	2153	8545	198	3772	21137
1972	5106	153	632	598	2313	8882	189	3908	21780
1973	5320	156	692	622	2526	9250	195	4046	22807
1974	5439	167	726	646	2657	9488	208	4148	23479
1975	5280	181	717	648	2740	9549	222	4165	23501
1976	5359	187	762	664	2930	9931	222	4271	24325
1977	5537	194	829	703	3169	10344	228	4452	25455
1978	5722	209	876	772	3509	10846	248	4676	26857
1979	5977	239	902	837	3860	11360	260	4975	28410
1980	6071	265	925	853	4075	11404	268	5160	29022
1981	6150	298	927	882	4285	11568	275	5298	29682
1982	6063	312	907	887	4378	11488	280	5340	29654
1983	5981	298	913	883	4693	11552	286	5467	30072
1984	6133	285	959	910	5222	12281	281	5665	31736
1985	6212	277	1010	913	5736	13084	304	5924	33460
1986	6163	238	1070	915	6164	13482	319	6305	34655
1987	6091	211	1107	920	6623	13626	323	6589	35490

Sources: See Appendix B, section B.4a

Table A.9   Revised estimates of productive labor by industry   (thousands of workers)

	MAN	MIN	CON	TPU	SER	WRT	AFF	GOV	Total
1950	12915	843	2142	2568	2776	3702	2495	534	27975
1960	13466	644	2574	2451	3249	4362	2088	670	29504
1970	15218	553	3072	2642	4527	6237	1492	851	34592
1980	15552	852	3513	2893	6973	7873	1770	910	40336

Sources: See Appendix B, section B.5a

Table A.10   Revised estimates of unproductive labor by industry (thousands of workers)

	MAN	MIN	CON	TPU	SER	WRT	GOV	FIN	Total
1950	2326	58	222	1466	850	5684	305	1888	12799
1960	3330	68	352	1553	1412	7029	425	2629	16798
1970	4149	70	516	1873	2699	8803	603	3645	22358
1980	4733	175	833	2253	5075	12437	709	5160	31375

Sources: See Appendix B, section B.5a

Table A.11   Detailed estimates of productive and unproductive labor (billions of hours)

	COM	FIN	CRC	SUP	UL*	COM CRC	CRC UL
1950	18.1	3.6	21.7	3.4	25.2	.83	.86
1960	22.5	4.9	27.4	4.7	32.2	.82	.85
1970	27.0	6.7	33.7	7.5	41.2	.80	.82
1980	35.7	9.4	45.1	10.2	55.3	.79	.82
Increase 1950–80	17.6	5.8	23.4	6.8	30.1		
% total increase of *UL*	58%	19%	78%	22%			

Notation
COM Commercial labor: unproductive labor in Wholesale and Retail
     Trade; sales workers in "productive industries" (i.e. all industries
     except wholesale and retail trade and finance, insurance and real
     estate); 75% of clerical workers in "productive industries"; total labor
     in Business Services

FIN Financial labor: total labor in finance, insurance, and real estate
CRC Circulation labor: commercial labor plus financial labor
SUP Supervisory labor: total unproductive labor minus circulation labor
UL* Revised estimates of total unproductive labor

Sources: see Appendix B, section B.5b.

Appendix B
Sources and Methods

B.1 NEW-VALUE

1. "Gross product of the Business sector" (*GBP*) is taken from *US National Income and Product Accounts* (*NIPAs*), table 1.7.
2. "Imputations in the Business sector" (*IMP*) is taken from *NIPAs*, table 8.9.
3. "Actual product of the Business sector" (*ABP*) is calculated by subtracting "Imputations in the Business sector" from "Gross product of the Business sector" (i.e. *ABP = GBP – IMP*).
4. "Capital consumption allowances (with capital consumption adjustment)" (*CCA*) is taken from *NIPAs*, table 1.9.
5. "Imputed capital consumption allowances" (ICA) is taken from *NIPAs*, table 8.9.
6. "Unproductive capital consumption allowances" (UCA) is calculated as the depreciation costs of the unproductive types of structures and equipment listed below in section B.3a (2) ("Constant Capital"), and is taken from the unpublished data provided by the Bureau of Economic Analysis cited in section B.3b.
7. "Depreciation charges" (*DEP*) is calculated as the difference between "Capital consumption allowances" and the sum of "Imputed capital consumption allowances" and "Unproductive capital consumption allowances" (i.e. *DEP = CCA – (ICA + UCA)*).
8. "Inventory evaluation adjustment" (*IVA*) is taken from *NIPAs*, table 6.16.
9. "Gross new-value" (*GN*) is calculated as the difference between "Actual business product" and the sum of "Depreciation charges" and "Inventory evaluation adjustment" (i.e. *GN = ABP – (DEP + IVA)*).
10. "Proprietor value" (*PV*) is calculated as the sum of "proprietor value" in the Agriculture, Services, and Construction industries, each of which is calculated in the following way:
    (a) For 1947 to 1982, "total hours" (*TH*) of all persons engaged in production in each of the above three industries is taken from *NIPAs*, table 6.11, and "employee hours" (*EH*) in each industry is taken from *NIPAs*, table 6.10.
    (b) "Proprietor hours" (*PH*) in each industry is taken as the difference between "total hours" and "employee hours" (i.e. *PH = TH – EH*).
    (c) "Net product" (*NP*) for each industry is taken from *NIPAs*, table 6.1.

172

(d) "Proprietor value" (PV) is calculated as the product of "net product" and the ratio of "proprietor hours" to "total hours" (i.e. $PV = NP \times PH/TH$).

(e) For the years after 1982, a similar procedure is used, based on the *number* of self-employed persons (PW), taken from *NIPAs*, table 6.9, and the *number* of persons engaged (TW), taken from *NIPAs*, table 6.10, rather than their respective *hours* (data for hours of all persons engaged was discontinued after 1982). For these years, "proprietor value" is calculated as the product of "net product" and the ratio PW/TW.

11. "New-value" (N) is calculated as the difference between "gross new-value" and "proprietor value" (i.e. $N = GN - PV$).

B.2 VARIABLE CAPITAL

The sources and methods used to derive estimates of variable capital are broadly similar to those used by Mage (1963).

1. "Compensation of employees" (COE) for each of the following eight industries is taken from *NIPAs* , table 6.4.

Manufacturing
Mining
Construction
Services
Transportation and public utilities
Wholesale and retail trade
Agriculture, forestry, and fisheries
Government enterprises

The industry totals are used except for the Services industry, for which the following subtotals are subtracted from the industry total: households and institutions, taken from *NIPAs*, table 1.12, and Business services (mostly circulation activities, such as advertising, credit collection, data processing, personnel supply, etc.), taken from *NIPAs*, table 6.4. The former subtotal is counted neither as variable capital nor as unproductive capital, since it refers to non-capitalist sectors of the economy; the latter subtotal is counted entirely as unproductive capital. The Finance, Insurance, and Real Estate industry is not included in the above list because I assume that all labor performed in this industry is unproductive, and thus that the total "compensation of employees" in this industry is unproductive capital.

2. "Corporate officers salaries" (COS) for each industry is taken from the Internal Revenue Service, *Statistics of Income, Corporate Income Tax Returns*, table 2.

3. "Gross labor costs" (GLC) for each industry is calculated as the difference between "compensation of employees" and "corporate officers salaries" (i.e. $GLC = COE - COS$).

4. "Variable capital" (V) for each industry is calculated as the product of a percentage (X) and the "gross labor costs" (i.e. $V = X \times GLC$). The percentage (X) is estimated for each industry in the following ways:

5. *Manufacturing*
    (a) "Wages of production workers" (WP) and "payroll of all employees" (PR) are taken from the *Census of Manufactures*, volume 1, table 1.[1]
    (b) "Total wages" (TW) is calculated by subtracting "corporate officers salaries" from "payroll of all employees" (i.e. $TW = PR - COS$).
    (c) The percentage (X) is calculated by dividing "wages of production workers" by "total wages" (i.e. $X = WP \,/\, TW$).

6. *Mining*
    (a) For the Census years 1954, 1958, 1963, 1972, 1977, 1982 and 1987: "wages of production workers" and "payroll of all employees" are taken from the *Census of Mineral Industries*, table 1. For these years, the percentage (X) is calculated in the same way as for Manufacturing.
    (b) For the early non-Census years between 1947 and 1953: the percentage (X) is calculated by extrapolation from the 1954 Census data, based on the ratio of "productive labor" (PL) to "all employees" (TL) taken from the Bureau of Labor Statistics, *Bulletin 1312*, according to the following equation:

$$X_t = \frac{X_{1954}}{(PL/TL)_{1954}} \times (PL/TL)_t$$

    where the subscript t refers to any non-Census year.
    (c) For the remaining non-Census years between 1955 and 1986: the percentage (X) is estimated by interpolation on the basis of the same ratio of "production workers" to "all employees", according to the following equation:

$$X_t = \frac{(X_b + X_s)\,/\,2}{((PL/TL)_b + (PL/TL)_s)\,/\,2} \times (PL/TL)_t$$

    where the subscript b refers to the nearest preceding Census year and the subscript s refers to the nearest succeeding Census year.

7. *Construction*
    (a) For the Census years, 1967, 1972, 1977, 1982, and 1987: "wages of construction workers" and "payroll of all employees" are taken from the *Census of Construction Industries*, table 1. For these years, the percentage (X) is calculated in the same way as for Manufacturing.
    (b) For the early non-Census years between 1947 and 1966: the percentage (X) is estimated by extrapolation from the 1967 Census data, using the same equation as for Mining in 6(b) above.

(c) For the remaining non-Census years between 1968 and 1986: the percentage (X) is estimated by interpolation, using the same equation as for Mining in 6(c) above.

8. *Transportation and public utilities*
   (a) "Productive labor" (*PL*) and "unproductive labor" (*UL*) are estimated as described below, section B.4a(2). "Total labor" (*TL*) is calculated as the sum of "productive labor" and "unproductive labor."
   (b) The percentage (X) is calculated for each year according to the following equation:

   $$X^t = \frac{X^m}{(PL/TL)^m} \times (PL/TL)^t$$

   where the superscripts t and m refer to the Transportation, etc. industry and the Manufacturing industry, respectively.

9. *Services*
   Essentially the same procedure as for the Transportation, etc. industry, except that "productive labor" and "unproductive labor" are estimated somewhat differently; see below, section B.4a(3).

10. *Wholesale and retail trade*
    Essentially the same procedure as for the Transportation, etc. industry, except that "productive labor" and "unproductive labor" are estimated somewhat differently; see below, section B.4a(4).

11. *Agriculture, forestry, and fisheries*
    The percentage (X) is assumed to be equal to 1.

12. *Government enterprises*
    The percentage (X) is assumed to be equal to the percentage (X) in the Transportation and public utilities industry.

B.3   CONSTANT CAPITAL

B.3a   Aggregate Estimates

1. "Net stock of fixed nonresidential private capital" (*NS*) (current cost) is taken from US Department of Commerce, *Fixed Reproducible Tangible Wealth in the United States, 1929–85* (*FRTW*), table A2.
2. "Net stock of unproductive fixed capital" (U_s) (current cost) is taken from *FRTW*, table A5, as the sum of the net fixed capital invested in the following types of structures and equipment:

   Structures: Commercial buildings × (0.50)
   Religious, educational, hospital, and
   institutional buildings

Equipment: Furniture and fixtures
            Office, computing, and accounting machines

3. "Net stock of fixed capital of government enterprises" *(GOV)* (current cost) is taken from *FRTW*, table A20.

4. "Fixed constant capital" *(FC)* is calculated as "net stock of fixed nonresidential private capital" minus "net stock of unproductive fixed capital" plus "net stock of fixed capital of government enterprises" (i.e. $FC = NS - U_s + GOV$).

5. "Circulating constant capital" *(CC)* is taken as the value of total business inventories (current cost), taken from *NIPAs*, table 5.10.

6. "Constant capital" *(C)* (current cost) is calculated as the sum of "fixed constant capital" and "circulating constant capital" (i.e. $C = FC + CC$).

B.3b Industry Estimates

All estimates are derived from unpublished data provided by the US Department of Commerce, Bureau of Economic Analysis. These data are similar to the data in *FRTW* described above, except that these data are also classified by industry.

1. For all industries except the Government enterprises industry and the Finance, Insurance, and Real Estate Industry:
    (a) "Fixed constant capital" is calculated as the difference between "net stock of fixed nonresidential private capital" and "net stock of unproductive fixed capital," estimated as above for the aggregate estimates.
    (b) "Circulating constant capital" is taken as the value of business inventories (current cost), taken from *NIPAs*, table 5.10, supplemented with more detailed data provided by the Bureau of Economic Analysis.

2. For the Government enterprises industry: "constant capital" is assumed to be equal to the "Net stock of fixed capital of government enterprises".

3. For the Finance, Insurance, and Real Estate industry: "constant capital" is assumed to be equal to zero.

B.4 PRODUCTIVE LABOR AND UNPRODUCTIVE LABOR

B.4a Workers

Estimates are derived primarily from the Bureau of Labor Statistics, *Bulletin 1312–12, Employment, Hours, and Earnings*, in the following way:

1. For the Manufacturing, Mining, and Construction industries: "productive labor" is assumed to be equal to the number of "production work-

ers", and "unproductive labor" is assumed to be equal to the remainder of "all employees".

2. For the Transportation and Public Utilities industry: "productive labor" is assumed to be equal to the number of "non-supervisory employees", and "unproductive labor" is assumed to be equal to the remainder of "all employees".

3. For the Services industry: "productive labor" is assumed to be equal to the number of "non-supervisory employees", except in Business services and in Non-profit institutions. The number of employees in Non-profit institutions (E_n) is estimated as the product of the total number of employees in the Services industry (E_s) and the ratio of "total employee compensation" for Non-profit institutions (TEC_n), taken from NIPAs, table 1.12, to "total employee compensation" for the Services industry (TEC_s), taken from *NIPAs*, table 6.4, i.e. $E_n = E_s \times (TEC_n)/(TEC_s)$. "Unproductive labor" is assumed to be equal to "all employees" of the Services industry minus employees in Non-profit institutions and minus "productive labor" (i.e. "unproductive labor" includes all labor in Business services).

4. For the Wholesale and retail trade industry: "productive labor" is assumed to be equal to the number of "non-supervisory employees" divided by two, and "unproductive labor" is assumed to be equal to the remainder of "all employees".

5. For the Finance, Insurance, and Real Estate industry: "productive labor" is assumed to be equal to zero and "unproductive labor" is assumed to be equal to "all employees".

6. For the Government enterprises industry: the ratio of "productive labor" to "total labor" is assumed to be equal to this ratio for the Transportation and Public Utilities industry. "Productive labor" in the Government enterprises is assumed to be equal to the product of this ratio and the number of "all employees", taken from the *NIPAs*, table 6.6, and "unproductive labor" is assumed to be equal to the remainder of "all employees."

7. For the Agriculture, Forestry and Fisheries industry: "productive labor" is assumed to be equal to "all employees", taken from the *NIPAs*, table 6.6, and "unproductive labor" is assumed to be equal to zero.

B.4b Hours

For each industry:

1. "Average weekly hours of production of non-supervisory workers" *(WHR)* is taken from *BLS Bulletin 1312–12*. For the Government enterprises industry, *WHR* is assumed to be equal to *WHR* of the Transportation and public utilities industry. For the Agriculture, etc. industry, see below, item 2.

2. "Annual hours of productive labor" (*PLH*) is calculated as the product of "average weekly hours of production of non-supervisory workers" times 50 weeks times the number of productive workers (*PLW*), as estimated above (i.e. *PLH* = *WHR* × 50 × *PLW*). For the Agriculture, etc. industry, *PLH* is taken directly from *NIPAs*, table 6.11.

3. "Annual hours of all employees" (*ALH*) is taken from unpublished data provided by the Bureau of Labor Statistics.

4. "Annual hours of unproductive labor" (*ULH*) is calculated as the difference between the "annual hours of all employees" and the "annual hours of productive labor" (i.e. *ULH* = *ALH* − *PLH*).

B.5 REVISED ESTIMATES OF PRODUCTIVE LABOR AND UNPRODUCTIVE LABOR

B.5a Workers

The estimates of productive labor and unproductive labor derived as described above are subject to bias due to the following discrepancies between these estimates and Marx's concepts:

(1) Technical workers (including engineers, scientists, and technicians) engaged in production activities in the Manufacturing, Mining, and Construction industries should be counted as productive labor, but are instead counted as unproductive labor.

(2) Sales and clerical workers in the Service and the Transportation, etc. industries should be counted as unproductive labor, but are instead counted as productive labor.

(3) The estimates of productive labor and unproductive labor in the Wholesale and Retail Trade industry are based on the arbitrary assumption that 50 per cent of non-supervisory employees is productive labor.

(4) Managers and supervisors who devote at least part of their labor to planning and coordinating production are counted entirely as unproductive labor.

In order to reduce these discrepancies between Marx's concepts of productive and unproductive labor and our estimates of these concepts, additional sources of data were utilized, besides those described in section B.4. No data exist which would enable us to divide the labor of managers and supervisors into productive and unproductive components, so the additional data address only the first three problems listed above.[2] The main source of additional data is the decennial *Census of the Population*. Thus these revised estimates are derived only for the four census years from 1950 to 1980. The specific sources and methods used to reduce each of the above conceptual problems are the following:

1. For the problem of technical workers in the Manufacturing, Mining, and Construction industries:

(a) for the years 1950, 1960, and 1970: the number of technical workers in each of these three industries was estimated as the sum of the number of engineers, scientists and technicians, taken from the Bureau of Labor Statistics, Bulletin 1781, *Employment of Scientists and Engineers 1950–70*, and Bulletin 1609, *Scientific and Technical Personnel in Industry, 1961–66.*

(b) for 1980: the number of technical workers in each of these industries was extrapolated forward from the data in (a), based on the ratio of technical workers to total non-production workers for the earlier years.

(c) for all years: the number of technical workers in each industry was added to the original estimate of "productive labor" and subtracted from the original estimate of "unproductive labor" .

2. For the problem of sales and clerical workers in the Service and Transportation, etc. industries:

(a) the number of sales and clerical workers in each of these two industries was estimated from the *Census of Population* (volume 2, part 7c, "Occupation by Industry").

(b) the number of sales and clerical workers in each industry was subtracted from the original estimate of "productive labor" and added to the original estimate of "unproductive labor".

3. For the problem of the arbitrary assumption in the Wholesale and Retail Trade industry:

(a) "Productive labor" was estimated as the sum of the number of craftsmen, operatives, laborers, and service workers, taken from the *Census of Population.*

(b) "Unproductive labor" was estimated as the difference between "all employees", taken from *BLS Bulletin 1312–12* as in section 4 above, and "productive labor".

B.5b Hours

Revised estimates of the annual hours of productive labor and unproductive labor are derived in the same way as the original estimates (see section B.4b), with the exception that the revised estimates of the number of productive workers are substituted for the original estimates of the number of productive workers.

Appendix C
Assessment of Bias in the Trends of the Marxian Variables

This appendix will consider the direction and extent of possible bias in the estimates of the Marxian variables presented in Chapter 2. The main concern will be whether or not there is a likely bias in the *trends* of these estimates; biases in the absolute levels of these estimates which do not affect the trends are of no concern.

C.1 BIAS IN TRENDS DUE TO CONCEPTUAL DISCREPANCIES

1. *Variable capital* The estimates of variable capital are subject to bias in their trend due to the following discrepancies between these estimates and Marx's concept of variable capital:

   (a) The compensation of technical workers engaged in production activities in the Manufacturing, Mining, and Construction industries should be included in the estimates, and is not included.
   (b) A part of the compensation of managers and supervisors who devote at least part of their labor to planning and coordinating production activities should be included in the estimates, and is not included.
   (c) The compensation of sales and clerical workers in the Services and the Transportation, etc. industries is included in the estimates, but should not be.
   (d) The estimates for the Wholesale and Retail Trade industry are based on the arbitrary assumption that 50 per cent of non-supervisory employees are engaged in production activities.

   Elsewhere (Moseley, 1985, appendix C), I have analyzed the possible bias in the trend of my estimates of the rate of surplus-value due to these discrepancies between Marx's concept of variable capital and my estimates of variable capital. I concluded that my estimates of the rate of surplus-value probably have a small upward bias in their trend, such that the "true" rate of surplus-value probably increased only 5–10 per cent, compared to the 15 per cent increase in my estimates. *Ceteris paribus*, a smaller increase in the rate of surplus-value would result in a proportionally greater decline in the rate of profit.

   However, this same underestimation of variable capital also imparts an upward bias to the trend in the value composition of capital, which partially offsets the upward bias in the rate of surplus-value. My calculations show that the net upward bias in the trend in the rate of profit from this source is probably not greater than 5 percentage points, such that the "true" rate of profit may have declined as much as 20 per cent, compared to the 15 per cent decline in my estimates.

2. *Constant capital*   The estimates of constant capital are much less vulnerable to bias because the stock of unproductive capital invested in buildings and equipment is much smaller in relation to constant capital than the flow of unproductive capital invested in wages in relation to variable capital. Even if *all* the fixed capital counted as unproductive capital in my estimates were instead counted as constant capital, the increase in the value composition of capital and the organic composition of capital would be only about 10 percentage points greater than in my estimates. *Ceteris paribus*, a greater increase in the composition of capital would result in a proportionally greater decline in the rate of profit.

3. *New-value*   The estimates of *new-value* are also considered to be fairly reliable, especially in terms of trends over time. The main source of possible bias in the estimates of new-value is a possible overestimation of "proprietor value", or the value produced by self-employed owners who perform productive functions (such as farmers, construction workers, doctors, etc.), because I assume that all of their labor is productive labor. If "proprietor value" is overestimated, then new-value is underestimated. More importantly, since "proprietor value" declined in relation to new-value over the postwar period, there may be upward biases in the trends of the rate of surplus-value and the rate of profit. This underestimation of new-value would also impart a downward bias in the trend of the estimates of the organic composition of capital, but have no effect on the trend of the estimates of the value composition of capital. However, once again the bias from this source cannot be greater than 10 percentage points.

Thus the conclusions of this assessment of bias in the trends of the key Marxian ratios due to conceptual discrepancies are:

(a)   The estimates of the rate of surplus-value probably have a small upward bias in their trend, due to biases in the estimates of variable capital and new-value.

(b)   The estimates of the value composition of capital probably have little or no bias in their trend, because biases in the estimates of constant capital and variable capital have offsetting effects.

(c)   The estimates of the organic composition of capital probably have a small downward bias in their trend, due to biases in the estimates of constant capital and new-value.

(d)   The estimates of the rate of profit probably have a small upward bias in their trend, due primarily to the upward bias in the estimates of the rate of surplus-value, such that the "true" rate of profit may have declined 5–10 percentage points more than the estimates. In other words, the "true" rate of profit probably declined 20–25 per cent, compared to the observed 15 per cent increase.

These conclusions lend slightly more empirical support to Marx's theory of the falling rate of profit. The rate of profit probably declined slightly more than the observed estimates; and the cause of this decline remains essentially the same: the composition of capital increased faster than the rate of surplus-value, as Marx hypothesized. The main alteration of the conclusions stated in Chapter 3 is that the rate of surplus-value probably increased less than the estimates, and perhaps did not increase at all, thus resulting in a greater decline in the rate of profit.[1]

C.2 BIAS IN TRENDS DUE TO LEVEL OF AGGREGATION ERROR

Another possible source of error in this empirical test of Marx's theory is that the level of aggregation to which Marx's theory most rigorously applies is the world capitalist economy as a whole, while the estimates presented here are for a single national economy, the US economy. The trends of the Marxian variables for the US economy may differ from the trends of these variables for the world capitalist economy. However, it is extremely difficult, and perhaps impossible, to derive estimates of the Marxian variables for the entire world capitalist economy. It is likely that some of the raw data necessary to derive estimates of the Marxian variables do not exist in some countries (especially data which distinguish between productive labor and unproductive labor). Thus we are left with the familiar alternative of treating the US economy as a closed economy, and estimating the Marxian variables more narrowly in terms of the US economy.

The most likely source of bias resulting from this procedure is that the composition of capital may have increased slower in the US than in the world capitalist economy. Reasons for suspecting such a bias are (i) the increase of the composition of capital in the US was rather slow, and (ii) the rest of the world probably experienced a faster pace of technological change in the postwar period. *Ceteris paribus*, a downward bias in the trend of the composition of capital would result in an upward bias in the trend of the rate of profit.

However, such a downward bias in the trend of the composition of capital would also result in a downward bias in the trend of the rate of surplus-value, due to changes in the international flows of value and surplus-value. According to Marx's theory, value is transferred from nations with a low composition of capital to those with a high composition of capital, such as the US (Carchedi, 1988). It follows from this that if the composition of capital in the US did increase slower than in the rest of the world during the postwar period, then the international transfer of value to the US would decline relatively over time, because the gap between the composition of capital in the US and in the rest of the world would diminish. This relative decline of the international inflow of value into the US would result in a smaller increase in the estimates of the rate of surplus-value than in the "true" rate of surplus-value, i.e. would result in a downward bias in the trend of the rate of surplus-value. These two downward biases in the composition of capital and the rate of surplus-value would have offsetting effects on the trend in the rate of profit. The opposite reasoning would apply if the composition of capital in the US increased faster than in the rest of the world.

Thus there would appear to be little or no bias in the trend of the rate of profit due to this level of aggregation error. The cause of the decline in the rate of profit remains essentially the same: the composition of capital increased faster than the rate of surplus-value. The only minor alterations of the conclusions stated in Chapter 3 are that the "true" composition of capital and rate of surplus-value may have increased slightly less than the estimates for the US.

Notes and References

1 MARX'S THEORY OF THE FALLING RATE OF PROFIT

1. See also C.III, 213–14.
2. A fourth theoretical issue which should be mentioned is the following: even if Marx demonstrated that the "value" rate of profit would decline as a result of technological change, does it necessarily follow that the "price" rate of profit will also decline? Or can the value rate of profit and the price rate of profit have different trends? Steedman (1977, pp.29–31) argues that one cannot assume that the value rate of profit will be a close approximation to the price rate of profit and thus that Marx's conclusion concerning the trend of the value rate of profit might not apply to the price rate of profit. Sweezy (1968, pp.127–28) presents the most common response to this argument, that although the trends in the value rate of profit and the price rate of profit may in theory be different, in actual fact they are not likely to be very different, because the trend of the composition of capital in luxury-goods industries is not likely to be very different from the trend of the composition of capital in wage-goods industries. Shaikh (1984, pp.59–64) argues that since both the price rate of profit and the value rate of profit are monotonically increasing functions of the rate of surplus-value, the two rates of profit will have the same trend. (This argument seems to be incomplete because it only allows for changes in the rate of surplus-value, i.e. it does not allow for changes in the composition of capital). Roemer (1977, pp.405–8) argues that for sufficiently large technological change, the two rates of profit will move in the same direction. My response is more fundamental: my interpretation of the determination of prices of production and the price rate of profit differs from the standard Bortkiewicz–Sweezy–Sraffa interpretation, which all the above writers share, and is based on Mattick Sr (1972), Mattick Jr (1981), and Carchedi (1984, 1988). According to this interpretation, the value rate of profit and the price rate of profit are identically equal and thus will always have identical trends. Thus Marx's theory of the rate of profit applies simultaneously to both the value rate of profit and the price rate of profit. My interpretation of the determination of prices of production and the price rate of profit is discussed at length in Moseley (1983, chapter 3) and (1991). Other writers who also argue that the value rate of profit and the price rate of profit are identically equal include Wolff, Roberts, and Callari (1982) and Kliman and McGlone (1988).
3. A similar interpretation of Marx's theory is presented by Mandel (1980).
4. Marx was not always clear about the distinction between the stock and flow of constant capital, and often made the simplifying assumption that all constant capital was entirely consumed and reproduced at each period

of production, i.e no fixed capital. But the stock of constant capital is clearly the more appropriate concept for an analysis of the rate of profit, the denominator of which is the stock of capital, not the periodic flow.

5. This equation can be derived as follows:

$$\frac{VCC}{OCC} = \frac{C/V}{C/(V+S)} = \frac{V+S}{V} = 1 + RS$$

6. In an earlier work, Fine and Harris (1976, pp.160–1) define the technical composition of capital essentially as I have above as "the ratio of means of production to living labor".

7. Marx's argument concerning an increase in the technical composition of capital discussed in the next subsection applies only to the *TCC*. An increased *TCC* does not necessarily imply an increased *TCC'*, since the latter also depends on changes in *WR*. Fine and Harris provide no argument as to why *TCC* should increase faster than *WR*. Thus, it remains unclear why Fine and Harris's definition of the technical composition of capital should increase.

8. We can see that according to these definitions, the trend in *OCC'* will always be the same as the the trend in the *TCC'*. However, since Fine and Harris do not provide a complete argument as to why *TCC'* should increase, they also do provide a complete theory of the trend in *OCC'*. We can also see from these equations that the trend in *OCC'* will be different from that in *VCC'* if and only if the ratio of the average values of the means of production and the means of subsistence changes over time as a result of technological change (i.e. if the rates of productivity growth in Department 1 and Department 2 are unequal).

9. The factor '*m*' as defined here is what Foley calls the "monetary expression of value" (1986b, chapter 2). To avoid confusion, please note that for Foley "*m*" stands for the inverse of the "monetary expression of value", or the "value of money". An extensive discussion of my interpretation of Marx's theory of value and surplus-value is presented in Moseley (1982, chapters 2 and 3).

10. We simplify here by assuming that the stock of variable capital is equal to zero. In actual fact, the stock of variable capital is negligibly small, since workers are generally paid only after they have worked for some period of time.

11. The rate of surplus-value also varies directly with the length of the working day and the intensity of labor. But Marx argued that these other two factors would in general mutually offset each other (a decline in the working day offset by an increase in the intensity of labor), so that the net effect of the trend of the rate of surplus-value would be minor.

12. For a further discussion of Marx's theory of the tendency of the rate of surplus-value to increase, see Moseley (1982, chapter 4).

13. The precise relation between *RS* and *SS* is: $RS/SS = 1 + RS$.

14. These two ratios may be obtained directly by: $RP = S/C = (S/N)/(C/N)$.

15. A model along these lines was presented by Mage (1963, pp.147–51).

16. Other assumptions included perfect competition and wages advanced prior to production.

17. Mandel (1981, pp.35–6) presents a similar argument.
18. As mentioned in note 2, my interpretation of the determination of prices of production and the price rate of profit differs from the standard Bortkiewicz–Sweezy–Sraffa interpretation, and is based on Mattick Sr (1972), Mattick Jr (1981), and Carchedi (1984, 1988).
19. Although Marx's theory does not provide a definite prediction concerning the trend in the rate of profit over time, it is by far the most substantial theory of the trend in the rate of profit in the history of economic theory; certainly much more substantial than the meager attention devoted to this subject by neo-classical theory. For example, neo-classical growth theory generally assumes that the rate of profit remains constant (e.g. Brems, 1977). Malinvaud (1984, p.61) has suggested that this assumption of a constant rate of profit is a major weakness and that growth theory should be further developed to allow the rate of profit to change over time.

2 CONCEPTUAL ISSUES IN THE ESTIMATION OF THE MARXIAN VARIABLES

1. In a review of *Capital*, Engels (1937, p.22) refers to the concept of capital as the "cardinal point in the whole book". Rosdolsky (1977) comments that the concept of capital is "the main subject of Marx's analysis (p.183; see the entire Chapter 11, "The Transition to Capital"). Foley (all references) also emphasizes the importance of Marx's concept of capital.
2. The dollar sign is substituted for the pound sign in all quotations from *Capital*.
3. It is immediately obvious that Marx's definition of capital differs fundamentally from the neo-classical concept of capital. The former is defined in terms of money and the latter is defined in terms of physical goods – goods used to produce other goods. The neo-classical concept of capital is confronted with the very difficult "aggregation problem", i.e. how to add together the heterogeneous types of "capital-goods". A discussion of this problem is beyond the scope of this book. But is is interesting to note, by way of comparison, that this difficult problem is not encountered by Marx's concept of capital, since this concept is defined in terms of money which clearly has a homogeneous unit of measure and thus can be added together in a straightforward manner.
4. Engels (1937, p.27) succinctly summarized Marx's definitions of capital and surplus-value in the following passages:

   > What is capital? Money which is changed into a commodity in order to be changed back from a commodity into more money than the original sum (p.22) . . . There must be more money drawn out from circulation than had been thrown into it. ... This ΔM, this increment (of money), Mr. Marx calls surplus-value.

5. Marx regarded this distinction between constant capital and variable capital to be one of his most important advances over previous economic

theory. None of the classical economists had clearly and explicitly made this distinction.

> Let me remind the reader that I was the first to use the categories "variable capital" and "constant capital." Political Economy since the time of A. Smith has confusedly mixed up the determining characteristics contained in these categories with the merely formal distinction, arising out of circulation, between fixed capital and circulating capital. (C.I, 760)

Marx argued that the classical economists were never able to explain the origin of surplus value adequately because they failed to clearly distinguish between constant capital and variable capital.

6. In actuality, the stock of variable capital is negligibly small, so that it is often assumed to be equal to zero in discussions of the theory of the rate of profit, as it is throughout this book.

7. "Government production" here refers to government agencies which provide services without specific charges to the public. Government enterprises which produce commodities for sale are treated essentially the same as capitalist enterprises, as they are in the US National Income and Product Accounts.

8. The concept of unproductive labor was also used by Marx in the broader sense to include labor employed in non-capitalist production, or "labor employed by revenue" (TSV.I, chapter 4 and addendum; C.I, 1038–49). Adam Smith used the concept of unproductive labor to refer only to labor employed in non-capitalist production, not to labor employed in non-production activities within capitalist enterprises. In this book, the term unproductive labor refers only to the latter category of capitalist employees employed in non-production activities.

9. It should be noted in passing that, in my opinion, Marx's concepts of productive and unproductive labor have no necessary implications for the definition of the "working class" or even in defining significant divisions within the working class. The working class does not consist solely of productive labor, but of all workers who have to sell their labor-power for a wage. Nor does the distinction between productive and unproductive labor divide the working class into opposing groups with conflicting interests. Nor does this distinction imply that productive workers are inherently more revolutionary than unproductive workers. All such questions are enormously complex and involve the interactions of many economic, political, and cultural factors which influence the lives of working people; they cannot be answered by simple inference from economic categories. The usefulness of the distinction between productive and unproductive labor is purely analytical. As this book aims to show, these concepts are necessary for the analysis of the production of surplus-value and the trends of the Marxian variables.

10. In a separate work, not devoted to an empirical test of Marx's theory of the falling rate of profit, Wolff (1987a) employs a distinction between productive labor and unproductive labor which is similar to the definitions adopted here, with the following significant exceptions: (i) Wolff's definition of productive labor includes most government employees

(those which produce use-values; e.g. education, health, infrastructure, etc.); and (ii) Wolff's definition of unproductive labor does not include the category of supervisory labor (although his estimates of unproductive labor include most of what I call supervisory labor).

11. In private correspondence, Weisskopf indicated that if he were to derive estimates for the total Business sector, he would include only tenant-occupied residential housing in his estimates of capital stock.

12. For a further discussion of this more complicated determination of the amount of variable capital, see Moseley (1982, pp.233–4).

13. See Chapter 4 for a further discussion of the differences between the Marxian rate of profit and the conventional rate of profit.

14. See Chapter 4 for an analysis of the trend of the conventional rate of profit in the postwar US economy.

15. Leadbeater concludes that "Marx's categories of productive and unproductive labor can also contribute much to applied studies of the actual patterns and trends of capitalist development" (p.617). The purpose of this book is to see what new insights are gained about the trends of the Marxian and the conventional rate of profit in the postwar US economy by an application of Marx's concepts of productive labor and unproductive labor.

16. Baran adopts this criterion in his definitions of productive labor and unproductive labor in order to demonstrate the irrationality of capitalism (especially the irrational use of the economic surplus), and Hunt concludes that Baran's criterion and purpose should be adopted in the definitions of productive and unproductive labor. This conclusion is, of course, justifiable, as long as one recognizes that Baran's definitions are different from Marx's definitions. However, in an empirical test of Marx's theory, which is the purpose of this book, one should adopt Marx's definitions as closely as possible.

17. Even though the surplus labor of unproductive workers does not result in the production of surplus-value, it does benefit capital in general because it reduces the costs of circulation and supervision and thus reduces the deductions from surplus-value which must be made in order to pay for these two unproductive functions. However, a saving in the necessary deductions from surplus-value is not the same as the production of additional surplus-value.

18. Rubin (1972, chapter 19) criticizes Hilferding for a similar interpretation of Marx's distinction between productive and unproductive labor.

3 ESTIMATIONS OF THE MARXIAN VARIABLES FOR THE POSTWAR US ECONOMY

1. Similar interpretations are presented by Mandel (1980) and Bowles, Gordon and Weisskopf (1983).

2. See Moseley (1982, chapter 6) for a further discussion of the differences between the Marxian concept of new-value and the national income accounting concept of net product.

3. For the determination of the secular trends of the three Marxian ratios over this period, it is not necessary to consider the effects of changing rates of capacity utilization, because the capacity utilization rate at the beginning of our period of study was almost approximately equal to the capacity utilization rate at the end of the period. Measured by the Federal Reserve Board's estimates, the capacity utilization rate in Manufacturing in 1947 was 82.0 per cent and in 1977 was 82.2 per cent. Similarly, in terms of five-year averages, the capacity utilization rate in Manufacturing in 1947–51 was 81.4 per cent and in 1973–7 was 81.2 per cent.

4. The advantage of regressing the natural logarithm of the rate of surplus-value, rather than the rate of surplus-value itself, is that in the former case the coefficient of time is an estimate of the average annual rate of change of the rate of surplus-value.

5. For these subperiods, the average annual rates of change were computed as the natural logarithm of the ratio of the last-year estimate to the first-year estimate (log (X_t/X_0)) divided by the number of years (t).

6. Weights are determined by the share of each component in the total constant capital.

7. The equation used to calculate the adjusted technical composition of capital is:

$$ATCC = TCC + b(CUR)$$

where b is the regression coefficient of the capacity utilization rate (CUR).

8. It should be noted that the cyclically adjusted estimates of the technical composition of capital show a slightly greater increase over the whole period (193 per cent compared to 177 per cent), in spite of the almost equal rates of capacity utilization in 1947 and 1977, because the cyclically adjusted estimate for the initial year 1947 is lower than the unadjusted estimate.

9. Unless otherwise noted, C always refers to the *stock* of constant capital and V always refers to the annual *flow* of variable capital.

10. Wolff (1987b) conducts a similar analysis of the effects of changes in the distribution of capital on the organic composition of capital. Wolff comes to the even stronger conclusion that structural change by itself reduced the organic composition of capital by 40 per cent. The differences in our conclusions result largely from different definitions of the organic composition of capital, as discussed in Chapter 2. However, we agree on the main point: changes in the distribution of capital and labor had a significant negative effect on the organic composition of capital in the postwar US economy.

11. Wolff (1987b) concludes from his analysis of the effects of changes in the distribution of labor and capital (Wolff does not consider the other two "other factors") that if this distribution remained constant, the rate of profit would have declined by an additional 10–15 percentage points.

12. This method is adopted from Denison (1969), which reconciles Denison's estimates of inputs and output in the US economy (1950–62) with Jorgenson and Griliches' estimates of these variables.

13. A striking difference between Weisskopf's and my estimates of the rate of surplus-value is the absolute levels of these estimates. The profit-to-wages ratio in the NFCB sector declined from 0.28 to 0.19. These estimates imply that the surplus-labor-time of workers in the postwar US economy was much smaller than necessary-labor-time. Assuming a working day of eight hours, surplus-labor-time was less than two hours throughout the period. By contrast, as discussed in section 3.1 of this chapter, my estimates of the rate of surplus-value imply that surplus-labor-time was almost five hours during this period.

14. Weisskopf actually uses the inverse of this ratio in his empirical analysis to fit his accounting framework.

15. In his article, Weisskopf does not report the absolute magnitudes of the composition of capital, but only the average annual rate of change, computed by running a regression of the natural logarithm of the composition of capital on time. The reported average annual rate of change is −0.02 per cent, which implies a 2 per cent decline in the composition of capital over the whole period. However, his actual estimates, replicated using Weisskopf's own raw data, which he kindly supplied to me (indirectly through Gerald Epstein), increased 12 per cent, as shown in Table 3.11.

16. Wolff's estimates are for only six years because he uses input–output tables to derive his estimates and these tables are available only for these six years during his period of study.

17. Yaffe (1973) makes a similar critique of Glyn and Sutcliffe's (1972) estimates of the Marxian variables for the postwar UK economy.

18. The capacity utilization rate was 81.4 in 1977 and 81.1 in 1987. In terms of five-year averages, the capacity utilization rate was 80.0 in 1973–7 and 79.1 in 1983–7.

4   THE DECLINE OF THE CONVENTIONAL RATE OF PROFIT

1. These estimates of the conventional rate of profit refer to the before-tax rate of profit, with which this chapter is solely concerned.

2. This decline in the rate of profit is a worldwide phenomenon; all major OECD nations experienced a similar decline over the postwar period (see Hill, 1979).

3. In the remainder of this chapter, the rate of profit refers to the *conventional* rate of profit, unless explicitly stated otherwise.

4. Wolff's estimates are actually for the inverse of the output–capital ratio, which declined slightly (almost 10 per cent).

5. Other examples of the "rising strength of labor" variant of the profit squeeze theory include Bowles, Gordon, and Weisskopf (1983) for the US and Glyn and Sutcliffe (1972) for the UK.

6. Weisskopf further modifies his estimates to take into account the effect of different capacity utilization rates on the wage share, but this modifica-

tion has little effect on the secular trends of the wage share, and so will be ignored here.

7. In a later article, Weisskopf (1981) made significant alternatives to his accounting framework and redefined several key variables, but his revised analysis leads to essentially the same conclusion as his original analysis: that the fundamental cause of the increase in the wage share was the relatively lower rates of unemployment in the postwar period. For a more complete discussion of this later article, see Moseley (1987).

8. Other examples of the "slower productivity growth" variant of the profit squeeze theory include Lipietz (1986) for the US and several European countries and Reati (1986, 1989) for West Germany and France, respectively.

9. Thus Wolff's estimates of the rate of profit actually differ significantly from the rate of profit as it is conventionally defined, because they include government "capital" in the denominator of the rate of profit.

10. Wolff's estimates of the total real wage and the total real output are actually measured in units of labor-hours, rather than constant prices, but this difference has little effect on the trends of the average real wage and the average productivity, and so will be ignored here.

11. A similar Marxian theory of the conventional rate of profit was presented by Gillman (1958, chapter 7). However, he mistakenly considers the trend in the conventional rate of profit an empirical test of Marx's theory of the falling rate of profit.

12. Profit is here defined broadly to include all forms of property income, including interest and rent.

13. The conventional concept of profit also differs from Marx's concept of surplus-value in the following minor respects which are ignored in this analysis: indirect business taxes are not included in profit and are included in surplus-value; and various imputations for non-market transactions are included in profit and are not included in surplus-value. These differences have very little effect on the trend in the conventional rate of profit.

14. Here again we make the simplifying assumption that the stock of capital invested in the wages of workers, this time both productive and unproductive workers, is equal to zero. As noted in Chapter 3, the stock of capital invested in wages is very small, since capitalists pay workers only after they have worked for some period of time.

15. In this chapter, the "composition of capital" refers to the *value* composition of capital.

16. The years 1947 to 1977 are initially chosen as my initial period of analysis for the same reasons as in Chapter 3: to analyze the causes of the decline in the conventional rate of profit during the postwar long-wave period of expansion, and to facilitate the comparison of my explanation of this decline presented here with Weisskopf's and Wolff's explanations discussed above. The trend in the conventional rate of profit since the mid-1970s will be examined in the final section in this chapter as a kind of post-period empirical test of these competing explanations of the decline in the rate of profit prior to the mid-1970s.

17. These estimates have not been adjusted for cyclical fluctuations because I am interested here solely in secular trends and the capacity utilization rate at the end of my period (e.g. 81.4 per cent in 1977 for Manufacturing) was very close to the capacity utilization rate at the beginning of the period (82.0 in 1947). Similarly, in terms of five-year averages, the utilization rate was 82.1 in 1948–52 and 81.9 in 1973–7. We can see from these measures of the capacity utilization rate that a reduction in utilization was not a cause of the decline in the rate of profit over this period. Since a decline in the utilization rate is often taken as evidence of a "realization problem" (e.g. Weisskopf), these estimates also suggest that such a "realization problem" did not exist during this period (Weisskopf and Wolff come to the same conclusion).

18. From 1947–65 to 1965–77, the productivity of productive labor, measured in terms of average annual rates of increase, declined 1.33 percentage points, from 3.36 to 2.03 per cent, and the productivity of all employees declined 1.85 percentage points, from 2.66 to 0.77 per cent.

19. It makes almost no difference in the trends of the ratio of unproductive labor to productive labor whether labor is measured in units of workers or hours.

20. Although Wolff's definitions of productive and unproductive labor differ somewhat from my definitions (see Chapter 2, note 10), the overall increase in Wolff's estimates of the ratio of unproductive labor to productive labor is very similar to my estimates (78 per cent from 1947 to 1976, compared to an 80 per cent increase in my estimates).

21. Also surprisingly, Wolff's theoretical model in this more recent book assumes a Cobb–Douglas production function in the productive sector (1987a, p.88). A Cobb-Douglas production function implies that the income shares between labor and capital remain constant, which was obviously not true in the postwar US economy.

22. For a further discussion of this Marxian explanation of the decline in the share of profit, see Moseley, 1985, 1987.

23. I use the Personal Consumption Expenditure Deflator as the index for the price of wage-goods, rather than the Consumer Price Index which Weisskopf uses, because the CPI has a significant upward bias from 1975 to 1985, for reasons explained in Moseley (1987).

24. For a more complete discussion of this implied prediction of Weisskopf's theory, see Moseley (1985, 1987). See also Weisskopf's reply to the former (Weisskopf, 1985).

25. Nordhaus's (1974) explanation of the decline in the share of profit in the postwar US economy also seems to imply that the profit share should have increased after 1975. Nordhaus argues that the fundamental cause of the decline in the profit share was a reduction of the risk premium included in profit, due to the perceived effectiveness of government economic policies to eliminate the risk of another severe depression. It seems fairly certain that the perceived risk of a severe depression has increased significantly since 1975. If this is so, then Nordhaus's theory would seem to imply the prediction that the risk premium should have increased since 1975, and thus that the profit share also should have increased.

26. The ratio *US* is ignored here because of its limited empirical significance.
27. This method consists essentially of two steps: (i) estimation of the effect of the capacity utilization rate on the rate (or the share) of profit by means of an *OLS* regression; (ii) calculation of the adjusted rate (or share) of profit by multiplying the regression coefficient of the capacity utilization rate times the capacity utilization rate for each year and adding this product to the actual rate (or share) or profit.

5 THE CAUSES OF THE INCREASE OF UNPRODUCTIVE LABOR

1. A similar model is employed in Fuchs (1968) in his analysis of sectoral shifts of employment (more precisely, of the relative increase of employment in Services and in Wholesale and Retail Trade in particular).
2. In fact, the BEA estimates show that output in Wholesale and Retail Trade and in Manufacturing increased at approximately the same rate over the postwar period. Given the implicit assumption of constant *S*, all these estimates show is that the percentage of manufactured goods distributed through Wholesale and Retail Trade remained essentially constant.
3. Data for *non-installment* consumer credit *extended* do not exist. Data for non-installment consumer credit *outstanding* (less appropriate for comparison to current consumer sales) do exist, but are judged to be so unreliable that they are no longer published by their source, the Federal Reserve Board. For what they are worth, these data indicate that: (i) non-installment credit has increased more slowly than installment credit, so that non-installment credit as a percentage of total consumer credit declined from 36 per cent in 1950 to 15 per cent in 1980; and (ii) the percentage of non-installment credit held by financial institutions increased from 43 per cent in 1950 to 75 per cent in 1980 (source: *Federal Reserve Bulletin*). Thus, as in the case of the more significant installment credit, most of the additional labor required to process non-installment credit was financial labor, not commercial labor.
4. National Commission of Electronic Fund Transfers, *Electronic Fund Transfer in the United States*, Washington, DC: Government Printing Office, 1977, p. 333.
5. A further question is whether even this small increase in the "sales effort", if it occurred, was due to a "realization problem", as elaborated by Baran and Sweezy (1966), or instead was due to increased non-price competition of this type for reasons other than a "realization problem". This question also applies to the increase of financial labor due to the credit-related "sales effort" discussed above. An answer to this question would require, to begin with, an empirical determination of whether or not such a "realization problem" in fact existed in the postwar US economy. In my opinion, such an empirical determination has never been adequately presented.

6. Other possible forms of an increased "sales effort" are traveling sales-persons, point-of-sale promotion, warranties, returns and adjustments, free trials, etc. I have not yet been able to obtain even indirect estimates of the labor employed in these other functions. It is my hypothesis at this point that there was no significant increase in the percentage of commercial labor employed in these other forms of the "sales effort" in the postwar US economy.

7. Brand and Duke's estimates are official Bureau of Labor Statistics estimates, which are regularly updated.

8. Brand and Duke suggest another possible cause of the rapid growth of checks: the increase of trading activity on security and commodity exchanges. Such trading usually involves multiple fund transfers through the banking system.

9. As a substitute for data for firms, Edwards uses data on the size of establishments to test the hypothesis that the larger size of firms was an important cause of the increase of non-production labor in US manufacturing. Edwards presents the following data on the ratio of non-production workers (N) to production workers (P) in manufacturing establishments, classified according to the number of employees per establishment, for the years 1954 and 1972:

Number of Employees	N/P 1954	1972
1– 499	0.24	0.32
500–2499	0.26	0.34
2500 +	0.36	0.44

These data clearly show that the largest establishments have the highest N/P ratio, with the largest category (greater than 2500 employees) having a significantly higher ratio than the two smaller categories. Presumably, similar data for *firms*, instead of *establishments*, would show an even greater increase in the ratio N/P, since it seems likely that firms which operate more than one establishment would have even greater "control problems" than single-establishment firms. These data also show that the ratio N/P increased significantly *within* each size category, thus suggesting that other factors besides increased size were also significant causes of the increase of this ratio.

10. I thank Gerard Dumenil for stimulating my thinking along these lines, although he would probably still disagree with my conclusions.

11. An area in which non-profit maximizing behaviour by managers clearly prevails is the managers' own salaries, perquisites, and expense accounts. Managers' salaries and managers' staffs would seem to be governed by similar self-interested motivations.

12. This "delayering" usually does not mean increased worker control, but rather decentralization and delegation of managerial authority.

13. The method used to derive these revised contributions was: (i) calculate what the rate of surplus-value and the two ratios UF and US would have been on the basis of the assumptions that the ratio of supervisory labor to productive labor remained constant and the decline in the rate of profit was the same as the actual decline; and (ii) use these hypothetical estimates to recalculate the contributions of the four Marxian determinants to the total decline of the rate of profit, using the same method as in Table 4.2 of Chapter 4.

6 CONCLUSION

1. For the purposes of these last two sections, no distinction need be made between the value and the organic composition of capital.
2. As early as the 1950s, Mattick predicted, almost alone among economic theorists, including Marxist ones, that sooner or later the effectiveness of Keynesian policies would come to an. end and that the postwar boom would be followed by yet another period of crisis and stagnation. The events of the last twenty years have largely confirmed the validity of Mattick's analysis.
3. Mattick emphasized that expansionary fiscal policy has the additional disadvantage of requiring that a greater portion of surplus-value must be borrowed to finance the government deficit, and thus a smaller portion of surplus-value is left over for purposes of capital accumulation. Thus expansionary fiscal policy exacerbates the problem of insufficient profitability, rather than solves it.

APPENDIX B: SOURCES AND METHODS

1. The Census data for the "Wages of production workers" cannot be used to estimate variable capital directly because these data do not include benefits and supplements to wages and salaries, mainly employer contributions to social security and to private benefit plans. But these Census data can be used to estimate the percentage of total compensation that is variable capital, on the assumption that these supplemental benefits are distributed between production workers and non-production workers in the same proportion as wages and salaries are distributed between these two groups of workers.
2. I derived an estimate of the remaining bias in the trend of the ratio of unproductive labor to productive labor resulting from the underestimation of the productive labor of managers and supervisors, by assuming that managers and supervisors devote 25 per cent of their labor to productive functions. The resulting ratio of unproductive to productive labor increased 67 per cent from 1950 to 1980, compared to the 70 per cent increase in the revised estimates of this ratio presented in table 5.1.

APPENDIX C: ASSESSMENT OF BIAS

1. It also seems safe to conclude that even with this alteration, the rate of surplus-value almost certainly did not decline significantly. Thus the secular "profit squeeze" interpretation of Marx's theory is still contradicted by the evidence for the postwar US economy.

Bibliography

Alberro, José and Joseph Persky (1981), "The Dynamics of Fixed Capital Revaluation and Scrapping", *Review of Radical Political Economics*, 13 (Summer): 32–7.

Attewell, Paul (1987), "The Deskilling Controversy", *Work and Occupations*, 14 (August): 323–46.

Baran, Paul (1957), *The Political Economy of Growth* (New York: Prometheus).

—————— and Paul Sweezy (1966), *Monopoly Capital* (New York: Monthly Review Press).

Barger, Harold (1955), *Distribution's Place in the American Economy since 1869* (Princeton, NJ: Princeton University Press).

Berle, A.A. and G.C. Means (1932), *The Modern Corporation and Private Property* (New York: Commerce Clearing House).

Blaug, Mark (1974), "Technical Change and Marxian Economics", in David Horowitz (ed.), *Marx and Modern Economics* (New York: Monthly Review Press).

—————— (1980), *The Methodology of Economics, or How Economists Explain* (New York: Cambridge University Press).

Blumberg, P. (1968), *Industrial Democracy: The Sociology of Participation* (London: Constable).

Bosworth, Barry (1982), "Capital Formation and Economic Policy", *Brookings Papers on Economic Activity* (1): 273–326.

Bowles, Samuel, David Gordon and Thomas Weisskopf (1983), *Beyond the Wasteland* (Garden City, New York: Doubleday).

Brand, Horst and John Duke (1982), "Productivity in Commercial Banking: Computers Spur the Advance", *Monthly Labor Review*, 105 (December): 19–27.

Braverman, Harry (1974), *Labor and Monopoly Capital* (New York: Monthly Review Press).

Brems, Hans (1977), "Reality and Neo-Classical Theory", *Journal of Economic Literature*, 15 (March): 72–83.

Caldwell, Bruce (1982), *Beyond Positivism: Economic Methodology in the Twentieth Century* (Boston: Allen & Unwin).

Carchedi, Guglielmo, (1984), "The Logic of Prices as Values", *Economy and Society*, 13 (4): 431–55.

—————— (1988), "Marxian Price Theory and Modern Capitalism", *International Journal of Political Economy*, 18 (Summer).

Chandler, Alfred (1962), *Strategy and Structure* (Cambridge, MA: MIT Press).

Christiansen, Jens (1976), "Marx and the Falling Rate of Profit", *American Economic Review*, 66 (May): 20–66.

Clark, Gregory (1984), "Authority and Efficiency: The Labor Market and the Managerial Revolution of the Late Nineteenth Century", *Journal of Economic History*, 44 (December): 1069–83.

Clawson, Dan (1980), *Bureaucracy and the Labor Process* (New York: Monthly Review Press).

Cogoy, Mario (1973), "The Fall of the Rate of Profit and the Theory of Accumulation: A Reply to Paul Sweezy", *Bulletin of the Conference of Socialist Economists*, no. 7 (Winter): 52–67.

—— (1987), "Neo-Marxist Theory, Marx, and the Accumulation of Capital", *International Journal of Political Economy*, 17 (Summer): 11–37.

Delaunay, Jean-Claude (1989), "Applied Research for the Case of France of the Marxist Theory of the Rate of Surplus-value, 1896–1980", *International Journal of Political Economy*, 19 (Spring): 33–47.

Denison, Edward F. (1969), "Some Major Issues in Productivity Analysis: An Examination of Estimates of Jorgenson and Griliches", *Survey of Current Business*, 49 (May, part II): 1–27.

Drago, Richard (1984–5), "New Use of an Old Technology: Growth of Worker Participation", *Journal of Post Keynesian Economics*, 7 (Winter): 153–67.

Dumas, Lloyd (1986), *The Overburdened Economy* (Berkeley: University of California Press).

Dumenil, Gerard (1983–4), "Beyond the Transformation Riddle: A Labor Theory of Value", *Science and Society*, 47 (Winter): 426–50.

Edwards, Richard (1979), *Contested Terrain* (New York: Basic Books).

Elger, Tony (1979), "Valorization and Deskilling: A Critique of Braverman", *Capital and Class*, 7 (Spring): 58–99.

Elson, Diane (1979), "The Value Form of Labor", in Elson (ed.), *Value: The Representation of Labor in Capitalism* (London: CSE Books).

Engels, Frederick (1937), *Engels on Capital* (New York: International Publishers.

Feldstein, Martin and Lawrence Summers (1977), "Is the Rate of Profit Falling?" *Brookings Papers on Economic Activity* (1): 211–28.

Feldstein, Martin, Louis Dicks-Mireaux, and James Poterba (1983), "The Effective Tax Rate and the Pretax Rate of Return", *Journal of Public Economics*, 21 (July): 129–58.

Fine, Ben (1973), "A Note on Productive and Unproductive Labor", *Bulletin of the Conference of Socialist Economists*, 6 (Autumn): 99–102.

—— and Laurence Harris (1979), *Rereading Capital* (London: Macmillan Press).

Foley, Duncan (1982a), "The Value of money, the Value of Labor-Power, and the Marxian Transformation Problem", *Review of Radical Political Economics*, 14 (Summer): 37–49.

—— (1982b), "Realization and Accumulation in a Marxian Model of the Circuit of Capital", *Journal of Economic Theory*, 28 (December): 300–19.

—— (1986a), *Money, Accumulation, and Crisis* (New York: Harwood Academic Press).

—— (1986b), *Understanding Capital: Marx's Economic Theory* (Cambridge: Harvard University Press).

Foss, Murray (1984), *Changing Utilization of Fixed Capital: An Element of Long-Term Growth* (Washington: American Enterprise Institute).

Freeman, Alan (1988), "The Social Wage and the Profit Rate in Britain, 1950–1986", presented at the International Conference on Accumulation and Profitability, New York University.

Fuchs, Victor (1968), *The Service Economy* (New York: Columbia University Press).

Gillman, Joseph (1958), *The Falling Rate of Profit* (New York: Carmen Associates).

Glyn, Andrew and Bob Sutcliffe (1972), *British Capitalism, Workers, and the Profit Squeeze* (Harmondsworth: Penguin Books).

Gordon, David (1976), "Capitalist Efficiency or Socialist Efficiency", *Monthly Review*, 28 (July–August): 19–39.

———, Richard Edwards and Michael Reich (1982) *Segmented Work, Divided Workers: The Historical Transformation of Labor in the United States* (New York: Cambridge University Press).

Gough, Ian (1972), "Marx's Theory of Productive and Unproductive Labor", *New Left Review*, No. 76 (November–December): 47–72.

Gouverneur, Jacques (1983), *Contemporary Capitalism and Marxist Economics* (Totowa, NJ: Barnes & Noble Books).

Harrison, John (1973), "Productive and Unproductive Labor in Marx's Political Economy", *Bulletin of the Conference of Socialist Economists* 6 (Autumn): 70–82.

Harvey, David (1985), "The Value-Creating Capacity of Skilled Labor in Marxian Economics", *Review of Radical Political Economics*, 17 (Spring–Summer): 83—102.

Heap, Shaun (1980), "World Profitability Crisis in the 1970's: Some Empirical Evidence", *Capital and Class* 12 (Winter): 66–84.

Hilferding, Rudolph (1949), "Bohm–Bawerk's Criticism of Marx", in Paul Sweezy (ed.), *Karl Marx and the Close of His System* (London: Merlin Press).

Hill, T.P. (1979), *Profits and Rates of Return* (Paris: Organisation for Co-operation and Development).

Hodgson, Geoffrey (1982–3), "Worker Participation and Macroeconomic Efficiency", *Journal of Post Keynesian Economics*, 5 (Winter): 267–75.

Holland, David M. and Stewart C. Meyers (1984), "Trends in Corporate Profitability and Capital Costs in the United States", in Holland (ed.), *Measuring Profitability and Capital Costs* (Lexington, MA: Lexington Books).

Hunt, E.K. (1979), "The Categories of Productive and Unproductive Labor in Marxist Economic Theory", *Science and Society*, 43 (Fall): 303–25.

Hunt, Ian (1983), "An Obituary of a New Life for the Tendency of the Rate of Profit to Fall?", *Review of Radical Political Economics*, 15 (Spring): 131–48.

Kliman, Andrew and Ted McGlone (1988), "The Transformation Non-Problem and the Non-Transformation Problem", *Capital and Class*, 35 (Summer): 56–83.

Laibman, David (1982a), "Technical Change, the Real Wage, and the Rate of Exploitation: The Falling Rate of Profit Reconsidered", *Review of Radical Political Economics*, 14 (Summer): 95–105.

200   *Bibliography*

—— (1982b), "Unproductive Labor: Critique of a Concept", in William Rowe (ed.), *Studies in Labor Theory and Practice, Studies in Marxism*, 12: 59–72.

Leadbeater, David (1985), "The Consistency of Marx's Categories of Productive Labor and Unproductive Labor", *History of Political Economy*, 17 (Winter): 591–619.

Lebowitz, Michael (1976), "Marx's Falling Rate of Profit: A Dialectical View", *Canadian Journal of Economics*, 9 (May): 232–54.

——(1982), "The General and the Specific in Marx's Theory of Crisis", *Studies in Political Economy*, no. 7 (Winter): 5–24.

Leibling, Herman (1980), *Corporate Profitability and Capital Formation: Are Rates of Return Sufficient?* (New York: Pergamon Press).

Lipietz, Alain (1982a), "The 'So-Called Transformation Problem' Revisited", *Journal of Economic Theory*, 26 (February): 59–88.

—— (1982b), "Credit Money: A Condition Permitting Inflationary Crisis", *Review of Radical Political Economics*, 14 (Summer): 49–58.

—— (1986), "Behind the Crisis: The Exhaustion of a Regime of Accumulation", *Review of Radical Political Economics*, 18 (Spring–Summer), 13–32.

Lovell, Michael (1978), "The Profit Picture: Trends and Cycles", *Brookings Papers on Economic Activity*, (3) 769–88.

Mack, Ruth (1959), "Inflation and Quasi-Elective Changes in Costs", *Review of Economics and Statistics* 41 (August) 225–31.

Mage, Shane (1963), *The Law of the Falling Tendency of the Rate of Profit*, Ph.D. dissertation, Columbia University.

Malinvaud, Edmond (1984), *Mass Unemployment* (New York: Basil Blackwell).

Mandel, Ernst (1980), *Long Waves of Capitalist Development* (New York: Cambridge University Press).

—— (1981), "Introduction" to Marx (1981)

Marglin, Stephen (1974), "What do Bosses Do?", *Review of Radical Political Economics*, 6 (Summer): 60–112.

Marx, Karl (1963, 1968, 1991), *Theories of Surplus Value*, Vols. 1, 2, 3 (Moscow: Progress Publishers).

—— (1970), *A Contribution to the Critique of Political Economy* (New York: International Publishers).

—— (1973), *Grundrisse* (Harmondsworth: Penguin Books).

—— (1977, 1978, 1981), *Capital*, Vols 1,2,3 (New York: Random House).

—— and Frederick Engels (1975), *Selected Correspondence* (Moscow: Progress Publishers).

—— (1988), *Marx–Engels Collected Works*, vol. 30 (New York: International Publishers.

Mattick, Paul Sr (1959), "Value Theory and Capital Accumulation", *Science and Society*, 23 (Winter) 27–51.

—— (1969), *Marx and Keynes: The Limits of the Mixed Economy*, (Boston: Porter Sargent).

—— (1972), "Samuelson's 'Transformation' of Marxism into Bourgeois Economics", *Science and Society*, 36 (Fall): 258–73.

Mattick, Paul Jr (1981), "Some Aspects of the Value-Price Problem", *Economies et Sociétés*, 15 (6–7): 275–81.

McCloskey, Donald (1985), *The Rhetoric of Economics* (Madison, WI: University of Wisconson Press).

Melman, Seymour (1951), "The Rise of Administrative Overhead in the Manufacturing Industries of the United States 1899–1947", *Oxford Economic Papers*, 3 (January): 62–112.

—— (1983), *Profits Without Production* (New York: Knopf).

Mohun, Simon (1984–5), "Abstract Labor and its Value-Form", *Science and Society*, 48 (Winter): 386–406.

Morishima, Michio (1973), *Marx's Economics* (New York: Cambridge University Press).

Moseley, Fred (1982), *The Rate of Surplus Value in the United States Economy, 1947–1977*, Ph.D. dissertation, University of Massachusetts.

—— (1983), "Marx's Concepts of Productive Labor and Unproductive Labor", *Eastern Economic Journal*, 9 (July–December) 180–9.

—— (1985), "The Rate of Surplus Value in the Postwar U.S. Economy: A Critique of Weisskopf's Estimates", *Cambridge Journal of Economics*, 9 (March) 180–9.

—— (1986), "Estimates of the Rate of Surplus Value in the Postwar U.S. Economy", *Review of Radical Political Economics*, 18 (Spring–Summer): 168–89.

—— (1987), "The Profit Share and the Rate of Surplus-value in the Postwar U.S. Economy, 1975–85", *Cambridge Journal of Economics*, 11 (December): 393–8.

—— (1988), "The Rate of Surplus-Value, the Organic Composition of Capital, and the General Rate of Profit in the U.S. Economy: A Critique and Update of Wolff's Estimates", *American Economic Review*, 78 (March): 298–303.

—— (1989), "The Decline of the Rate of Profit in the Postwar US Economy: Marxian and Regulation Explanations", *International Journal of Political Economy* 19 (Spring): 48–66.

—— (1991), "Marx's Logical Method and the Transformation Problem", paper presented at ASSA Annual Convention.

Nordhaus, William (1974), "The Falling Share of Profits", *Brookings Papers on Economic Activity*, (1): 169–217.

Oi, Walter (1987), "The Indirect Effect of Technology on Retail Trade", in Richard Cyert and David Mowery (eds), *Technology and Employment: Innovation and Growth in the US Economy* (Washington: National Academy Press).

Okishio, Nobuo (1961), "Technical Change and the Rate of Profit", *Kobe University Economic Review*, 7: 86–99.

Parijs, P. van (1980), "The Falling Rate of Profit: An Obituary", *Review of Radical Political Economics*, 12 (Spring): 1–16.

Perelman, Michael (1985), "Marx, Malthus, and the Organic Composition of Capital", *History of Political Economy*, 17 (Fall): 461–90.

Reati, Angelo (1986), "The Rate of Profit and the Organic Composition of Capital in West German Industry from 1960 to 1981", *Review of Radical Political Economics*, 18 (Spring–Summer) 56–86.

———— (1989), "The Rate of Profit and the Organic Composition of Capital in the Long Postwar Cycle: The Case of French Industry from 1959 to 1981", *International Journal of Political Economy*, 19 (Spring): 10–32.

Reuten, Geert and Michael Williams (1989), *Value-Form and the State: The Tendencies of Accumulation and the Determination of Economic Policy in Capitalist Society* (London: Routledge).

Ricardo, David (1977), *The Principles of Political Economy and Taxation* (New York: Everyman's Library).

Robinson, Joan (1966), *An Essay on Marxian Economics* (London: Macmillan).

Roemer, John (1977), "Technical Change and the 'Tendency of the Rate of Profit to Fall", *Journal of Economic Theory*, 16 (December): 403–24.

———— (1979), "Continuing Controversy on the Falling Rate of Profit: Fixed Capital and Other Issues", *Cambridge Journal of Economics*, 3 (September): 379–98.

Roncaglia, Alessandro (1974), "The Reduction of Complex Labor to Simple Labor", *Bulletin of the Conference of Socialist Economists* 9 (Autumn) 1–12.

Rosdolsky, Roman (1977), *The Making of Marx's Capital* (London: Pluto Press).

Rowthorn, Bob (1974), "Skilled Labor in the Marxist System", *Bulletin of Conference of Socialist Economists*, 8 (Spring) 25–45.

Rubin, I.I. (1972), *Essays on Marx's Theory of Value* (Detroit: Black and Red Press).

Salvadori, Neri (1981), "Falling Rate of Profit with a Constant Real Wage: An Example", *Cambridge Journal of Economics*, 5 (March) 59–66.

Sanderson, Susan R. and Lawrence Schein (1986), "Sizing Up the Down-Sizing Era", *Across the Board*, (November): 15–18.

Shaikh, Anwar (1978a), "Political Economy and Capitalism: Notes on Dobb's Theory of Crisis", *Cambridge Journal of Economics*, 2 (June): 233–51.

———— (1978b), "National Income Accounts and Marxian Categories", New School for Social Research, mimeograph.

———— (1980), "Marxian Competition vs. Perfect Competition: Further Comments on the So-Called Choice of Technique", *Cambridge Journal of Economics*, 4 (December): 75–83.

———— (1984), "The Transformation of Marx to Sraffa", in Ernst Mandel and Alan Freeman (eds.), *Ricardo, Marx, Sraffa* (London: Verso).

Smith, Adam (1965), *An Inquiry into the Causes of the Wealth of Nations* (New York: Modern Library).

Speagle, Richard and Leo Silverman (1953), "The Banking Income Dilemma", *Review of Economic and Statistics*, 35 (May) 128–39.

Speagle, Richard and Ernest Kohn (1958), "Employment and Output in Banking", *Review of Economic and Statistics*, 40 (February): 22–35.

Sraffa, Piero (1960), *The Production of Commodities by Means of Commodities* (New York: Cambridge University Press).

Steedman, Ian (1977), *Marx After Sraffa* (London: New Left Books).

Stone, Katherine (1974), "The Origins of Job Structures in the Steel Industry", *Review of Radical Political Economics*, 6 (Summer): 113–73.

Sweezy, Paul (1968), *The Theory of Capitalist Development* (New York: Monthly Review Press).

Tomasko, Robert M. (1987), *Downsizing: Reshaping the Corporation for the Future* (New York: Amacom).

Tortasada, R. (1977), "A Note on the Reduction of Complex Labor to Simple Labor", *Capital and Class*, 1 (Spring): 106–16.

US Bureau of the Census (1988), *1987 Census of Construction Industries*, Vol. 1. (Washington, DC: US Government Printing Office).

—— (1988), *1987 Census of Manufacturing*, Vol. 1 (Washington, DC: US Government Printing Office.

—— (1988), *1987 Census of Mineral Industries*, Vol. 1 (Washington, DC: US Government Printing Office).

—— (1982), *1980 Census of the Population*, Vol. 2 (Washington, DC: US Government Printing Office).

US Bureau of Labor Statistics (1968), *Scientific and Technical Personnel in Industry, 1961–66*, Bulletin 1609 (Washington, DC: US Government Printing Office).

—— (1973), *Employment of Scientists and Engineers, 1950–70*, Bulletin 1781 (Washington, DC: US Government Printing Office).

—— (1985), *Employment, Earnings, and Hours, United States, 1909–84*, Bulletin 1312–12 (Washington, DC: US Government Printing Office).

—— (1985–87), *Employment and Earnings*, March issues (Washington, DC: US Government Printing Office).

US Department of Commerce (1954), *Survey of Current Business, National Income Supplement* (Washington, DC: US Government Printing Office).

—— (1986), *The National Income and Product Accounts of the United States, 1929–82* (Washington, DC: US Government Printing Office).

—— (1987), *Fixed Reproducible Wealth in the United States, 1929–85* (Washington, DC: US Government Printing Office).

—— (1984–88), *Survey of Current Business*, July and August issues (Washington, DC: US Government Printing Office).

US Internal Revenue Service (1948–77), *Statistics of Income, Corporate Income Tax Returns* (Washington, DC: US Government Printing Office).

Usher, Dan (1980), *The Measurement of Capital* (Chicago: University of Chicago Press).

Vroey, Michel de (1981), "Value, Production, and Exchange", in Ian Steedman (ed.), *The Value Controversy* (London: New Left Books).

—— (1982), "On the Obsolescence of the Marxian Theory of Value", *Capital and Class*, 17 (Summer): 34–59.

Warburton, Clark (1958), "Financial Intermediaries", in *A Critique of the United States Income and Product Accounts* (Princeton, NJ: Princeton University Press).

Ward, Michael (1976), *The Measurement of Capital* (Paris: Organization for Economic Cooperation and Development).

Weeks, John (1981), *Capital and Exploitation* (Princeton, NJ: Princeton University Press).

Weisskopf, Thomas E. (1979), "Marxian Crisis Theory and the Rate of Profit in the Postwar U.S. Economy", *Cambridge Journal of Economics*, 3 (December): 341–78.

—— (1981), "Wages, Salaries, and the Profit Share: A Rejoinder", *Cambridge Journal of Economics*, 5 (June): 175–82.

———— (1985), "The Rate of Surplus-Value in the U.S. Economy: A Response to Moseley's Critique", *Cambridge Journal of Economics* 9 (March): 80–4.

Williamson, Oliver (1963), "Managerial Discretion and Business Behavior", *American Economic Review*, 53 (December) 10032–57.

———— (1967), "Hierarchical Control and Optimum Firm Size", *Journal of Political Economy*, 75 (February): 123–38.

———— (1970), *Corporate Control and Business Behavior* (Englewood Cliffs, NJ: Prentice Hall).

Wolff, Edward N. (1979), "The Rate of Surplus Value, the Organic Composition of Capital, and the General Rate of Profit in the U.S. Economy, 1947–1967", *American Economic Review*, 69 (June): 329–41.

———— (1986), "The Productivity Slowdown and the Fall in the Rate of Profit, 1947–76", *Review of Radical Political Economics*, 18 (Spring–Summer): 87–109.

———— (1987a), *Growth, Accumulation, and Unproductive Activity* (New York: Cambridge University Press).

———— (1987b), "Structural Change and the Rate of Profit in the U.S. Economy, 1947–76", presented at the ASSA Annual Convention.

Wolff, Richard, Bruce Roberts and Antonio Callari (1982), "Marx's (not Ricardo's) Transformation Problem: A Radical Reconceptualization", *History of Political Economy*, 14: 564–82.

Work Relations Group (prepared by Jeremy Brecher) (1978), "Uncovering the Hidden History of the American Workplace", *Review of Radical Political Economics*, 10 (Winter): 1–23.

Yaffe, David (1972), "The Marxian Theory of Crisis, Capital, and the State", *Bulletin of the Conference of Socialist Economists*, 4 (Winter) 5–58.

———— (1973), "The Crisis of Profitability: A Critique of the Glyn-Sutcliffe Thesis", *New Left Review*, no. 80 (July–August) 45–61.

Zimbalist, Andrew (ed.) (1979), *Case Studies in the Labor Process* (New York: Monthly Review Press).

Name Index

Subject Index

[Key references have been set in **bold**.]

see also organic composition of
capital, technical composition
of capital
variable capital, 26, **28–30**, 32, **37**,
39–40, **41**, 43, 116, 156, 187n.5
estimates of, **50–1**, 56, 61; sources
and methods, 173–5
possible bias in estimates, 180–1
see also wages of unproductive
labor

wages
of productive labor, *see* variable
capital
of total labor, 110, 116
of unproductive labor, *see*
unproductive capital
working day, 9, 12, 14, 17,
185n.11
world capitalist economy, 49,
182–3